Rachel Josefowitz Siegel
Ellen Cole
Susan Steinberg-Oren
Editors

D0781413

Jewish Mothers
Tell Their Stories
Acts of Love and Courage

"**T**his is a book to be read, imbibed, tasted, and cherished. No jokes here about the stereotyped Jewish mother. These are serious essays—honest, revealing, often riveting, and passionate. From feminists like Israeli Alice Shalvi reminiscing about sharing a bed with her grandmother to Phyllis Chesler, a single mother dealing with her son, to Shulamit Reinharz discovering 'our children, ourselves,' *Jewish Mothers Tell Their Stories* is a roadmap to understanding and cherishing our Jewish mothers with heart, body, and soul."

Ruth Gruber, PhD
Author of *Haven, Exodus 1947,*
and *Raquela: A Woman of Israel*

"**F**inally, a collection of personal stories that present the experience of Jewish mothers without stereotypes and without self-serving jokes! Most of all, I appreciate the wide range of authors and the variety of perspectives. At the end I felt that I was not told how to be a Jewish mother, but rather offered permission to celebrate who and how I am. The book made me laugh, cry, and reflect on my own and my family's experiences. I look forward to discussing it with my daughters, my daughter-in-law, and my grandchildren."

Sylvia Rimm, PhD
Author, *See Jane Win*

"**I**n a gentle and understated way, this is a very moving book. Take three dozen thoughtful, introspective, and totally honest writers, charge them with a topic that evokes intense feeling, and not surprisingly you come up with a work of power and poignancy.

Reading each piece, I could not help but paraphrase the Talmudic insight about an individual life: each mother–daughter/son relationship is a whole world; I could not help but think of Jewish children of the Holocaust and children all over the world who grew up bereft of their mothers; I could not help but think how I, a relatively good daughter and mother, might have done things differently. Not at all preachy but generously taking the reader into the writer's own universe, this is a book that should be read by Jewish mothers and fathers along their own complex, exhilarating, challenging parental journeys."

Blu Greenberg
Author, *Women and Judaism:
A View from Tradition*
and *How to Run a Traditional
Jewish Household*

Jewish Mothers Tell Their Stories
Acts of Love and Courage

Jewish Mothers
Tell Their Stories
Acts of Love and Courage

Rachel Josefowitz Siegel
Ellen Cole
Susan Steinberg-Oren
Editors

The Haworth Press®
New York • London • Oxford

The Haworth Press, Inc., 10 Alice Street, Binghamton, NY 13904-1580

Publication of Chapter 3, "Traditions," by Chawwa Wijnberg and Janine Beulink, translated by Johanna H. Prins and Johanna W. Prins, has been made possible with financial support from the Foundation for the Production and Translation of Dutch Literature.

Cover design by Marylouise E. Doyle.

Library of Congress Cataloging-in-Publication Data

Jewish mothers tell their stories : acts of love and courage / Rachel Josefowitz Siegel, Ellen Cole, Susan Steinberg-Oren, editors.
    p. cm.
  ISBN 0-7890-1099-2 (hard : alk. paper) — ISBN 0-7890-1100-X (pbk : alk. paper)
  1. Jewish women. 2. Mothers. 3. Jews—Identity. I. Siegel, Rachel Josefowitz. II. Cole, Ellen. III. Steinberg-Oren, Susan.

HQ1172 .J47 2000
306.874′3′089924—dc21

00-027606

We dedicate this book to all Jewish mothers,
named and unnamed, past, present, and future.

Rachel Josefowitz Siegel lovingly remembers her mother,
Frieda Shur Josefowitz, her mother-in-law, Pauline Siegel,
and her grandmothers, Rochel Gitel Shur and Chaya Josefowitz.

Ellen Cole lovingly dedicates this book to her mother,
Shirley Salzman Strauss,
and honors the memory of her grandmothers,
Lena Persky Salzman and Fannye Mothner Strauss.

Susan Steinberg-Oren dedicates this book with great love
and appreciation to her mother, Cynthia Sherman Steinberg,
her mother-in-law, Fenia Oren, her grandmother, Goldie Steinberg,
and to the memory of her nana, Celia Marcus Sherman,
who died at the age of 101 as we were completing this book.

CONTENTS

ABOUT THE EDITORS

Rachel Josefowitz Siegel, MSW, has lectured and written extensively about Jewish women and aging. In 1994, she received the First Annual Award for Distinguished Contributions to the Field of Jewish Women in Psychology, presented by the Association for Women in Psychology. A 1995 issue of the journal *Women & Therapy* was dedicated to Ms. Siegel on the occasion of her 70th birthday, and she was included in *Feminist Foremothers in Women's Studies, Psychology, and Mental Health* (Chester, Rothblum, and Cole, 1995). Retired from her private practice in feminist psychotherapy, she continues to write and give lectures. Born in Berlin, of Ashkenazi Lithuanian background, Ms. Siegel moved to Switzerland before immigrating to the United States in 1939. She started her professional career after twenty-five years of raising two sons and a daughter in an observant, Conservative home in Ithaca, New York. Now widowed, she balances her work and volunteer activities with family visits and yearly adventurous trips with her grown grandchildren.

Ellen Cole, PhD, is Professor of Psychology and Director of the Master of Science in Counseling Psychology Program at Alaska Pacific University in Anchorage. The former editor of the journal *Women & Therapy* and the Haworth Press book program Innovations in Feminist Studies, she has written and edited numerous publications about human sexuality and women's mental health. Dr. Cole received a Distinguished Publication Award from the Association for Women and Psychology in

1987. In 1998, she and Rachel Josefowitz Siegel received the Award for Jewish Scholarship from the association's Jewish Caucus. Ellen was born into a nonobservant Reform Jewish family in the New York City borough of Queens. Until she went to college in 1958, nearly everyone with whom she had contact was also Jewish. Since then, she has lived in Plainfield, Vermont; Prescott, Arizona; and Anchorage, Alaska; areas with small Jewish populations. She says she nearly lost track of herself as a Jewish woman until beginning the collaboration with Rachel Josefowitz Siegel that resulted in their first book. It is Rachel and the many Jewish women they have published that she credits with her return to her roots.

Susan Steinberg-Oren, PhD, is a VA Staff Psychologist; Assistant Clinical Professor at the University of California at Los Angeles and Fuller Theological Seminary Graduate Clinical Psychology Program; and a Clinical Psychologist in private practice in Los Angeles, California. She has published numerous articles about emotion, psychotherapy, and feminist psychology, including a chapter in two prior books by Rachel Josefowitz Siegel and Ellen Cole. *Jewish Mothers* has offered her another opportunity to combine her personal and professional interests in the areas of Judaism, parenting, and the psychology of women. Susan grew up within the tradition of American Conservative Judaism. She married an Israeli, and together they enjoy passing their heritage on to their two young children.

CONTRIBUTORS

 **Jane Ariel, PhD,** is a family therapist in Oakland, California. She grew up in Scarsdale, New York, attended Oberlin College, and moved to Israel when she was twenty-five. There she married and had two children. As executive director of a research institute at the Hebrew University of Jerusalem, she dealt with the educational and social gap between Ashkenazi and Sephardic Jews. She returned to the United States in 1980, where she earned her PhD at the California Graduate School of Family Psychology. Brought up as a nonpracticing Jew, she is still unaffiliated. She serves on the board of Chochmat haLev, Wisdom of the Heart, an organization dedicated to developing the meditative and spiritual aspects of Judaism.

 **Susan Berrin, MSW,** is the editor of *Sh'ma,* a monthly journal addressing the cutting-edge issues facing North American Jewry. She is also the editor of two landmark Jewish anthologies, *Celebrating the New Moon: A Rosh Chodesh Anthology* and *A Heart of Wisdom: Making the Jewish Journey from Midlife Through the Elder Years.* She lectures frequently on Rosh Chodesh, Jewish midlife issues, and aging with integrity. Susan lives with her husband and three children in Newton, Massachusetts.

 **Rabbi Lenore Bohm** is an American Reform Rabbi and the author of numerous articles, as well as the books *Holiday Study Guide* and *Rosh Chodesh Study Guide.* She teaches Judaism from a feminist perspective and is a popular speaker on women in religion, spirituality, Jewish parenting, and theology. She lives in San Diego County with her husband, Dr. Paul Goodman, and their four school-age children. She was raised in a Reform background in New York and Atlanta, in the shadows of her Viennese parents' refugee experiences.

Gayle Brandeis is a widely published, award-winning writer and dancer living in Riverside, California, with her husband and their two children. Her book *Fruit-flesh: Luscious Lessons for Women Writers* is forthcoming, as is her anthology, *Towards a Center of Voices: Women Poets on Women Poets and the Poetic Process.* Her family tree is rooted in Russian Jewish soil on both sides; she herself is trying to get more rooted to her heritage in the sandy, and not very Jewish, California desert.

Sandra Butler turned away from a middle-class Reform Judaism of the 1950s that allowed neither questions nor spontaneity. She spent decades searching for faith and meaning in the vocabularies of feminist psychology and activist politics. Now both are synthesized and embedded in her involvement in the Jewish Renewal movement. She continues to write and teach with an emphasis on violence against women and the politics of women's health. She is the author of *Conspiracy of Silence: The Trauma of Incest* and co-author of *Cancer in Two Voices.*

Paula J. Caplan, PhD, is a nonfiction writer, playwright, actor, psychologist, and social activist who was born and raised in Springfield, Missouri, in the heart of the Bible Belt, attended Harvard University, and lived in Toronto for twenty years before returning to the United States. She is the author of books that include *The Myth of Women's Masochism*; *Don't Blame Mother: Mending the Mother-Daughter Relationship*; *Thinking Critically About Research on Sex and Gender*—co-authored with her son, Jeremy, and line edited by her daughter, Emily; and *They Say You're Crazy: How the World's Most Powerful Psychiatrists Decide Who's Normal.* She recently wrote an award-winning play, *Call Me Crazy.* Her heritage is a combination of Lithuanian/Polish and maybe Russian. She recently compiled *Labors of Love: A Rabinowitz Family Cookbook* as one way to preserve the heritage of her women (and some men) ancestors.

 **Phyllis Chesler, PhD,** is the author of nine books, including *Women and Madness* and, most recently, *Letters to a Young Feminist.* She is a cofounder of the Association for Women in Psychology and the National Women's Health Network, and a founding board member of the International Committee for Women of the Wall. She is currently co-editing a volume for the Brandeis University Press that will document Jewish women's eleven-year struggle to pray at the Kotel.

 **Michele Clark, MEd, LCMHC,** teaches in the graduate counseling program at Goddard College. She is also a graduate student in Near Eastern and Judaic Studies at Brandeis University, where her research interests focus on the current Jewish American community. She grew up in a moderately observant Conservative household. She attends services regularly in an eclectic, unaffiliated synagogue.

 **Liz Cordonnier** is a writer of fiction, essays, and editorials. Her work has appeared in such literary periodicals as *Messages from the Heart,* and in newspapers such as the *Hartford Courant.* Raised in Philadelphia, she is a graduate of Syracuse University, and currently resides in Connecticut with her husband and two children. She and her family do not formally practice a single religion, but use the ethics and values of their separate backgrounds to guide their children on a moral and spiritual path.

 **Pamela Cravez, JD,** is a writer who moved to Anchorage, Alaska, eighteen years ago with her husband. They are continuing a family tradition of resettlement. Whereas earlier generations in her family moved from Eastern Europe to the Midwest and then to all corners of the globe, her husband's family has traveled from Russia to Cuba to Miami all within a generation. Their two boys already have an avid interest in travel and geography. There's no telling where the family will end up next.

Laurie Davis, a consultant and writer, lives in the country with her partner, their two daughters, and a number of cats, dogs, horses, and hens.

Karen Engel is a freelance radio journalist who lives with her Austrian non-Jewish husband, Uwe Schaflinger, in Graz, Austria. They have three children. Her father, born in Danzig, emigrated to the United States after World War II, and most of her immediate family were from assimilated Polish Jewish or German Jewish backgrounds. Her mother's family has lived in North America for generations. Karen and Uwe observe most of the Jewish holidays and identify mainly with progressive Judaism, although they sometimes find more meaning and authenticity in traditional or Orthodox Jewish thought.

Linda Stone Fish, PhD, is the Program Director and an Associate Professor in the Marriage and Family Therapy Program at Syracuse University. She has been teaching, conducting research, and practicing family therapy for over fifteen years. She is a Conservative Jew, is married, and has four children.

Annette B. Fromm, PhD, is a culturally active Jew living in Miami Beach, Florida, where she is Director of Education at the Jewish Museum of Florida. As a child of a mixed marriage, Greek Jewish and Ashkenazi, she was raised with an appreciation of cultural diversity. She has worked in a number of capacities in different kinds of museums, including a multiethnic museum in Cleveland, Ohio, and a regional Jewish museum in Tulsa, Oklahoma. She also developed Native American exhibits for a major natural history museum.

Helen Gardner, PhD, is an Australian who started her career as a research biochemist and moved into computer programming and systems analysis. In 1989, she decided she would rather work with people than with things and became a Community Development Officer and Coordinator of Volunteers for a Jewish Welfare Agency. She completed a doctorate in family psychology in 1996 and currently teaches research methodology to postgraduate counseling students at La Trobe University. Although Jewish by birth, she was reared as a devout Christian in a rural setting by a paid nanny. She returned to live as a Jew with her mother at age nine. She is currently an observant Jew living in metropolitan Melbourne, Australia.

Born in 1957, **Celia Gartenberg, MA,** lives in Seattle, Washington, with her husband, Dov, a Conservative congregational rabbi, and three children, Zachary, Moriel, and Fay. She is the Director of Development and Marketing for Jewish Family Service, occasionally acting as cantorial soloist for local congregations and training Bar/Bat Mitzvah students. Her mother is a convert. Celia was raised in the Reform movement of Judaism. As a young adult, she underwent an Orthodox conversion and is now a practicing Conservative Jew.

Naomi Graetz, BHL, MA, is a former native Manhattanite who has lived in Israel since 1967. She teaches English at Ben Gurion University of the Negev in Beersheba, Israel. She is the author of *S/He Created Them: Feminist Retellings of Biblical Stories* (Professional Press, 1993), a collection of her original midrashim, and *Silence is Deadly: Judaism Confronts Wifebeating* (Jason Aronson, 1998). She is a Masorti (Conservative) Jewish woman whose husband is a pulpit rabbi. She is one of the regular Torah readers and runs a Rosh Hodesh group for women in her congregation. Her novel, *The Rabbi's Wife Plays at Tennis,* is in search of a publisher.

Barbara Green, MA, JD, is a retired lawyer, community organizer, peace activist, and secular Jew living in Washington, DC. She serves on the international board of the New Israel Fund and occasionally attends services at the Havurah Fabrangen.

Marjorie Hoffman, MA, MS, was raised in the Bronx in the 1950s and 1960s, in a predominantly Jewish neighborhood. Her mother, an artist and art teacher, greatly influenced her, and Marjorie followed directly in her footsteps. She is a sculptor and teacher. However, she sees herself primarily as a parent. Her father, who discarded his Orthodox upbringing as a young man, gave Marjorie a strong Jewish identity but nothing in the way of religious or cultural education. Marjorie first learned about such holidays as Purim and Simhas Torah when she met her husband. Marrying into a more religious family and having her own children set her on her present path of seeking greater connection to Judaism.

Barbara D. Holender is a seventy-two-year-old mother of two, grandmother of three, and author of three books of poetry and a children's book in Hebrew. Her family belonged to a Conservative synagogue until Barbara's teen years, when they joined Reform Temple Beth Zion in Buffalo, New York, to which she still belongs. Her background was strongly Zionist, focused then and now on Jewish education and observance, community service, and Israel. (Photo © Layle Silbert, 1995)

Ellen Narotzky Kennedy earned her PhD in Marketing from the University of Minnesota and is completing a doctorate in sociology. She is currently Professor of Marketing at the University of St. Thomas in St. Paul, Minnesota. Ellen was raised as a Reform Jew in Ishpeming, a small town in northern Michigan. Her father was a first-generation American raised in Ishpeming in an Orthodox Jewish household, and her mother, from the East Coast, was Reform. All four grandparents were Eastern European immigrants. Ellen is the divorced mother of two children whose father is not Jewish. She is very involved in Reform Jewish life through synagogue participation and leadership as well as research and speaking on current issues in Judaism.

Sharla Green Kibel is a thirty-nine-year-old Jewish mother married to a Jewish husband. They were both raised in southern Africa and have two daughters, ages six and two. Sharla's grandparents were Ashkenazi Jews from Poland, Lithuania, and Russia, and she was educated at a Hebrew day school within a white, middle-class South African community. Most Jews of her childhood called themselves Orthodox but in practice behaved like American Conservative Jews. Sharla now lives and works as a psychotherapist in the Bay Area in California, where she has been able to experience a rich diversity of Jewish practice. As an adult, Sharla has affiliated with Reconstructionist and Reform congregations. She thinks of herself as a postdenominational Jew, who wishes to drink from all the wells available.

Michele Landsberg is the author of three books, an award-winning staff columnist for the *Toronto Star,* and a noted Canadian feminist. Her father was born in Toronto in 1894 into the Katznelson family of Russian left-wing Zionist renown. Her mother, smuggled out of Russia as an infant, came to Canada later as a child. Michele joined a Reconstructionist congregation in Toronto when her children were young. She is now formally unaffiliated, except with Esther Broner's Feminist Seder, which was her pathway back to meaningful Jewish ritual.

Amia Lieblich, PhD, was born in Tel Aviv, Israel, and has lived most of her life in Jerusalem. She has two sons and a daughter. She is a psychologist and a writer, and teaches at the Hebrew University of Jerusalem. Raised in a Jewish Orthodox home by parents who immigrated from Poland in 1936, she is, however, a secular woman today. Among her recent books is

Conversations with Dvora (1997), a psychobiography of Jewish author Dvora Baron.

Mira Morgenstern, PhD, was brought up in the Orthodox Jewish community, in which she continues to live with her family. Her education, like that of her children, has always proceeded along double tracks. She received an Orthodox day school education that included in-depth study of biblical texts as well as a college-preparatory curriculum. She completed the course for the Hebrew Teachers' Diploma at Yeshiva University, and also received her doctorate in political theory from Princeton University. She has published a feminist reading of Rousseau, *Rousseau and the Politics of Ambiguity,* and is currently working on a study of the concept of political community in the Hebrew Bible.

Stephanie Palladino, MEd, initially had a professional career as a high school teacher of Spanish language and literature. In 1990 she received certification as an elementary-school counselor and now works in that capacity at a small elementary school in rural western Massachusetts. As the product of a secular Jewish upbringing, she was surprised and later pleased by her teenage daughter's seemingly spontaneous interest in Judaism. A strong desire to explore her Jewish identity eventually led her daughter to Auschwitz, which she visited as a participant in The March of the Living. Her experience there stimulated Stephanie to examine facets of her own Jewish identity, which she previously had overlooked. Her prose poem in this volume documents part of that process.

Shulamit Reinharz, PhD, is Professor of Sociology, Director of Women's Studies, and Founding Director of the Hadassah Research Institute on Jewish Women, all at Brandeis University, and mother of Yael (twenty-two) and Naomi (seventeen).

Shelley Peterman Schwarz, BS, lives in Madison, Wisconsin, with David, her husband of thirty years. They are both active members of Temple Beth El, a Reform congregation. Shelley has distinguished herself by meeting the personal and professional challenges of living and working with multiple sclerosis. An award-winning writer, businesswoman, and professional motivational speaker, Ms. Schwarz uses her experiences to help others challenged by life's ups and downs.

Alice Shalvi was born in Germany in 1926 into a modern-Orthodox Zionist family. Educated in England, she emigrated to Israel in 1949. She was a faculty member in the English Department at Hebrew University of Jerusalem from 1950 to 1990, Principal of Pelech Experimental High School for girls from 1975 to 1990, and has been Founding Chairwoman of the Israel Women's Network since 1984. A lifelong feminist whose desire for an egalitarian religious framework led her to Conservative Judaism, she has, since 1997, been the Rector of the Schechter Institute for Jewish Studies, the Jerusalem affiliate of the Jewish Theological Seminary of America. Professor Shalvi married Moshe Shalvi in 1950; they have three sons, three daughters, and numerous grandchildren. (Photo © Joan Roth)

Sharon L. Siegel, PhD, MFT, is a Jewish old Crone. She is a feminist psychotherapist in private practice in West Hollywood, California, Clinical Coordinator at an agency for the homeless in Los Angeles, and is very active in the Association for Women in Psychology. Fluently bilingual and biliteral in Spanish, Siegel lives in the multicultural fast lane. She was a peace activist during the Vietnam War, present in the United Farmworker strikes, and remains involved in Touch in Peace, an organization of Israeli Jewish and Palestinian Arab professionals. She is a member of Congregation Kol Ami, a lesbian/gay Reform synagogue. Bat Mitzvahed at age forty-three, she enjoys a deep spring of various spiritualities. Siegel resonates with the Goddess-centered rituals of Feminist Dianic Traditions and insists that tikkun olam (the Jewish ethic of repairing the world) is actually handled quite well by many kinds of people.

Marcia Cohn Spiegel, MA, earned her degree in Jewish Communal Service from Hebrew Union College–Jewish Institute of Religion. She is working to create change in the attitudes of the Jewish community toward addiction, violence, and sexual abuse. She is the founder of the Alcoholism/Drug Action Program of Jewish Family Service, Los Angeles, as well as L'Chaim: 12 Steps to Recovery. She is author of *The Heritage of Noah: Alcoholism in the Jewish Community Today,* and co-author of *The Jewish Women's Awareness Guide* and *Women Speak to God: The Poems and Prayers of Jewish Women.* Her Lithuanian grandparents were Orthodox; her parents were Conservative. She is a member of a Conservative synagogue, but feels most at home in Jewish Renewal or Reconstructionist settings. She is a member of B'not Esh and Shabbat Shenit, feminist spiritual communities.

Béatrice Steinberg was raised as a Catholic in France. After marrying her American Jewish husband, she committed to live in the United States and raise their children Jewish. The family became active in a Reform congregation. Béatrice eventually converted to Judaism and recently celebrated her adult Bat Mitzvah. She is a full-time Chief Financial Officer with an art publishing company and lives in Boston with her husband and their two daughters.

Marlena Thompson, MLS, a former Director of Judaic Studies in a day school, has published over 100 articles in magazines and newspapers and has had short stories and essays anthologized. In 1998 Behrman House published her collection of children's poems, *Let's Discover God,* which will soon be followed by her children's poems about values. Her first novel, *A Rare & Deadly Issue,* will be published in 2001. She is of Eastern European extraction with a diluted, but still honored, Sephardic heritage, and is currently unaffiliated with any synagogue or denomination.

Chawwa Wijnberg, born in 1942, was hidden with her mother in a small village near Amsterdam during World War II. Her father, a resistance fighter, was shot dead in 1943. Trained as a sculptor, she married and lived in Israel from 1965 to 1974. The mother of two, she started writing in 1980 and has published two books of poetry. She is now divorced and lives with her woman friend in Kockengen, near Utrecht. Chawwa's daughter, **Janine Beulink, MA,** was born in Tel Aviv in 1970. She studied film and television in Amsterdam and Canterbury, England. She is currently working as a journalist for the *Dutch Jewish Weekly* and as an editor for its monthly youth supplement. The letters in this book make up the first chapter of a book of letters they plan to publish. (Photo © Jaime R. Halegua)

 **Lois Young-Tulin** lives in the Philadelphia area. A writer and teacher, she has published numerous poems and articles, as well as the book *Escape Roots* (1994), and has recently completed a book about her relationship with Sophie Tucker, a third cousin. Her father's family were Russian Jews who immigrated to America in the late 1880s. She is a fourth-generation American-born Dutch Jew on her mother's side.

Introduction

Rachel Josefowitz Siegel
Ellen Cole
Susan Steinberg-Oren

THE BEGINNING

Susan: The idea for this book flashed in my head as I was packing for my brother-in-law's wedding in Israel. I had just finished reading *Celebrating the Lives of Jewish Women: Patterns in a Feminist Sampler*, edited by Rachel and Ellen (Siegel and Cole, 1997) in which I was one of the authors. I had also contributed a chapter to *Jewish Women in Therapy: Seen but Not Heard* (Siegel and Cole, 1991). It seemed to me that many essays in both books touched on motherhood, but the theme of Jewish mothering was not highlighted. What about a collection of essays pertaining to Jewish mothers, the topic nearest and dearest to my heart? When I saw Rachel in Israel, the project was born.

Rachel: Sue approached me in April 1998 with her idea. She had in mind a collection of personal articles about Jewish mothers, written in the Jewish mother's own voice. Sue's idea appealed to me immediately, and when I shared it with Ellen she was equally enthusiastic. So our trusted team of Siegel and Cole has become Siegel, Cole, and Steinberg-Oren. We invited a handful of writers whose work we admire and put out a wide call for proposals. We were nearly overwhelmed with responses—close to 100 proposals from Jewish mothers all over the world, in various kinds of Jewish, interfaith, and intercultural families, including writers, poets, teachers, artists, mental health practitioners, and academic scholars.

Ellen: Rachel and I have worked together for ten years, first focusing on mental health issues of Jewish women and then on a celebration of their (and our) lives, paralleling a shift in psychology itself, from a problem-centered discipline to one that also looks at life satisfaction and well-being. When I was offered the opportunity to work with Rachel and Sue on a third book in what is now a trilogy about Jewish women, I jumped at the chance. What could be more central to life than the growing of lives? What could be more central to the very idea of Jewishness than the Jewish mother herself?

THE STEREOTYPE: VILIFIED AND IDEALIZED

I can remember the first time I referred to myself as a Jewish mother. We had just moved into a predominantly non-Jewish neighborhood. I was describing my worries about my son and daughter's adjustment to their new preschools and community, as well as a transition to kindergarten in a couple of months. Excusing my anxious thoughts to my new non-Jewish friend, I said, "What can I say—I'm a Jewish mother." We both laughed, but the statement jolted me. By birth, I am a Jewish mother, but what did I really mean? Was I overprotective, anxious, and intrusive, as my internalized negative stereotype implied, at least to me? Then I began to wonder whether the concept of Jewish mother even continues to be relevant for my generation, for mothers of young children at the beginning of the twenty-first century. What does the term mean to non-Jews? To Jews? As a Jewish mother today, who am I?

Susan Steinberg-Oren

What does the term "Jewish mother" suggest to Jews and non-Jews today? To begin to explore this question, Ellen conducted a ministudy in Anchorage, Alaska, a city with a small Jewish population. A non-Jewish graduate student, Shelley Wilson-Schoessler, went to a popular shopping mall and asked 100 people at random to respond to the following question: "What is the first thing that goes through your mind when I say the term 'Jewish mother'? Please don't censor."

Responses fell roughly into three categories. About a third of the respondents gave more or less neutral answers, saying things such as: they had no idea, Jewish mothers are just like anybody else, they didn't know any Jewish people, "healthy and married," "steeped in tradition," "wearing a robe and taking care of children," "chicken soup," and "a peasant woman, rag on her head, in the kitchen feeding everyone."

Another third gave positive responses, including the following: "A strong worker with family support." "Kind." "Strong family ties." "A little round jolly person, good worker, wants to make everybody happy." "A momma who loves her children and protects them, gives them good counsel and cares about what they do; intelligent." "Caring, respected, loving, religious, and smart." "Passionate, a good wife, involved with her children." "Caring and playful." "They're great mothers; family oriented, traditional, loved, and compassionate." "Caring eyes, interested in what I have to say."

Mildly negative responses included "worrying about everything" and "someone nagging who makes you eat all the time." Some of the more strongly negative responses included: "Condescending—their children are better than my children." "Overprotective and pushy, Yiddish accent, makes others feel guilty." "Passive-aggressive; someone not to have against you." "Bitch, guilt, clinging, I've yet to meet a submissive Jewish mother" (this response was from one of only a few Jews in the sample). "A bitch, ruling everybody's life, can't stand it if she's not in charge." "Big and overweight, trying to interfere." "Strict and mean to children." "She is oppressed and so is everyone around her." "Bitchy penny-pincher, won't spend for anything, runs everything and everybody, like Seinfeld's mother." "Big nose, nagging, and nosy." "Spoiled, rich, nagging, and domineering." And so on. The stereotype is alive and well, at least in one urban area.

Turning to the literature, only a few articles have been published about the Jewish Mother stereotype (Beck, 1991; Siegel, 1987, 1999). From Ellen's ministudy, these and other writings, and our own experiences and observations, it became clear to us that biased attitudes toward Jewish mothers continue to exist. Furthermore, these attitudes comingle with anti-Semitic stereotypes about Jews in general, such as "all Jews are rich and stingy," or "smart and paranoid."

Derogatory remarks about Jewish mothers are so commonly unquestioned and so pervasive that it is easy to ignore the underlying insult. Furthermore, objections to the negative caricature are frequently met with replies such as, "Well, you haven't met *my* mother," followed by a list of negative traits that are supposed to prove that Jewish mothers really are overprotective, anxious, intrusive, controlling, and possessive. Or they are met with the defense that Jewish mothers are really honored and admired among Jews, a statement that conveys the idealized version of the stereotype and denies the reality of the insult.

Vilified or idealized, stereotypical assumptions about Jewish mothers are two sides of the same coin. What is admired in one is rejected and ridiculed in the other as being excessive, not fitting into mainstream American culture, not fitting into the gender roles that are assigned to women and men in America. Both of these stereotypes have a profound impact on all Jewish mothers and Jewish women. They usually make us feel bad.

Jewish women who are not mothers feel bad because the idealization of Jewish mothers leaves no room for any other female role within a Jewish context. Jewish mothers who do not live up to the idealized image feel bad because they think that they should be able to. On the other hand, Jewish mothers who are generously loving, proud of their children, and devoted to their families feel bad because they are haunted by the fear of being or appearing to be like the ridiculed negative caricature. We may stifle our creativity, warmth, caring, and expressiveness for fear of being called a Jewish Mother. Furthermore, having absorbed these images into our own view of Jewish mothers, having internalized these oppressive messages, we judge one another by that measure. We judge ourselves, our own mothers, our sisters, our friends.

A large number of the proposals for our book started with the author's assessment of how far she had or had wanted to deviate from a generic, ill-defined Jewish Mother image. This image contained elements of the idealized Jewish Mother that could be traced to Jewish tradition or to personal memories of a loving Bobbe, an all-accepting, unconditionally loving grandmother. The image also contained elements of the caricature that could be traced to frequently heard and commonly accepted jokes or to the personal experience of an imperfect mother with unacceptable traits. Some of these authors used the Jewish mother stereotype as a kind of yardstick by which to measure themselves. They wondered, "Am I as good as the idealized Jewish mother?" or "Am I as bad as the caricature?"

To some extent, many of us have absorbed the gender norms and family values that are historically rooted in the Jewish experience of ghetto life and persecution. These ethnocultural patterns can surely be acknowledged without being turned into the viciously blaming caricatures that are proclaimed by some Jewish men, by some non-Jews, and even by mental health professionals. In fact, what we found most touching were the accounts of Jewish mothers who looked beyond the stereotype and wrote lovingly about what they had learned to do or not to do from their own Jewish mothers, separating the traits they admired from the ones they tried to reject.

While some of the qualities that are assigned to Jewish mothers are true of some Jewish mothers, they are also true of other mothers, especially immigrant mothers, and may even be found among men. Also, among all mothers, including Jewish mothers, there are some who are mean, cold, neglectful, and even abusive. But the recognition of such behaviors does not justify the anger, ridicule, and abuse heaped upon Jewish mothers in general.

The big question is, why are there so many jokes about Jewish mothers? The only possible explanation is that it is OK in our culture to express anti-Semitism when it is combined with woman-hating and not directed at Jewish men, and perhaps also to express woman-hating when it is combined with anti-Semitism and not directed at non-Jewish women. Far too many Jews will laugh at the sexism and far too many women will laugh at the anti-Semitism. Such jokes would never be tolerated if used about another ethnic or religious group, nor would they be tolerated if used against Jewish men. We need to keep this in mind when we laugh at or repeat jokes about Jewish mothers.

BEYOND THE STEREOTYPES

In this book, we wanted to get beyond the stereotypes by presenting the stories of real Jewish mothers at the turn of this century, in their diversity and with the complexities of their lives. When we have told people that we are editing a book about Jewish mothers, the response has generally been predictable. First there is a slightly puzzled, slightly deprecating smile. Then, when they understand that this is not a collection of Jewish Mother jokes, come the questions. "Why Jewish mothers? Do you really think that Jewish mothers are different?" And then, perhaps, from some more thoughtful people, "Well, what kind of Jewish mothers are you talking about?" These are actually good questions, although they sometimes reflect the same male-centered attitudes that caused people in earlier decades to ask, "Why are you focusing on women?" "What's so special or so different about women?" "What kind of women?" Only now it is an attitude that is not only male-centered, but ignorant or naive about Jews, and possibly anti-Semitic. These questions are about the validity of spending time and energy on a topic that others consider to be nothing but a joke, and a bad one at that.

Ellyn Kaschak (1997) said, "First there are the questions." Questions are clearly important and legitimate. Even when we cannot give any answers, or when the answers keep shifting, we must keep asking the questions. We, as editors, amassed a long list of questions in the early stages, for the work could not proceed without them:

- Who are we, those of us who are Jewish mothers?
- Do we have identifiable characteristics?
- What is Jewish about Jewish mothers?
- What is Jewish about our mothering?
- How do we differ from mothers who are not Jewish?
- How do we differ from Jewish women who are not mothers?
- How do we differ from one another?
- What issues do we have in common?
- What are the external circumstances that affect our lives?
- Upon what internal resources do we draw?
- Do we share similar Jewish values, rituals, historic memories?
- Do we agree on politics?
- Do we agree on anything at all?

We ask you, the reader, to keep these questions in mind while reading this book, for you will find partial answers in each essay, while complete answers remain elusive. Human nature is endlessly complex.

ISSUES AND THEMES

While each of us came to this project with years of thinking, reading, and talking with and about Jewish women and Jewish mothers, we now have a deeper and richer understanding of what Jewish mothers are feeling, thinking about, and wanting to write about. Granted this is a skewed sample, based on mothers who had the skills, the inclination, and the urge to respond to our call for papers. And while we shall continue to refer to "mothers" as the book's organizing principle, it is important to note that our contributors include a Jewish lesbian writing about how the Jewish motherhood imperative affects the lives of Jewish women who are not mothers. We are more aware than ever of the impossibility of including all aspects of Jewish mothers' experiences in any one book or even trying to convey the complexities and diversities of our Jewish cultural backgrounds. Yet some themes have emerged that indicate commonality.

Most but not all Jewish mothers in our collection refer to their Jewishness in terms of religious observance, assigning less importance to the broad range of secular Jewish activities and interests that express their ethnic, historical, cultural, political, culinary, and emotional Jewishness.

The Jewish identity of Jewish mothers, on the whole, seems to be fluid over the course of a lifetime, consisting of a continuing process of growth and change, frequently but not always in response to our children's perceived needs and our children's choices. Even where the authors indicate that they continue to live within the Reform, Conservative, Orthodox, or secular tradition of their parents, they write about an evolving inner consciousness and a maturing concurrent change in the external expression of their Jewishness. We can assume that there are others who do not deviate from the ways of their childhood, but they did not write to us.

Anti-Semitism is a pervasive reality in the mothering decisions that Jewish mothers make. Our authors are emotionally affected in ways that may alter their behavior as Jewish mothers by exposure to ignorant assumptions by non-Jewish neighbors or teachers, isolated fairly mild anti-Semitic incidents, and haunting Holocaust memories. Another driving force in Jewish mothering is the isolation of

Jewish families in predominantly non-Jewish environments. Although these negative factors can drive Jewish mothers toward observance of Jewish rituals, and toward creating or invigorating Jewish communities, the sexism and exclusivity of some Jewish congregations may drive others away from organized Judaism.

Many of the Jewish mothers in this collection honor the cultural and geographic backgrounds of their own Jewish mothers as factors that still have an impact on their attitudes and behaviors, whether or not they have chosen to reject some of their mothers' traits or ways of interacting in the world.

Authors in this collection have written about raising children in the Diaspora (outside of Israel), living in the shadow of the Holocaust, raising soldier-sons in Israel, living with disabilities, the significance of Jewish values, tikkun olam (healing or repairing the world), the importance of religion, spirituality, and feminism in their lives, conversion to Judaism, coming to terms with their own and their children's unconventional choices, "mixed" marriages, conscious Jewish identification, ways to mother, and even the effect of bureaucracy on raising children. They write of the "unbinding love" that makes it possible to make painful or unpopular decisions as a Jewish mother.

Words have different meanings to different people and in different contexts. The words "Jewish mother" and "Jewish family" have different meanings today than they did even some twenty years ago. Betty Friedan, in a recent Cornell University talk about American families, stressed the importance of changing the paradigm. The same can be said about Jewish families and Jewish mothers. Today's Jewish mothers, as reflected in this volume, are nearly always working mothers. Many are divorced, some are openly lesbian or bisexual, some are single mothers. Many are married to non-Jews. (An article in *Forward* [Gootman, 1999, pp. 1, 2] reported that "52% of Jews getting married between 1985 and 1990 were marrying non-Jews.") Jewish mothers may or may not be observant in their religious practices and, if they are observant, their beliefs and practices take many forms.

With the editing of this book, we have concluded that the problem with speaking about Jewish mothers is that few generalizations about them hold up across the board. We can make observations about some of the external factors that affect Jewish mothers, and we can identify some of the cultural and historic messages that shape the inner landscape of our psyches. But even here we find great variations. We have brought together the voices of Jewish mothers to tell their own stories, to tell anecdotes and vignettes about what is Jewishly significant to them in their own lives. And, indeed, these stories contain some of the answers, some of the differences and similarities among us, some of the issues and themes that are important to us as Jewish mothers.

IN CONCLUSION

During our combined ninety-seven years as Jewish mothers (Rachel, fifty-five years; Ellen, thirty-four years; Sue, eight years), we have lived through many changes in the expression of our Jewishness, and so have our children. What feels important is that the Jewish dimensions of our lives, however we may express them, continue to be important to each of us.

Jewish mothers have held a strange and special place in the Jewish history that was written by Jewish men. We have been revered and idealized as Foremothers, Sarah, Rebekah, Rachel, and Leah, yet unnamed and unsung in biblical genealogies. Few have been honored while many have been made invisible.

Today, in our own lifetimes, something extraordinary is happening. Jewish women and Jewish mothers have begun to document our own history, to speak and write in our own voices, to truly honor ourselves, our mothers, and our daughters. May we keep asking our own questions and writing our own wisdom. May we go from strength to strength, l'dor v'dor.

As editors, we are grateful to our contributors, individually and as a group, for entrusting us with their personal stories, vignettes, poems, prayers, and sermons. They have made us cry, and laugh, and feel, and think more deeply. We hope that you, the reader, will savor each contribution on its own, and let it touch your soul.

REFERENCES

Beck, Evelyn Torton. (1991). Therapy's double dilemma: Antisemitism and misogyny. In R.J. Siegel and E. Cole (Eds.), *Jewish women in therapy: Seen but not heard* (pp. 19-30). Binghamton, NY: Harrington Park Press.

Gootman, Elissa. (1999). 2000 census will explore renaissance: Queries to focus on identity. *Forward*, Vol. C11, No. 31224 (February 19): 1-2.

Kaschak, Ellyn. (1997). First there are the questions. In R.J. Siegel and E. Cole (Eds.), *Celebrating the lives of Jewish women: Patterns in a feminist sampler* (pp. 247-258). Binghamton, NY: Harrington Park Press.

Siegel, Rachel Josefowitz. (1987). Antisemitism and sexism in stereotypes of Jewish women. In D. Howard (Ed.), *Dynamics of feminist therapy* (pp. 249-257). Binghamton, NY: The Haworth Press.

Siegel, Rachel Josefowitz. (1999). *Jewish mothers: Beyond the stereotype.* Unpublished invited address upon accepting the 1998 Jewish Caucus Award for Ellen Cole and Rachel Josefowitz Siegel, Association for Women in Psychology Annual Meeting, Providence, RI.

Siegel, Rachel Josefowitz and Cole, Ellen (Eds.). (1991). *Jewish women in therapy: Seen but not heard.* Binghamton, NY: Harrington Park Press.

Siegel, Rachel Josefowitz and Cole, Ellen (Eds.). (1997). *Celebrating the lives of Jewish women: Patterns in a feminist sampler.* Binghamton, NY: Harrington Park Press.

SECTION I:
TRADITIONS

1

From Generation to Generation

Alice Shalvi

THE BEST PART OF THE DAY

Looking back at my childhood—as I now do with increasing frequency and ever-growing intensity—I realize that many of the functions usually performed by mothers were, in my case, carried out primarily by my mother's mother, who lived with my parents from their marriage in 1920 until her death eighteen years later.

My grandmother was not a jovial woman. Her passport photo—the only likeness of her that survives, apart from the small one that peers out of the large family group photograph taken at my parents' wedding—shows a long, rather lugubrious, wrinkled face, sad eyes, an unsmiling mouth—all perhaps indicative of the poverty, the hardship, the losses, the suffering she had endured in the Galician shtetl where she gave birth to her five children. There she had run a small grocery store while her husband, a devout scholar, sat both days and many nights studying in the beit midrash. Thence she had been deported together with her family, during World War I, to be returned there once the territory was recaptured. In the bitter winter of the transportation she had lost one of her three daughters to typhoid fever. During that same war, her youngest son, an ardent communist who every Friday stole one of the challot she had baked to give to someone poorer, had run away to join the revolutionary forces in Russia. At the end of the war, her husband died. An older son and daughter were already married and had moved elsewhere. She was left alone with my mother.

My father, her nephew, who had fought in the Austrian army, made a detour on his way home to Germany from captivity in

Russia, to see how his relatives were faring. He met my mother. The next year he sent for her and they married. She brought her mother with her, either because she herself wanted the support of someone who knew and loved her as she entered a new phase of her life, became acquainted with a new country, a new family, a new culture; or because, a dutiful daughter, she did not want to leave her mother to struggle on alone. Germany spelled, perhaps, hope.

My grandmother amply repaid my parents' welcoming hospitality—though I am certain none of them ever perceived their relationship in this cold, reckoning way. While my mother partnered my father in their small wholesale business, my grandmother took over the cooking and baking, at which she excelled. I particularly recall the little challah rolls—one round, the other long and plaited—which she made for my brother and myself every Friday, in addition to the two large and splendid ones that provided for the rest of those at table. And her cherry cake—a flat baking tin of pastry, piled with luscious, sweet-smelling fruit, oozing its purple-red juices. . . .

For most of the years of my childhood, until her death, we shared a bedroom, so that I became acquainted with her most intimate habits.

She kept her scanty belongings in a cardboard box under her bed, rather than in a cupboard, perhaps in order to facilitate removal should she ever again have to flee from home. Here she kept her two wigs—the everyday one and the "best" one for Shabbat and Yomtov; the kerchiefs which she wore on top on her wig; her siddur and her Yiddish Teitsch-Humash, a thick volume bound in rich dark-red leather, decorated on the front cover with a gilt centerpiece on which were engraved the Hebrew words of its title—Torah, Nevi'im, Ketuvim.

Every morning, as I lazed in bed, half-awake, half-asleep, I would watch as she carefully combed her wispy silver hair, donned the wig, tied over it the kerchief of her choice, and went over to the corner of the room to recite the morning prayers.

Often, in the afternoons, I would ask her to tell me stories. Then she would amuse me with tales of the shtetl, singling out various of her customers who were distinguished either because of some vagary or because they committed some deed—brave or foolish—worthy of record in a kind of folk narrative, a saga that she composed for my benefit. Interestingly enough, many of these narratives were marked by a humor which, given the sadness of her portrait, one would not have supposed her to possess. I never tired of hearing these stories and very soon some of their key phrases became catchwords in our conversational exchanges, a kind of secret code that my older brother could not comprehend.

But the best part of the day came once I was in bed. Then my grandmother would take out her Teitsch-Humash and, opening it at one of the numerous reproductions of etchings and engravings, which served as illustrations, would tell me The Story. Fascinated, I would listen, relating to the characters as though they, too, had been part of the shtetl experience, people my grandmother had met and known intimately. Nonetheless, even as a young child I was aware that the characters of The Book, unlike those of my grandmother's strictly oral narratives, had an aura of holiness about them that derived precisely from their being enshrined in a real book, in pictures as well as text, not merely in my grandmother's memory. Yet Moishe Rabbenu, majestically stretching out his rod to part the waters of the Red Sea, was as real to me as Yossel der Roiter who, in his eagerness to steal a pushke of meat while my grandmother's back was turned, foolishly picked a can at the foot of the display, toppling the entire pyramid down on his luckless self.

Finally, when the evening's episode came to an end, my grandmother, sitting on the bed by my side, would recite the Shema with me, carefully intoning each word for me to repeat until, by the age of about four, I was able to say the prayer by myself, as she listened to check that I'd got all the words right. The clear, though never explicitly stated, implication was that if one recited these words before falling asleep, no harm would befall one during the night. So, having intoned the prayer, I would close my eyes and, firmly clasping my grandmother's hand for further reassurance, would settle down to sleep. A favorite ruse of mine was to *pretend* to be asleep, to wait till my grandmother began slowly, gently, carefully to withdraw her hand, and then to snatch it back. I was afraid of the dark and needed the reassurance of her presence, but I couldn't bring myself to confess what I assume she in any case realized, that I was scared of being alone, even if I *had* said the Shema. And so I kept her at my side with this "practical joke," in which she (I hope willingly) colluded.

*   *   *

Today, I once again live in a three-generational household. My youngest daughter, named Pnina after my mother, and her husband and little daughter live with us, inhabiting what were once our children's rooms.

I speak English to my beloved Batsheva (who is named after her great-grandmother, my husband's mother). I read her English nursery rhymes and other children's classics that were never part of my own childhood. But, as my greatest pleasure of the day, I recite the Shema to her when she seems ready to go to sleep. She follows my lips closely as I bend over her. Recently she has begun, as yet soundlessly, to articulate the words herself. I am longing for the day when she will echo them.

The Teitsch-Humash, unfortunately, has disappeared. I am searching for a suitable replacement—a fat volume with impressive illustrations—but I doubt whether I shall find anything as beautiful or evocative as that red-leather-bound gold-engraved book from which I derived my first awareness of being a part of the Jewish people and its history.

BEGGING TO DIFFER

My mother was a worrier. Like the proverbial Yiddishe Mamme she bustled about us, like a fussy hen around her chicks, expressing concern with numerous clucks—of anxiety, disapproval, wise (as I now realize) counsel, warning. Her excessive attention frequently irritated my brother and me, who longed for greater independence, the right to learn from our own mistakes, to live our own lives.

She was especially critical of the people to whom we were sexually attracted. My brother, sensibly, never brought any girlfriends home, but somehow—intuitively, it would seem—my mother managed to learn a great deal about them. Needless to say, none was good enough for her gifted firstborn. Either they were too lowborn, or they were arrogant, or they weren't moral. No wonder he never married during her lifetime. In any case, she took care of what she considered his every need. She cooked, she baked, she mended. When she had what proved to be her final, near-fatal stroke while she was on a visit to us in Jerusalem, her only concern was that she *must* return to London, for who would send his shirts to the laundry on time? Similarly, as she lay on her deathbed at Hadassah Hospital, tubes protruding from nose and veins, she turned to me to remind me there was no bread in the house for the next day's school sandwiches. They were her last words to me.

I was less cautious than my brother and did bring my boyfriends home, only for them to be subjected to precisely the same kind of critical scrutiny. Nobody was wholly satisfactory, though some proved more eligible than others. My own desires were swept aside as the product of foolish, immature, romantic sentimentalism.

Meanwhile, like my brother, I enjoyed all the fruits of my mother's labors. Every Friday while I was at college in Cambridge I would receive a carefully packed parcel of roast chicken and my mother's wonderful rogalkes, delicious little cakes stuffed with cinnamon and raisins. Every week I would send home a parcel of laundry to be washed and ironed.

When I returned from Israel during the summers to visit my parents, the first meal I was served consisted of all my favorite foods, unobtainable, undreamed of, in the austerity of Israel's early statehood: salmon, asparagus, and strawberries and cream. Just as earlier in my childhood, my mother would sit at the other side of the table, watching me with evident vicarious enjoyment, delighting in my pleasure.

She seldom ate an entire meal herself. She was busy in the kitchen, busy serving us, busy ensuring that our plates—and those of guests—were instantly replenished once the first serving had been consumed. Because she tended to gain weight easily, she thought that by not eating she would remain slimmer. But since she also hated to see any food go to waste (a permanent source of distress for any of us who have ever endured food shortages and rationing), she would later, surreptitiously, finish off all the edible scraps brought into the kitchen.

I loved my mother, but early on I determined not to be like her. I would not go around dusting and polishing while my family were peacefully sitting in the living room trying to read or listen to music. I would have a profession other than homemaking. I would not interfere in my children's private lives, not criticize their friends as unsuitable.

But oh, dear! What have I come to realize? Concern for one's children is all too natural a phenomenon (see Genesis, passim). One does want to see them well-nourished, eating wholesome home cooking rather than fast food. One wants them to go out looking respectable, decently dressed, well-kempt, with handkerchiefs in their pockets. Not to smoke, not to get drunk, not to marry the wrong person. One's children are, as it were, an advertisement for oneself as a parent. Bearing our names, they are like athletes whose shorts or shirts bear the logo of their sponsors. I am my daughter's Adidas, my son's Nike. And so I find myself replicating my mother, more than I ever thought I would. I am not quite so single-minded, because I do have a profession; I do have many extrafamilial interests. But, as I have painfully discovered, my children, too, frequently think of me as a clucking hen.

"Control yourself," I say to myself. "Keep out of it." But my mother's (*any* mother's?) innermost feelings all too often overcome me. Just as the face I see in my mirror increasingly resembles hers, so does my maternal concern. Perhaps that is just an inevitable fact of being a mother, of being a daughter.

I wonder, are my daughters like *me*?

2

How I Learned to Be a Jewish Mother

Michele Landsberg

My four-year-old son sat at the kitchen table and asked innocently, "Does a Jewish nose have more red blood corpuscles than a gentile nose?" He had, it seems, been puzzling it out, all by himself. The woman next door, in our leafy new neighborhood in a Toronto suburb, had told him that you could always tell a Jew by his nose. As he explained it to me now, he reasoned that size or shape could not be the telltale sign, because these varied so dramatically. Therefore, it must be color. But how could the color of a nose differ from person to person? It must be the amount of red blood. This conclusion was baffling to him, however, since none of us seemed to have a red nose, so he brought his philosophic musings to me. I struggled between rage and wonder. To see this sweetly solemn child bringing to bear all the rational and scientific thinking of which he was capable—on a piece of moronic bigotry!

For years, in the 1960s and now at the beginning of the 1970s, I had blithely and perhaps willfully believed that the virulent anti-Semitism of my Toronto childhood was a thing of the past. Now, in a flash, I determined that my own three children would not suffer the shame and the hurt that marred my own primary-school years.

My parents observed the holidays in cursory fashion. A tin menorah, a couple of quarters and a lead dreidl, with no stories or songs to accompany them, did not make much of a bulwark against the red and green enchantments of the Christmas season that engulfed us. The daily anti-Semitism to which I was subjected at school, the forced hymn singing, the hateful remarks of principal and teachers, all hurt me deeply but also kindled my defiant loyalty to Jewishness. It was not, however, a particularly joyful allegiance.

If anti-Semitism still smoldered and burned—and we soon learned that it was endemic in this all-white, all-gentile suburb where most residents, both working and middle class, had an English ancestry—I would equip my children gloriously to soar above it, unsinged.

Problem: I was too left-wing, too agnostic, too feminist, to find any comfortable niche for my children in the stolidly conformist Jewish synagogues of those days. No alternative or progressive havurot or day schools existed in Toronto at that time. Second problem: my husband had grown up in a distinguished Bundist household (his father, David Lewis, was a founder and leader of Canada's third party, the social democratic New Democratic Party), where his parents spoke literary Yiddish but refused to celebrate holidays. He had little knowledge of Jewish practice. I was on my own. Well, not entirely: my parents had sent me, for ten years, to the Sunday school of the improbably named Holy Blossom Temple, Toronto's first Reform synagogue. This was where I had first conceived a profound distaste for materialistic display, watery grape juice in paper cups, and a social pecking order based on mink and cashmere (of which I had neither). At least I had learned something of the ritual year.

Even more fortunate was my youthful rebellion, which had led me into the arms of the Zionist youth movement. Zionism, in the eyes of the upwardly mobile Holy Blossomites of the 1950s, was a boat-rocking disgrace and a dangerous provocation to the surrounding gentiles. To me, it was an intellectual haven. Judaism was snatched back from the fur-bearing middle class and made vibrant again by our ardent readings of Zionist philosophers.

We pranced about in flowing costumes, performing Israeli folk dances to which we memorized the intricate steps; we summered at bare-bones tent camps where we pretended to be pioneers; we conducted Third Seders; eventually, many of us spent a post-high school year in Israel, studying at the Institute for Youth Leaders from Abroad, where I picked up the Hebrew that was reserved for boys at Holy Blossom. Despite my cynicism about religion—sharpened by youthful encounters with the foetid misogyny of Jerusalem's Hasidim—I enthusiastically self-identified as a "tribal" Jew.

Now, as a resolute Jewish-mother-in-training, I delved back into these various sources of fragmentary knowledge to see what could be borrowed, adapted, appropriated into progressive practice. And, I soon discovered, Judaism is tailor-made for appropriation. Almost all the festivals are centered on the home (No wonder Jewish identity is matrilineal! Without us, the whole enterprise would collapse.) and rich in symbolism.

Havdalah! I learned how to observe it by scrabbling through my old books, found a shop that sold elegantly twisted candles and silver spice boxes, and made a sensual celebration of every Saturday night. We sipped wine, sniffed cinnamon and cloves, and took turns sizzling out the flame in the wine. The prayer that thanks God for making a difference between night and day, Shabbat and the other days, Jews and the other nations, was a weekly source of lively discussion—and a way to remind my attentive little ones that we cherished our difference. I didn't miss the chance, as well, to point out that Judaism validates the glory of sensual pleasure.

On Succoth, we riotously built wobbly structures out of straw mats and poles, festooned them with strings of cranberries and grapes and danced about with lulavim we made from reeds, and later used to fight off marauding raccoons who gobbled the decorations.

Purim, I remembered from my time on kibbutz, was an occasion to give sweets to one's friends. My children and I made woven baskets out of dough, baked them golden, filled them with cakes and invitations to a Purim carnival, and delivered them to neighborhood friends. Our carnival (complete with megillah play, noisemakers, costumes, and carnival games with prizes) must have mystified our gentile friends, but we had a ball. Vashti, I taught the children, was a real feminist, refusing to dance naked for the drunken king. I knew the message had gotten through when our son, then six, made a sign for his Purim costume that read: "Ahashuerus was an MCP." He was astonished when his friends didn't know that was short for "male chauvinist pig."

Although by now the children were at a local public school, and being tormented by an anti-Semitic boy who hung swastikas over their desks and organized a gang to beat them up in the schoolyard, the Jewish calendar was still proving a rich cornucopia of delights to offset the pain of being targeted by bigots. Shamelessly, we turned Chanukah into an eight-night extravaganza of latkes, presents, prizes, and spinning dreidls. Despite the dazzle of Christmas lights, and trees, and carols, and school decorations and pageants and choirs and commercials and. . . . Despite the overwhelmingly and unselfconsciously Christian nature of a Toronto December, we made Chanukah even more wonderful.

Ah, but Passover. That was the highlight of the year, and completely, happily, hectically mad. Here, too, I found rituals that mesmerized the children with drama: the night before Passover, we organized a search for chametz. We turned off all the lights, took flashlights, and hunted through the excitingly darkened house for the carefully placed crumbs I had left on windowsills. Then we burned them in the fireplace, the flames throwing a warm light around the dark room.

My mother, a gifted cook, always helped with the dinner, arriving at our house with peppery gefilte fish and cloudlike Passover sponge cakes. Still, it was up to me to conduct the Seder as best I could, while dashing back and forth to the kitchen to check the matzo balls, stir the soup, turn the potatoes that were roasting to a deep caramel brown with the slow-simmering brisket. Since my mother could read no more Hebrew than my husband, it was I who read the Haggadah, coached the children in asking the Four Questions, chose the readings and orchestrated the entire event.

You can see the possibilities. This was a self-invented Passover, faithful to the spirit of the holiday, but with generous helpings of left-wing discussion, historic memory, and feminist interpretation.

Gradually, my husband joined in with his wonderful singing voice, contributing Yiddish versions of the "Peat Bog Soldiers" and freedom songs that became mandatory elements of our annual Seder. His musicality was a piece of luck: my own singing skills are lamentable. In later years, when we escaped from suburb to city and my children associated with other Jews as they prepared for their Bat and Bar Mitzvoth, they teased me that they had unknowingly absorbed from me some weirdly off-key versions of all the blessings—an anomaly they discovered only when they joined in the Shabbat prayers at friends' houses.

I know that Judaism, like feminism, is a belief system that you cannot really practice alone. Jewish rules dictate that you can't even pray unless you have a minyan. But at that time I considered myself in exile from a community that didn't count me as one of the required ten for a minyan. I refused either to participate in sexist rituals, or to cede my Jewishness.

To the fanatics of the ultra-Orthodox cults, I would probably not even be considered a Jew. But who gave them the right to define Jewishness? My version, rich in argument, prophetic ideals, and a lifetime of emotional affiliation, is equally authentic. In vowing to help my children feel that to be Jewish was a privilege, a treasure, and a joy, I not only protected them as best I could from the harm of anti-Semitic wounds, but preserved one more generation of proudly Jewish-identified young people who look forward to recreating the same practices with their own future progeny.

Then came the year that my mother, shockingly, died in a house fire one snowy night. As I labored through my grief, salvaging what I could from her ruined house, I began to dread the upcoming Seder, so imbued with family memories. I cry easily at the best of times; how would I make it through the Haggadah?

In tribute to my dearly loved mother, I recreated all her most triumphant recipes. A desperate and mourning love lent magic to my hands; for the first time, I made her gefilte fish, her horseradish (everything from scratch, of course), her sponge cake with its tangy lemon sauce. It was all perfect. Her candlesticks, her best table-cloth, even her crystal glasses—how strange that they survived the fire that took her breath away forever—made the table gleam. The food was ready, and I sat down.

Quietly, and with perfect tact and confidence, my two daughters and my son, all teenagers now, took over the Seder, reading, singing, chanting Hebrew, leading discussion.

This was how I learned to be a Jewish mother, and this was how I learned I had succeeded.

3

Traditions

Chawwa Wijnberg
Janine Beulink
Translated by Johanna H. Prins and Johanna W. Prins

LETTER TO A DAUGHTER
Chawwa Wijnberg

My dearest,

If only we Jews could be like swans. Floating around stately white, carefree and proud. Having large families without feeling guilty about overpopulation. With air in our feathers and no human fears because we aren't like ordinary birds or ducks.

What you want frightens me. I understand you don't want to tie your Jewish identity to what Meyer Sluyser calls "the deep sorrow." That's what my mother spooned into me along with the chicken soup. But then again, despite everything, she loved life. I'm not like that. Although my mind blurs when I try to explain it to you, I would like to tell you stories. Tall tales, like the ones my mother told about her mother. Our family history, my mother's. I know too little about my father and his history.

Why do I need you to understand that I still weep endlessly because my father was shot dead? Why do I want my neighbors to fly their flag at half-mast on the Fourth of May?* A few days later it hardly matters to me anymore. But on that day I think that nobody can or will ever want to understand me. I often lose myself in frozen time. How do you manage to distance yourself from all that?

---

*The Fourth of May is Commemoration Day in the Netherlands for the victims of World War II.

Why am I asking you how I should live? I am the mother. You are not mine. But I'm the one with the questions and it seems like you have the answers. Is that true?

Says John to Moshe: "You Jews always answer a question with another question."

Says Moshe: "Do we?"

That's what I do. You want to know about Judaism and I ask questions. That's how I was taught. It's not about the answers, but about asking questions. But according to tradition the child poses the questions. What makes this mother different from all other mothers?

What I really mean is, why aren't you afraid? You are open about being Jewish, but you don't have to be. I gave you a tall blond goy as a father. You have a safe non-Jewish name. Only those blue eyes don't look goy enough. Interested in traditions. Jewish traditions.

You tell me you attended the memorial for the dead with many, many Jews all around you, and it gave you a strong and happy feeling. I get nauseated thinking it takes only one lunatic with a machine gun to turn it into a blood bath.

To answer the question you didn't ask, yes, I do like many things, but Jewish traditions are too close for comfort.

Did I ever tell you why Mama willed herself to survive the war?

As a child around seven years old, she often complained at home about headaches. One day her little sister Greta said: "She has headaches because the teacher keeps knocking her head against the wall."

The story doesn't mention if the anti-Semitic teacher was fired, only that Mama was sent to a psychiatrist. That man taught her that she should never again let herself be terrorized by anybody. Whenever Mama told that story, she beamed. "I didn't want Hitler to have that pleasure."

Other times I got to hear: "I was on the verge of joining the deportation," or "If I'd gotten a chance to trade you in to get your father back, I would have done it." Or, "They would never have been able to lay their hands on you—I personally would have wrung your neck first." I can't say these remarks put me at ease.

When I asked Mama how she could handle so much grief, parents gone, sister gone, husband gone, in-laws, sister-in-law, brother-in-law, and their two children, she answered, opening the palms of her hands: "Come, life, come."

How she could do that filled me with desperate admiration.

Before the war Mama led an affluent life. That fortune was stolen from us. On my bad days I think of that with bitterness.

Mama's father had one of the first cars. When they took a ride, the children counted the cars they met on the way. Can you imagine that? Her mother would stay for six weeks at Scheveningen with the children and a servant. She was seventeen when she met Bob, my father, the love of her life. They were idealists, socialists, and Zionists. Not religious.

She read a lot. Her parents adored her and as a young bride she even got a servant to ward off boredom.

They did observe holidays, baked the butter cake, and don't forget, there was my grandmother's chickenchickenrooster soup, which I would have loved to taste.

The way people ate then. You take twenty eggs. . . .

As soon as there is any mention of food, I get distracted. By the way, eating that food was our tradition. And telling stories. Do you know the story of Leni and the hamantaschen? Someday I'll tell you about it.

Everything is related to the people who aren't here anymore. The absence that has to be filled with lots and lots of food.

The smugness of the religious Jews drives me up the wall. The right-wing politics. The homophobia bothers me, of course. The kitsch, not real art, that they collect. The pedantry of being the chosen people. My mother accused me of Judische Selbsthasse, Jewish self-hatred.

But I do not want to hate. Not myself. Not myself as a Jew. And not others. I can understand Jewish political adversaries, but when they persecute others out of ignorance or impotence, it makes me sick.

"You Jews should know better."

But why should Jews learn to know better, from something as horrible as the Second World War? Could it be that we have become the chosen people after all? At least in the eyes of those who call us "you Jews"?

As I have taught you and your brother: Your freedom ends where somebody else's begins. . . . So if the Palestinians say they are a nation, they are a nation. That's what my decent common sense says. My feelings don't always agree. Especially not right after an assault.

But the same applies to them when we, the Jews, the Israelis, kill yet another rock-throwing child. But who are we?

My mother was so dead-certain of everything. Like not wanting to play the role of grandmother: "Don't think I will baby-sit for your children." Her mother didn't do it for her and so I didn't get my mother as a grandmama for you.

How I have longed for a Jewish family. Where do I belong? Where do I want to belong? Sometimes I don't want to belong anywhere at all. For years I searched for somebody like me. Until I realized I didn't want to meet her. And when I finally met her, in someone with a similar history, also born in the war, also gone into hiding, also with a difficult mama, I was bitterly disappointed. As the ad campaign goes: You can take a child out of the war, but how can you take the war out of a child? And that war child goes on, wide awake and scared to death, as a postwar adult . . .

My face in the mirror shows a patient. A neurotic person. A pedantic person. An egocentric person. Someone holding a grudge. May people like me remain an exception.

Are there healthy Jews, I mean, people who have not been affected by wars, persecutions, and the insanity of those who hate us?

I'll tell you the story of a doll, Elleke.

> The doll Elleke was broken, the head shattered.
>
> The mother tries to console the child: "Let's take her to the doll doctor."
>
> The child, anxious: "Can the doll doctor make her better?"
>
> "Yes, of course, sweetheart."
>
> The mother is always right and the father is dead, so the child hopes against all odds that the father will return by a miracle. Perhaps the father has lost his way and can't remember anything.

The doll returns with another head.

The child thinks: "You see, it isn't possible," and bursts out in tears, inconsolably.

The mother gets impatient. Irritated, she says: "Crocodile tears. Save your tears for something worse."

The child is offended. She is crying about the worst thing that could happen. About Elleke, who was also taken away. Elleke from the photo album. The five-year-old bridesmaid. Elleke, the girl in the butterfly dress. The cousin. Elleke, the daughter of Marth and Mau.

The child had named the doll after her. And nobody can make Elleke live again, not even the doll doctor.

The child withdraws to the attic with her great grief and thinks that adults are stupid. She doesn't want to become like that. She decides to remain a child always.

And that child had children. She felt happy and comforted in their presence. Family. Just like a real family.

My doll Elleke. My family. And I myself will play the part of the doll doctor.

How can you enjoy life if you don't distance yourself from the meshugene person who is raising you? What's a Jewish mother without her daughter? How can I let you go without binding you to me through guilt?

Says John to Peter: "If you do it with a girl, make sure she isn't Jewish. A Catholic girl screams: 'Jesus! Maria! Joseph!' But a Jewish girl screams: 'Mama!' And she will appear!"

So what would you do without me?

Like the other day, when the police came after the break-in at your house. . . . Although still in tears, you told the law you were not in need of victim assistance: "My mother is coming!"

You know I take walks these days. Time to reflect. Once around the village. An hour eastbound or an hour westbound. Along the water because, thank God, it's everywhere. And then I look at all the interesting plants that are growing. Horsetail, which in its early stage looks like tiny towers of Babel. Giant fescue, I looked it up, and couch grass. Barren brome, false-brome, mousetail, and grass in the shape of little hands. Sweet, don't you think? It has five fingers, yes, but can it talk?

It turned out to be a yellow meadow star, a lousy yellow star of a plant. They always have it in for us Jews. Did you know there is something called mercyweed?

Whenever I imagine all these different green plants as people, I want to be the wild wormwood. Or the little cattail. And as far as I'm concerned, the Palestinians can be creeping vines. And all the pious ones are coltsfoot. Fundamentalists. Practically impossible to remove from my garden.

Buttercups, Queen Anne's lace, so many beautiful and unbeliev- ably different plants growing everywhere. And I know this: I taught you that everything, all that lives, all that breathes, has a right to exist. You and I, the golden oat grass, ryegrass, small and large mallow, pepperwort, hoary plantain, and each dandelion scattering itself in the wind.

If my father had been deeply religious, and not a hero in the resis- tance, then after the war, even as a nonbeliever, I would have become an obedient, pious woman. As a tribute. But my father was leftist. He ate pork. He did. You don't. So be it. In the past you didn't want Hebrew school, now you do. Omayn v'omayn, they used to say at the shul in Dordrecht.

And one more thing.

1805. From the diary of a wine merchant. Events in the life of Hendrik Brouwer, 1769-1817. On the subject of the vaccination of "our little Daughter."

> We pray to God that He will bless this artful undertaking as protection against children's disease, and that this undertaking will not cause fainting spells, the fear of which unto this day had caused our wavering hearts to refrain from action.

You understand that the wavering hearts speak to me most elo- quently. (Dearest, may you never become one of those weeds, a maiden's tear or a bleeding heart.)

Love, and a poem too, from
        your mother.

SWAN

Swan, on black water
you float, so clean, so
monday laundry day white
what use would you have
for the thoughts of a human
listen

whisper
you might sink
under the surface
might have to stand
on your webbed toes in the mud
the sucking mud
thanking god
for your long neck
so you might yet
catch a breath of air

you do not think of that, swan
when you see me, you puff up your sleeves
proudly you sail forth, certain
that the water and the sky
will carry you

it goes without saying
you have air and power in your wings
ruler of the sky and
the broad stream
where so effortlessly
so monday laundry day white
you float, white swan
my daughter floats
also strong also
on black water

AFTER THE ICE AGE
Janine Beulink

Dearest Mama,

Frozen time, you can't get lost in it. You crash into it and stick to the ice. And if nobody comes by with a heating unit, there is little chance to thaw out. You get lost in the freezer, and occasionally I turn the heat on. For a moment you peek out over the edge, but you quickly return to your spot between the frozen chickens. The great sorrow paralyzes you. And you know the chickens.

But I haven't been formally introduced to those chickens and imagine I'm a swan: large and strong on dangerous waters. I love long necks and laundry-day white. I'm not at all ready for subfreezing temperatures. I have power in my wings. The pike doesn't scare me. And if someone dares to touch my children, I'd kill him. Because I am the mother. Are you the child?

The girl was around seven years old. Dark blond, big green-brown eyes. She had just stormed into the kitchen through the backdoor. Angry and confused. "Dirty Jew," they called her at school. She looked at her mother with distaste. "I'm not a Jew, am I?"

That was the moment that you realized you'd have to let me and my brother know. We were Jewish in a small Christian village. But what made us Jews, and what that meant, you didn't explain. What made us different from all the other people I knew?

A circle was drawn with chalk on the pavement of the schoolyard. It was subdivided in segments. Every part was a country, and belonged to someone. The one who thought of playing the game "I Declare War" chose to be the Netherlands. Grudgingly the other children chose countries they knew: Belgium, Germany, England. With pounding heart the girl wrote "Israel" on her part of the circle. The country she came from. Afraid and proud at the same time. Afraid she would be "different," proud she had something special. She hadn't yet realized how strange it must have sounded when the neighbor boy from Germany called: "I declare war on . . . Israel!"

That I was born in Israel, I already understood as a small child. My passport showed it. But aside from the scent of rain on dry earth, I couldn't remember a thing. For a long time I thought only my birthplace made me different from others.

It was that blond boy with the crew cut and a slack-jawed mouth. A bit too big and too strong for his age. His remarks were like that too. The girl was a little scared of him. Often she came home from school crying.

And then you got angry at his mother. And not a little. Crying and screaming you clutched the telephone, you tried to explain hysterically why her son couldn't say "those things!" Because your family is gone. Because this is exactly how the war had begun. I stood there and sank through the floor in shame. Scolding hurts, but this was worse. Now I understand your reaction better. The story about your mother and her anti-Semitic teacher, I didn't know.

The girl realized it must have had something to do with The Past. With being afraid. That handsome man in the old photograph, that was her grandfather. She looked at his eyes, his ears. Did hers look like his? She didn't ask her mother. She would certainly start crying. And when her mother cried, she couldn't keep her own tears back either.

The girl visited her grandmother. It was the mother of her non-Jewish father, a real lady in a flowered dress. In a shining polished cabinet, behind closed doors, stood the cookie tin. The girl didn't understand it at all. Why were cookies kept in tins? And why didn't the doors open more often? Wasn't it a festive occasion that they were there? At home, and at her other grandmother's, things were different. She didn't dare to ask why.

At least we knew how to have a party. And if there was nobody who had a birthday or passed an exam, we would make up an excuse. Cookies, chocolate, nuts, all served out at once. No leftovers, please. When we did it, we did it well. Like the way we ate chicken with french fries every Friday. Ha, that didn't happen at my girl-friends'! But why not, I didn't understand. Were we really normal? Why didn't you look like the neighbor and why didn't our yard look like theirs? Why wasn't I allowed to join the majorettes? Why didn't we go to church wearing hats?

During vacations in Israel, when I visited friends and families, I recognized things from home. Indulging in sweets, chicken on Friday. The excitement, the heated debates. I wanted to know more. I didn't know other Jewish children in the Netherlands. I read. Singer, Potok, Malamud. In *The Assistant,* the main character, Frank, undergoes circumcision, as the last phase of converting. I was sixteen and deeply impressed. If someone was willing to learn so much about this and even submit to a painful operation, it must mean that being Jewish is great. And although you had selected a "safe" non-Jewish name for me on purpose, it wouldn't help. There is no choice. I *am* Jewish.

I began to fit myself into a garment of feathers. Without a swimming diploma I stuck out my neck. Looking for other swans like me, I joined a Jewish youth club. The first time I went under. It was at a Friday night supper. I imitated all the gestures of my tablemates and looked like the only one who had no notion of the meaning of it. My white outfit didn't feel so comfortable yet.

I changed to other waterways. The ditches in the polder became the canals in Amsterdam and I let myself become web-toed. Now it was impossible to sink down in the mud. I took swimming lessons. Followed a course to relearn the language I had spoken until my third year. Familiarized myself with the customs of eating kosher, the holidays and memorial days. Made new friends with whom I had a good time swimming. They knew the canals where I felt at home, in a rather detached way.

You look at me from the shore. I see your fear, your sorrow. But I refuse to stay put. I use that fear to do courageous things. For instance, I travel in full state to the other side of the world. With pain in my heart I steer my own course. Joining the rescue team makes no sense. How can a child console her mother?

I don't want to fill up emptiness with food, the way you do. Eating was and is part of the Jewish culture. The way it is part of any culture. That may be the only thing left for you. But I don't mind being more Jewish than just chicken soup.

You ask yourself how I can enjoy life if I don't break the ties with a meshugene parent. But Mama, raising children is over. Now you're just my mother. Someone who pours tea when her daughter comes to visit.

I know, often it's different when we are together. Then I'm the mother and you're the child. That's the way it has developed. Your behavior and my character. I made you cups of tea and helped you to get out of the house. Prepared my own sandwiches when I was seven. Took your hand while crossing the street and protected you from buses, trams, and bicycles. And now I'm telling you how I want to celebrate Pesach. And you're asking questions and feel sad. I am comforting you. You're peeking over the edge of the freezer.

But when I'm by myself, I reverse the roles. Then I am the child who asks questions and is afraid. Because who says I know where I'm going? "A trembling compass needle," you once wrote. The only thing I know is that I want to know more. I still have so many questions. How do I prepare your chicken soup? How did you celebrate the Seder at home in the past? There are still so many stories I don't know. Tell me the stories. Make them mine. Only then will they be preserved. Because what are young swans without stories?

Your daughter.

– 4 –

My Mother Is Greek

Annette B. Fromm

I married when I was thirty-eight years old, after years of adventures, education, and professional achievement. Perhaps the greatest achievement of all was the birth of our daughter on a Shabbat evening in the Rosh Hashanah season when I was forty years old.

A secondary achievement, attained several months earlier, was the completion of my doctoral dissertation. Only recently did I realize how much my dissertation was an academic quest that was personally tied to my Jewish motherhood. The research for that academic tome took me to the community in Greece that my maternal grandparents had left early in the twentieth century to come to America. It certainly provided me with a historical context to understand the values my mother gave to me. Education, arts, individualism, independence, and pride in our distinct heritage are examples of those values.

These values are not necessarily uniquely Greek Jewish. They are, however, part of my character, and I endeavor to instill them into the young, still incompletely shaped character of our daughter, Miriam Shana. The fact that my mother now lives with us helps me transmit these values to Miriam, just as my mother originally transmitted them to me.

My husband and I have introduced Miriam to many art forms. Books are scattered across our home and read time and time again. During High Holy Day services in our small community in Oklahoma she reveled in reading to the younger children who were bored by the proceedings. She and I took advantage of as many volunteer situations in the community as we could. Thus, we are able to enter the activity without paying, a reflection of lessons of Depression-era frugality passed on by my mother. Through these activities our daughter is also gaining a Jewish sense of participating in community and working for the aid of others.

Luckily, we are in a different financial situation than my parents were. I continue to work as a museum professional and occasional university professor. What a surprise one day when Miriam pronounced that I am a "teaching doctor," as a means to explain why I am Doctor Fromm and do not heal people. She takes great pride in showing off the museums where I have worked and work to friends, family, and classmates.

Miriam accompanied me on a week-long trip to Athens when she was seven years old for the opening of the Jewish Museum of Greece, an organization to which I serve as consultant. She met family living there and old family friends. We visited museums and parks. The memories are indelible, reinforcing an identity of which she was already very aware. Athens has become her favorite place in the world, to which everything and all trips can be compared.

Now when we take road trips, Greek tapes echo throughout the car interior to reinforce that Greek Jewish heritage which measures one-quarter of Miriam's mixed-up Jewish American background. I have started speaking Greek to her so she will remember the linguistic music she heard on our short trip. And we try to visit local Greek festivals to experience the music, dance, colors, and food that we share.

As a mother, it is now my turn to follow my mother's example. My daughter is the palette to which I apply the sense of being in the line of Greek Jewish women. It is my joy to observe her as she grows and flourishes. I have no choice but to allow her to be an individual and carry on our tradition of independence. But the lessons that I impart are taken from my mother. To understand my mothering skills, my mother's story must be told. It is from her that I have derived my own sense of right and wrong, my own deep-seated values.

My mother is Greek—and Jewish. My maternal grandparents were Jews from northwestern Greece. They emigrated to the United States from Ioannina, a northern provincial capital. The Jewish population of Ioannina predates the massive wave of fifteenth-century immigrants from the Iberian Peninsula. Unlike most other Balkan Jewish communities, they were minimally influenced by the

Sephardic Jewish refugees and maintained a distinct Greek Jewish traditional culture and minhag.

The world from which my grandparents came was one of the last vestiges of the Ottoman Empire. Among the many attributes of that 500-year-old regime was ethnic pluralism. Muslims, Christians, Jews, Gypsies, Vlachs, and others lived together in northwestern Greece. They were allowed some measure of autonomy as long as their taxes were paid to the administrative Ottomans. While the members of distinct communities in Ioannina were socially segregated, this separation was not enforced by the ruling powers. Ghettos were not part of the landscape of Ottoman Greece. Distinct neighborhoods existed, but a few families of different backgrounds also lived among the Jews. Individuals of diverse backgrounds interacted daily in the marketplace. This history imbued my grandparents with a knowledge and a tolerance of others.

My mother is an independent, intelligent daughter of the Ottoman Empire. She was the youngest daughter, born and raised in an extended family enclave in New York City, in a microcosm of Ioannina in exile. In the early decades of the twentieth century approximately 2,000 Jews left Ioannina in response to political and economic changes as northwestern Greece was absorbed into the modern Greek state. The majority resettled in New York City, but my branch of the family tree moved to Pittsburgh, Pennsylvania. Yes, Squirrel Hill, the heart of Jewish Pittsburgh. There, in the 1950s, my pride in our unique heritage led me to frequently explain that Jewish people had also lived in Greece. At the time, very few Ashkenazi Jews were aware or appreciative of their Sephardic co-religionists. Actually, I am a member of a double minority group in America, a Greek Jewish minority within a Sephardic Jewish minority.

Despite the fact that we were physically distant from most of our relatives, my childhood was filled with vivid reminders of our distinctiveness. Greek food was frequently found on our table. I often accompanied my mother on shopping trips to the Greek wholesalers to buy the ingredients for those delicacies that were not widely available as they are now. Mr. Stamoulis greeted me in Greek, pinched my cheeks, and plied me with Jordan almonds before he and Mom struck a bargain agreeable to both.

Greek phrases were frequently heard at home. My mother spoke them in anger and love, to hasten or caution us, or just to keep them alive in her mind. Not only were they the commonly spoken demotic Greek, but also certain phrases that were idiomatic of early twentieth-century Ioannina. Greek music was ever present as we listened to phonograph records and *Greek Hour* on the radio. A Greek Orthodox woman from Smyrna, who lived on the next street up the hill, was my fictive godmother. My mother had family from Smyrna, and instantly our families were related, despite the difference in our faiths. I attended Hebrew school and Sunday School at the Ashkenazi shul down the street from my elementary school. But, three days a week, I took the bus to the magnificent Greek Orthodox Church near the public library for Greek school. There I received instruction in language and culture. By an arrangement with the priest, however, I did not receive the religion lessons. In fact, those pages in the schoolbooks, which I still have, are heavily crossed out in pencil. "Bravo," exclaimed the Papa when my mother enrolled me. He was proud that a Greek Jew was sending her daughter to reclaim a part of her heritage.

Later in life, as I conducted fieldwork among Greek and Lebanese Orthodox community members in Cleveland, Ohio, I was emphatically told a number of times that we were the same people despite the differences in our faiths. The geographic heritage was a strong tie that united us.

This sense of cultural interrelationships can be viewed as a relic of the Ottoman experience and a part of Greek Jewish identity. It was an intensely pluralistic society where Jews had few imposed feelings of oppression. I always heard from my mother that as a young woman she felt more comfortable with Italians than with Ashkenazi Jews. Today Miriam enjoys local Greek festivals, fully aware that Greek culture is a part of her heritage, too. When I cautioned her to respectful silence inside a church sanctuary, explaining that Greek people are quiet in worship as we are, she quipped that, "We're Greek, too, only Jewish!" I remember hearing that phrase often as I was growing up.

As a result of my upbringing and our personal tastes, Miriam has met many people from many nations around the world. Angolan, Mongolian, French, Finnish, Christian, Muslim, and Native American are but a few of the diverse cultures welcomed into our home and our family. I worked extensively with American Indian people in Oklahoma. At one of the last Cheyenne dances we attended before leaving Oklahoma, our then eight-year-old daughter rhetorically asked, "Mom, are we great friends of the Indians?" "Tell her you are great friends of the Indians," the wife of one of the elders kindly and gently instructed me to respond.

When we traveled to New York to visit my grandparents, Nona and Pappou, we were smothered in a Greek, Ottoman, and Jewish environment. The Jewish part was not very visible. We were rarely there for Jewish holidays, as they fell during the school year, and our visits were in the summer. I remember very few Judaica objects in the home, maybe brass Shabbat candlesticks or a Chanukah menorah. But Judaism lived there in the values and ethics projected by my grandmother.

My grandparents were working-class people who instilled work-related ethics into my mother and her siblings. Mom was a sweatshop seamstress. She often worked in factories owned by a compatriot of my grandparents. Unlike the other "girls," she had a thirst for learning and carried books with her to the shop. During lunch hour she chose to read rather than discuss the latest movie stars. Her level head saved them in more than one situation, like the time a machine motor caught fire. As the other workers responded to the emergency in a panic, my mother calmly unplugged the machine and then tended to the flames. This sort of action, I believe, set the example for me to look for solutions and approach situations as a problem solver rather than dwelling on details.

My mother was a union activist in New York City in the late 1930s, often the only woman taking part in leadership roles in meetings. After my father died, my brothers and I explored old records and diplomas. There we found a small, browned, undated handbill announcing a union rally led by Congressman Vito Marcantonio. Mollie Bacola, our mother, was the only officiating woman among a long list of men listed along the sides in small print. This treasured memento of her work ethic and her drive for fairness and equality now hangs framed in our home.

My mother's love of learning and education has left me with an indelible image of the ideal female. Even though education is not often a driving force among entrepreneurial non-Ashkenazi Jews, my brothers and I were regularly taken to the great reading rooms of Pittsburgh's Carnegie Library. I remember listening to children's programs there while my mother searched for recent works of fiction and nonfiction for herself. While she worked in her own seamstress shop she always found time to go to the library for speakers or special programs. To this day my mother remains an avid reader. Is this why I instruct my daughter that near and distant worlds are available in books? And she is absorbing the lesson; her preferred destination after an appointment with the dentist is a bookstore, not the local ice cream shop. She sets herself ambitious summer reading goals, then surpasses them.

While I attended college in the 1970s I listened to feminists who questioned the contributions of housewives, women who stayed at home to raise their baby-boomer children. My mother followed her own path. She was primarily a housewife, yet her work was often relied upon when the family income was diminished. My vivid memories place her not in front of television soap operas, but seeking out and attending lectures about current affairs, history, art, and other topics of the mind.

Art was a necessity in our lives. How many times did my mother tell me about the operas and music in New York's Metropolitan Opera House that she enjoyed as a young woman? I'm thrilled now when I see my daughter crawl into her Nona's lap to watch opera on *Great Performances.* While not uniquely Greek Jewish values, the appreciation of culture, the arts, languages, and books led to the expansion of my horizons. By exposing my daughter to these treasures I hope she will also reach for the stars.

As I grow older and independent in my own right, I have come to appreciate that through my Greek Jewish mother's sensitive management, along with my father's approval, my brothers and I were allowed to develop into three unique yet related individuals. Rarely were we told that we could not engage in some activity, yet my mother steered us toward those activities that she somehow recognized would meet our interests. I was in high school and college during the height of the hippie years. As a senior in high school, I painted a small, discreet black and white daisy on my face and often wore dresses I made from Indian print tablecloths. We still were a family of limited income. My mother fielded a number of parental phone calls that questioned my behavior by countering that my individuality caused no one any harm.

Now I encourage my daughter to express her own individuality in many ways. I try my best not to stifle her, not knowing in what direction her actions will lead. In the years following the toddler stage a favorite piece of clothing was the "cow nightgown crown," as she called her invention. What child doesn't leave a quickly removed pullover suspended around her head, imagining who knows what? What mother allowed the child to let the "crown" remain in place on the way to day care? Yes, that was me. Why not be unconventional and express yourself through clothing? Her creativity brought her such pleasure, and confusion to the teachers! As she prepares to enter the third grade and is falling prey to peer pressure, I cringe at the thought of allowing her to dress like her classmates. I am thrilled to see her subtle and sometimes not-too-subtle gestures of individuality.

And so, our daughter is another Greek Jewish young woman. Yes, part of her heritage reflects Jewish traditions from other parts of Europe and the United States through the influence of my non-Greek father and my husband. And I am passing on to Miriam the many positive influences that my mother so lovingly offered to my brothers and me.

Perhaps none of these parenting approaches is unique to Greek Jews. They reflect, however, a particular response to living in culturally plural communities such as the Ioannina of my grandmother and the New York City of my mother. An additional quality which no doubt is also a result of matriarchal influences is the Ottoman self-effacement instilled in women. This quality was modeled by my mother, and leads me to recognize the achievements of others while downplaying my own strides, professionally and personally.

It is interesting that Miriam is a strongly independent soul who can only be pointed in a direction, not taken there. The guidance I received from my mother in child rearing was to suggest, not to force, to guide children to a path that will suit them. Then to let go, to see where they lead themselves, and to be there along the way to comfort and congratulate.

Mandelbrot, Rugelach, and a Family Quilt

Lois Young-Tulin

"Mom, come on down. I'm ready to start baking!" my daughter Karen calls to me from the kitchen. It is Friday afternoon of the last weekend of her visit. Karen is visiting us for two weeks, fourteen days, which includes celebrating my mother's eighty-ninth birthday.

As a birthday gift, Karen is baking mandelbrot, literally almond bread, and rugelach, a crescent-shaped cookie that comes from the Yiddish rugel or royal. It is something I have never done for my mother.

When I enter the kitchen I am struck by how well organized Karen is. The kitchen table is covered with wax paper. On the wax paper are small custard cups filled with the necessary ingredients: minced nuts, powdered sugar, apricot jelly, and raspberry jelly. She has prepared the dough in advance. A can of Pam takes the place of a rolling pin since we cannot find mine. We stand side by side and take turns rolling the dough and spooning the fillings into each rugela. As one batch bakes in the oven, we prepare another. The sweet smell of baked goods fills the air. With flour on our faces and jelly on our fingers, we embrace.

"This is so much fun," Karen says, hugging me.

I nod, tears stinging my eyes.

A mere six months earlier, I had helped my daughter and her partner move to their new home in Pacifica, California, and joined them as they nailed a mezuzah to their door post. I thought about the journey we had taken and are still taking together, the mother/

daughter implications, the Jewish traditions, and the new paths we were forging as other life stages presented themselves.

A year earlier, I had taken part in a wedding ceremony as my daughter and her partner were "married" in a Jewish and African-American ceremony. Two months later, on the East Coast, my husband and I hosted a party in honor of the couple. We invited our friends and relatives. In a sense, it had also been our coming-out party as parents of a gay child. It was an important leg of my unconventional journey as a Jewish mother of a lesbian daughter.

The journey had begun when I birthed a daughter thirty-odd years ago. Karen's early years included Hebrew school, Purim party costumes, Hanukkah candle lightings, the Four Questions at Passover, her Bat Mitzvah at thirteen, and her first trip to Israel.

As my daughter had grown into womanhood in the 1960s and 1970s, so had my own consciousness and activism in the feminist movement. When my daughter came out to me as a lesbian during her senior year in college, I was faced with my own homophobia, as well as the old blame/shame/blame syndrome.

It was hard to determine what the source of my initial embarrassment was. Was it homophobia alone? How much of my initial response was culturally specific? Judaism places great emphasis on family, children, and the future, which is assured by the continuation of family. As a Jewish mother, I had certain hopes and dreams for my daughter, which included her marrying a nice Jewish boy and giving me Jewish grandchildren. I had wanted to dance the hora at my daughter's wedding and cry during my grandchild's Bar/Bat Mitzvah. I felt the tug of the Jewish childbearing imperative, and I had falsely assumed that if my daughter is a lesbian, there would be no grandchildren.

Intellectually, I had accepted Karen's sexual orientation, but emotionally, my reaction shocked even me! Hadn't she always loved boys, worried about dates and being popular? I was disappointed in myself for being upset. After all, I was a fierce supporter of lesbian rights, and my own women's group was made up of lesbians as well as straight women. I was devastated, nevertheless. My daughter? I wondered what I had done wrong. Did my own feminism cause Karen to rebel by being more outrageous and declaring herself a lesbian? I was convinced she was merely going through a phase, that she would play it out and then return to heterosexuality. I talked to no one about her coming out to me, afraid that telling someone would make it a fact and would mark her for life. If she changed back to men it would be too late once word got around. How homophobic I was! Looking back, I am both shocked and ashamed of these reactions. But they were my real feelings and thoughts, and, if nothing else, I was being honest with myself.

After her graduation from college, Karen moved back in with me. Although I confessed to her that I was reading a few books for parents of gay children, I still hoped her lesbianism would go away. I knew better objectively, but emotionally I was coping poorly, buying into the homophobia around me. Emotionally I was stuck. I was deeply in the closet as the mother of a gay child. I felt ashamed, fearful, guilty, all wrapped into one package—silence and mourning were my masks for anger and self-blame.

That year was full of change. With each passing month, I felt less denial, less mourning, and more acceptance as the mother of a lesbian. Soon Karen began dating and bringing women home. That July she had a birthday party in my house, and I liked most of the guests. They were wonderful and close friends to Karen, bright, caring, loving women of varied ages and cultural backgrounds. I began to feel good about her sexual orientation. Karen was more open with me about her relationships, and I became more accepting.

Occasionally things still come up, moments of initial awkwardness when I interrupt another person's homophobic joke, the risk I sometimes feel when I come out to an older-generation aunt, but the truthfulness sits well with my sense of integrity and pride, and my love for my daughter.

With hard work and soul searching, including attending a group called PFLAG, Parents and Friends of Lesbians and Gays, I have been able to not only accept my daughter's sexual orientation, but also to embrace her and the women in her life who give her love and joy.

Now here we are, in my kitchen, cooking for my mother's eighty-ninth birthday, three generations of Jewish women represented in the very act of baking. When the last batch of rugelach is cooling, I take off my apron.

"Come with me, Karen," I say, leading her into the dining room. I reach for a pair of brass candlesticks on top of the walnut break-front and hand them to her. "These belonged to my great-grand-mother, my grandmother, and my mother before I got them. Now I want you to have them. Take them back to California with you," I say.

"Really?" Karen says, running her fingers over the shiny brass.

"Yes, I want you to have them."

"Thanks, Ma. They're wonderful."

When I had told my mother that Karen was gay, she surprised me by not acting surprised. My youngest son had already told her, she confessed, and added, "I wondered when you would get around to talking to me about it."

"Well," I said, "Here I am now, talking to you."

"I think this whole thing is due to Karen's having lived with her college boyfriend when she was too young, and then his breaking her heart," my mother said.

"I don't think so," I answered. "This is not something that some-one causes," I explained.

"How do you feel about it?" my mother asked.

"I'm supportive of Karen's choices. I didn't dream this would be the case, but now it's a fact, and I love my daughter very much. I want her to find love and to be happy, whatever it takes," I said, hating the way this sounded as soon as the words left my mouth.

"If you're okay with it, then I am," my mother said, and then she was ready to change the subject, so we did.

This past year Karen and her partner Jana had their first Passover Seder. They had gone to Seders at other people's homes before, but this would be theirs. They would have a multicultural women's Seder. They wrote their own Haggadah and sent invitations to many of their friends. Karen really wanted me to be there and sent me an invitation. She and Jana were determined to make it happen. Finally, the morning of the Seder, Karen called and spoke to my husband, David, her stepdad.

"You're the spontaneous one. What could I say to get her to come?" she asked him. David called around to a handful of airlines and found a flight that was leaving in one hour that would get me to California on time.

"Please, Mom, please. You don't even have to stay longer than twenty-four hours. I understand that you have to go to work on Monday and everything," Karen begged and pleaded. Finally she came up with the best offer. "Mom, I'll go to the sperm bank on Monday if you come for the Seder!" Karen knew how important it was to me to one day be a grandmother. Even though I knew she was joking, that joke conveyed to me how important it was to her to have me at her first Seder.

"Okay, I'll do it." I literally threw my stuff in a suitcase, drove out to the airport, and ran through the terminal to make the flight. Six hours later Karen met me at the airport, just in time for the Seder.

By the time we reached her house, her friends had already arrived. We received a warm and wonderful welcome. Many of Karen and Jana's friends had heard about me but had never met me. I could see the joy in Karen's eyes as she introduced me to her friends. Many of the women said that they couldn't imagine their own mothers doing what I had just done. I wanted to weep for them.

As part of the Seder, Karen and Jana invited people to share their own individual stories of personal liberation, to remind each other that the Passover story is universal in many ways. We went around the table, and when it was my turn, I told the story about my first PFLAG meeting.

My friend Bernice, the mother of a gay son, was contacted by the local PFLAG chapter about doing a workshop for the PFLAG board of directors, who were grappling with some important issues. Bernice was the on-call therapist to PFLAG. She called and invited me to colead the workshop with her. Our first meeting took place on a Friday afternoon on the first floor of an old church in Germantown, Pennsylvania. Bernice and I entered a sparsely furnished room set up with a circle of old chairs, run-down couches, and cushions arranged in the middle of the room. Eight women were already seated.

"Please come in and join us," asked a stately woman with beautiful white hair done up in a bun atop her head. Bernice took a seat next to her, and I sat down next to Bernice.

A small, dark-haired woman began. "My name is Eve [not her real name] and my son is gay. I'm the president of the Philadelphia

PFLAG chapter. I'm out as the mother of a gay son to my family and friends, but not at work where I'm a public school principal."

A tall rosy-cheeked woman was next. "My name is Carol [not her real name]. My daughter is a lesbian. She lives in Seattle with her German girlfriend. I'm out both professionally and personally."

Around they went, telling us their names and their relationships to their gay children or friends. Bernice was next.

"I'm Bernice. Some of you know me since I'm the on-call shrink. My son is gay."

I was next. For the first time I didn't hesitate. I felt safe. "I'm Lois. My daughter is a lesbian." Once the words were out of my mouth I felt a tremendous sense of relief. Here were others struggling with the issues I was. It was the beginning of my turnaround, the start of my own personal liberation.

This was the story I told at that Seder. Many of Karen's friends had tears in their eyes when I finished. A few commented on how much they wished that their parents would go to a PFLAG meeting. Many of them were estranged from their families because of their sexual orientation.

It is now more than ten years since Karen came out. Karen, Jana, and I get along famously, and I call myself Jana's mother-in-law. I have marched in gay rights parades; I support gay and lesbian rights, and I am open about being the mother of a lesbian. Ordinarily, Jana comes to all our family events; I wouldn't dream of excluding her. She is as much a part of our family as my son's wife. Karen loves Jana, so we love Jana, too. It is very simple.

Because Karen is out, I feel free to speak up when I hear a homophobic comment. I educate where I hear lack of information, and I support where I sense a need. My life has been enriched. Never have I been so close to my daughter, or so able to be honest with her. My daughter is living a rich, rewarding life with the same level of energy and capability she has always displayed, and with the solid assurance that she has her mother's admiring support.

When the time comes for Karen to have a child, adopt a child, or raise a child, I know it will bring up issues with many people. I know that I am not ashamed of her. I am very proud of her and who she is.

On the Friday night of her visit, I cook chicken soup, roasted chicken, and baked potatoes, make a salad, and steam asparagus. It is two days before Karen flies back to California. We invite her friends Janice and Lonnie, a lesbian couple, for Shabbat dinner.

At sundown, I ask Karen to say the prayer and light the Shabbat candles. We all say the blessing over the wine, and Lonnie breaks off a piece of challah and chants hamotzi, the prayer thanking God for the food we are about to eat. For dessert, we serve some of the rugelach that Karen baked earlier for her grandmother.

The next day, we pack the car and head to New York City for my mother's birthday party. With us are the mandelbrot and rugelach that Karen baked and the family quilt made by a woman artist, custom designed for my mother. It is made of scraps of material taken from clothes my mother once owned and family photographs transposed onto fabric. We are all there, in the quilt: my sister's children and their spouses/partners, her granddaughter, my mother's sister and her husband, my great-grandmother, my parents, and my three children, including my son's wife and my daughter's wife. Yes, my daughter's wife.

After a sumptuous birthday dinner, we present my mother with the quilt. Her eyes grow larger as a grin spreads across her eighty-nine-year-old face. She likes it. As her fingers touch each detail of the quilt she calls out, "My whole family is here in this quilt. There's Lois and Judith, and . . ." She names her grandchildren and great-granddaughter, and then their spouses, including Jana.

Karen's eyes meet mine. The circle is complete. The family is intact. Four generations of females sit together and ooh and aah over the quilt as we devour Karen's delicious rugelach and mandelbrot.

SECTION II:
UNBINDING LOVE

– 6 –

Unbinding Love

Celia Gartenberg

And Abraham took the wood for the offering and placed it upon his son Yitzhak, and took into his hand the fire and the knife, and so they went, both of them, together.

Genesis, The Binding of Isaac, 22:6

We've already chosen his name: Moriel, Hebrew for "G-d is my teacher." Minutes after giving birth, I study his sweet, placid features—the angelic mouth that, for the moment, asks nothing of me, the faintly irregular shape of his slate-blue eyes. Something about the slant of them makes me uneasy. "Is he retarded?" This, abruptly, to the nurse. "Of course not—he's just fine!" she retorts blithely, with just a hint of exasperated indulgence.

Six months later, I'm reading a Dr. Seuss book to my two-year-old, the baby nestled in the crook of my arm. "ABCDEFGHIJKLM-NO . . ." Turn the page. "P!" I blow the sound in their faces. They burst simultaneously into gleeful chortles. They often look at books together, the older "reading" to the younger. The baby laughs and squeals and bounces.

Just past his first birthday, we moved to Seattle, where my husband had taken a position as a congregational rabbi. I was housebound in a new city and pregnant with my third child. While my oldest was in preschool, I attempted quality time with the baby. Somewhere along the way he had gradually stopped playing games; wouldn't respond, wouldn't laugh. I stopped trying to engage him and took to my bed while he meandered absently around the room, never checking back to see where I was. I felt profoundly disconnected from him and wondered what was wrong with me. "You're depressed," my family said. "He won't play pat-a-cake with me," I fretted to the pediatrician. "Try not to compare him to his older sibling," she advised dismissively.

Later, in the office of a new pediatrician, I staged a sit-in, determined not to leave until the doctor admitted that something was wrong with my child. He did. He ordered many tests. I bore my toddler home, perversely triumphant, vindicated.

Months passed. No diagnosis was to be had from the tests. Moriel was now enrolled in the local university's laboratory preschool for children with special needs. My husband and I would routinely interrogate the teachers for clues. *Why has he stopped talking? Why does he keep doing the same weird things over and over?* We were mystified. Behind the one-way mirror of the viewing booth, we'd stand with other parents, clinically comparing symptoms, behaviors, idiosyncrasies. After a number of these conversations, we were convinced that our child was autistic.

And so he is. We have a $500 document, written and signed by an eminent diagnostician, to prove it. The diagnosis of autism, initially so clarifying (finally we'd know what to *do*!), soon gave way to overwhelming confusion. Not the stereotypically withdrawn youngster who is content to spin plates for hours, who will leave you alone if you leave him alone, our son was "severely behaviorally disturbed"—a tiny terror most of the time.

In the rare moments when he would melt into my arms for a cuddle, it was possible to forget, briefly, the frequency with which he screamed uncontrollably, banged his head on the floor, tore curtain rods out of the ceiling and screens from the doors, picked the stuffing out of his mattress, drank from the toilet, smeared his feces on walls, climbed out of windows to run down busy streets, threw his food on the floor or ground it into the upholstery, bent hangers, ate plants, and snatched soda cans out of strangers' hands in airports and ice cream from the cones of his brother's friends. He brilliantly outmaneuvered all my attempts to bar him from the refrigerator, the contents of which were an obsession, by watchfully

calculating any lapses in vigilance on my part, and then construct-
ing makeshift scaffolding from dining room chairs.

Letting him out of my sight even for seconds guaranteed fresh
disaster, or at least major disruption. I lived in constant, enervated
amazement at the havoc he could wreak in the time it took to turn
away from him and back again. I saw my life slipping away as the
days became consumed with reacting. There was no energy left for
my other two children: Zachary, the eldest by just eighteen months,
and the baby, Fay. Fay was a special gift, conceived and born before
we had Mori's diagnosis and everything changed. If the timing had
been different, I would not have risked another child. Even so, I
remember almost nothing of her infancy or early childhood, consumed as I was by Mori's pressing needs and demands and my
frantic desire to make him better. Dazed though I was, my recollec-
tions are vivid with running: running after a child out of control,
running away emotionally, running out of patience, running around.
I made countless trips to practitioners for numerous therapeutic
interventions: cranial-sacral, speech, sensory integration, auditory
integration, occupational, acupuncture, special-needs horseback-
riding, nutritional supplementation. . . .

Three-year-old Mori lies on his back, head held firmly but gently
by my mother and arms pinned to his sides by me, as I straddle him
in an attempt to insert a dropper of B vitamins into his rigidly
clenched mouth. He is fifty writhing, tensile pounds of complete
resistance. I am determined to get the vitamins down him, as I have
recently read about some research correlating B vitamins with im-
provement in autistic children. This is not the first time Mori and I
have been through this desperate drill, this battle of wills; there is
always something new to try. But Mori's fearsome resolve not to be
"done to" seems to distort all my attempts to nurture and care for
him, until they feel like force and aggression. There are no little
tricks ("Open up the hangar and let the airplane in!") to cajole him
into compliance. This time, as he flails against our ambivalent re-
straint, a pent-up scream somehow escaping the two steel bars that
are his shut-tight lips, something inside me snaps. He *will not* let me
help him. He *will not* accept my ministrations. He *will not* allow me
to get him well. He *will not* let me love him. I watch outside myself

as my hand arcs up, then crashes down to slam the carpeting next to his head. Not believing what I have almost done, I stare at my mother in stunned recognition of my limits. I get up. I give up.

I began to withdraw from the enormity of parenting three small children close in age ("one of whom is autistic!" as I always made sure to mention), and finally became severely depressed. There were times I did not love this child; wished he'd never been born. Fruit of my womb, whom I yet adored with a great, yearning passion. A fallen angel with one broken wing. A boy of ethereal beauty, no words, and quirky, irksome, infuriating ways.

Trapped, helpless, and frustrated, I recited my litany of woes to sympathetic friends. Some of them had lost children through illness or accident. In their eternal grief, they were the only ones who seemed to understand the way I felt about my son. Knowing what it was like to have a phantom child, they could comfortably encourage me to vivify his presence, sensing that it was okay to laugh when I related a humorous anecdote about him. Others with normal children would nod compassionately, yet from a distance, barely masking their relief at having been spared the nightmare that haunts every pregnant woman. Oddly, it was the parents with disabled children of their own who were often the least empathetic, the most judgmental. Each of us had a stake in a particular set of methods and solutions that was sure to wrest his or her child from the grip of disability; no one dared risk the taint of ineptitude or, God forbid, failure.

Around the time of Mori's seventh birthday, my husband's sabbatical came due. We had always planned to spend an academic year in Israel, but we knew it would be impossible to travel with our little wild man. (I had clear visions of our being ejected from the plane in midflight.) It was just at that time, to our great fortune, that we were made aware of an opening in a local highly regarded home for children with severe disabilities. We decided to place Mori there for the year and we took our other son and daughter to Jerusalem.

Israel is a very child-oriented place, and Israelis tend to be openly curious. I was always asked how many children I have. When I'd say three, but they saw only two, they wanted to know where the other one was. In a tumble of apologies, I would explain the circumstances. Most people didn't know what to say, didn't know how to commiserate. Should they acknowledge my longing to be with him or my relief at not having to take care of him? For it was clear that I reveled in the opportunity I now had for unimpeded connection with Fay and Zachary. I was finally able to relax into the humble dailiness of mothering—walking the kids to school, baking brownies, staging sleepovers, singing lullabies. I took them on trips, attempted some part-time home schooling with Zach, and attended to Fay's complex social calendar.

Those months were sweet with the emerging discovery of these two children. Yet I lived in a constant state of psychological triage as this discovery implacably forced me to work through the choice I knew I needed to make. If Mori did well in his "out-of-home placement," if he seemed happy there, I would keep him there and elect a life of normalcy, of prosaic parenting that precluded the heroism of caring for a severely disabled child.

Three months into the sabbatical, I sit in this apartment of Jerusalem stone, waiting for the kids to come home from school. The branches of the beech trees outside my window look like bleached bones splayed across a brilliant blue sky. Their round leaves, agitated by the wind, remind me of coins circling a belly dancer's undulating waist. The iron-grated window across the way weeps rust down the side of the building. I have been trying for days to respond to a request from Nancy, who is now caring for Mori. She suggests sending a video or cassette tape from our family. An innocent, simple request, yet it rankles, causes panic, sends me to the refrigerator for something to buffer the anxiety in the pit of my stomach. A tape—a plastic package of false cheer? For my son—my flesh, blood, tissue, sinew, and bone? It is not enough. Nothing will ever be enough. He is not at summer camp; he is in exile, as am I.

I knew within the first hour of meeting Nancy that she had the gift of truly seeing past the jarring, mangled surface of Mori's disability to the neshama (soul-essence) buried deep within. Since there is such a person in this world, I reason, then he is surely hers. Who am I to give him anything less than he deserves? After all, I only want the best for my children, even if the best doesn't happen to be me.

Though Nancy would have many moments of reckoning, my son's episodes would not immobilize her, would not reduce her to near-catatonia as they did me. She would know better than to believe that his every act was a personal indictment of her. I saw that she and her husband Ed had the measured, orderly, decisive temperament to provide the routine and structure Mori needed so badly—the very things that I and my frenetic, spontaneous household could not. I noted her resolve to advocate on behalf of "her" children in the face of an educational system that simply cowed me with its intransigence. I felt understood and respected by her, and I knew Mori would be loved.

Thus, five years after the sabbatical, Mori remains with Nancy and Ed and will until he is grown. Fiercely maternal and thoroughly absorbed in the lives of my other two children, I know that I cannot be their mother and his in the same lifetime. I, the person who, upon reading about child victims of war, poverty, abuse, or neglect, fancy that I would be ready to adopt unlimited numbers of them in a heartbeat, have willingly given up my child to another woman. I relinquish my changeling child to his fairy godmother. Nancy will be the one to take him to the doctor, attend his school conferences, monitor his medications, plan his summers, post his artwork on the refrigerator door, share firsthand his triumphs and tribulations. He'll get in *her* hair and under *her* skin.

Mori visits on weekends and school breaks, and between visits I talk about him to anyone who will listen. He sits with us at Passover Seders and Friday night dinners, devouring challah or matzah. Though he cannot talk, we are delighted with his vigorous attempts to communicate; he simultaneously combines his complete arsenal of awkward communications—a sign language tap on the chest, an explosive "Puh . . . " for "Please," and a vigorous nodding of the head—to get more of his favorite foods. He and I are profoundly content to sit together on the couch, as he twirls strands of my long hair; we walk to the park or to shul, his arm looped through the crook of my elbow in a gesture of gentlemanly escort and sweet possession.

But then he goes home, and I resume the life I have made without him, the tableau in which he peeks out from behind the curtain, standing in shadows. It is a tableau of thwarted expectations and unexpected blessings waiting to be recognized. I stand at its center, the strangest of cultural oxymorons: a Jewish mother who has chosen to give up her child. The protagonist in a maternal version of the *Akedah*, the story of the binding of Isaac, I feel bound up forever with Abraham in the almost-sacrifice of sons. After their traumatic encounter, Isaac continued on the journey alongside Abraham, weighted though his steps were by the understanding that his father had been ready to slay him. In the same way, Mori is ever my fellow traveler and constant companion, accepting my limitations and embracing my presence even in the face of the decision I have made.

As the years go by, I often reconsider my decision, frequently yearning to have Mori back. I believe I am strong enough now to handle the hard times, and, anyway, my boy is (most of the time) indescribably sweet and reasonably self-contained. But then I remember that it hasn't been me who's brought him to this point. As any mother knows, the deepest kind of love possible on this planet is forged only from the minute-by-minute tedium of parenting. It is Nancy who has earned that love, battling in the trenches at home and at school, fighting both him and the system for a better way, believing in him always and never backing down.

Mori opens the door without knocking and heads straight for the bathroom down the hall, always his first stop after returning to Nancy's home from a twice-monthly weekend visit with us. He appears very sure of the routine, described step by step in a row of small plastic picture cards velcroed onto a strip over the sink. After he has washed and dried his hands, he commandeers the comfortable living room sofa. Pristine white carpeting and several delicate knick-knacks on display at first make it hard to believe that this house is home to four severely disabled children, or to any children for that matter. Though everything always seems to be in place, numerous handmade craft projects—dried flower wreaths, dolls in crocheted skirts, candles nestled in gilt paper—create a comforting, homey atmosphere. For a while, Nancy and I stand in the doorway, chatting enthusiastically about "our boy," kvelling over his steady gains at home and school. As I leave, Mori and I exchange a very bouncy hug and he offers his forehead to be kissed. He slaps the air in a perfunctory good-bye gesture and I wave back, contented, knowing I'll see him again soon.

Am I selfish or selfless? Others might ask that question, but I no longer do. I resolutely defend my decision as the best one I could have made for each member of my family, Mori most of all. And what of my other two children? The ones who, in the normalcy of their accomplishments, are supposed to vindicate the quality of my parenting? From the time I was fortunate enough to find someone who could take on the special burden of caring for Mori, I have been free to fully immerse myself in nurturing all the "little talents and possibilities," as the novelist E. Annie Proulx describes it, of my other children. I tirelessly ferret out their unique interests and capabilities, providing them with opportunities to develop and grow, attending diligently to their own sets of special needs and challenges (surprise! . . . they have some too). But it is through Moriel that they have learned the deepest lessons about what it is to be human—the lessons I would most like them to learn but which are the most difficult to teach.

Along with twenty or so of the friends and family joining us for Passover Seder this year are Nancy, Ed, and the children who live with them. They've also brought along Andrew, a young man to whom they provide occasional respite care. Andrew is strapped into a wheelchair, unable to walk, and blind from self-inflicted blows to the head. Every so often, he emits an ominous-sounding chuckle. Most grown-ups might feel very uncomfortable in Andrew's presence, let alone any child. But Fay is utterly unfazed, finding him amusing and endearing. She discovers that he enjoys having his arm stroked and that he laughs delightedly when she blows into his face. She adopts him for the evening and later talks excitedly about how cute and fun he was to play with.

It is a year in which Zachary has briefly been the center of attention in our family and our community, as he has recently authored a children's book (Gartenberg, 1997) describing what it is like to be the sibling of a child with a severe disability. He has written it in an effort to make sense of the experience for himself, and, as he puts it, "to help people understand that someone like Mori is a real and wonderful person." Because it is also his Bar Mitzvah year, we check in with Fay every so often, asking gingerly how she feels about all the attention and praise (and presents) Zachary is getting. She firmly reassures us that she is very happy for Zach; he deserves it, and she knows her time will come. How could we think it would bother her? She loves her brother!

After the Bar Mitzvah, Zachary takes her out to dinner (it's his idea) to show his appreciation for her support and lack of jealousy. It's to be just the two of them, thank you, but I can't resist a peek in at the restaurant window. They sit happily dipping their bread in olive oil, engaged in friendly conversation. I can't help but marvel at their uncommon bond, and I know that Mori is their silent partner in creating it. Their open affection for and admiration of each other shines through me, dissolving the residues of guilt and ambivalence I carry inside. My husband and I have managed after all to guide them through extraordinary circumstances—not unscathed, but certainly the better for it.

Zach and Fay adore Mori. Adept by now at handling his outbursts and helping him with his routines, they understand that when they are grown, and we are gone, they will be responsible for him. I am reassured that, should either or both of them have a child like Mori (a genetically significant risk), they will have it in them, as I did not, to raise such a child with love and skill. But if they feel they cannot, I have at least shown them that, with the help of God, giving up can be a form of giving.

REFERENCE

Gartenberg, Zachary (1997). *Mori's Story: A Book About a Boy with Autism.* Photographs by Jerry Gay. Minneapolis: Lerner Publications Company.

How a Paper Clip Changed Our Lives

Shelley Peterman Schwarz

My fourteen-year-old daughter Jamie was standing at the door waiting for me to return. Her eyes were red and swollen; tears rolled down her cheeks. In her fist, she held a piece of paper that she waved in my face. "I found this in your desk. It sounds like you're going to kill yourself. Is that what you're planning? Tell me the truth!" She was angry, scared, and determined to get some answers.

I felt as if someone had hit me with a sledgehammer. A sharp pain pierced my heart. In her hand, Jamie clutched the "good-bye" letter I had been writing. What was I going to say to her? How could I distill years of suffering and increasing disability into words a child could understand and accept? How could I explain that in my mind I was failing miserably as a Jewish mother?

My childhood had been rather uneventful. My parents loved each other and there was no question that my brothers and I were loved equally and unconditionally. We were all healthy and so were all our grandparents, aunts, uncles, and cousins. We were a typical Jewish family of the 1950s. We celebrated Passover and the High Holidays together. And even though we didn't attend services on a regular basis, we knew we were Jewish.

My parents worked together in a restaurant that they owned and my brothers and I worked after school helping out in the business. My mother and I were particularly close, and as I was growing up I thought of her as my best friend.

I know my close family ties provided me with strong role models for living a Jewish life. Volunteering, fund-raising, visiting the sick, learning, sharing, and caring were just a few of the ways the women in my family, individually and collectively, tried to make a difference. These Jewish mothers were talented, thoughtful, capable, independent, energetic, loving, and giving.

What kind of a role model could I be? I wasn't anything like the women in my family. I fell painfully short in all areas.

It all started out rather idyllically. I married a wonderful man whose father was a Reform rabbi. My mother-in-law was the epitome of a rebbetzin. She was active in Jewish as well as community organizations. Her house and heart were always open. When David and I married, we brought together two wonderful families.

I taught deaf children in the public schools while David went to law school. We joined the temple in Madison, Wisconsin, where we lived, and we began to get involved. After David graduated and got a job, we bought a house and began thinking about starting a family. Jamie, our daughter, was born a year later. Andy, our son, followed nineteen months after that. Our little family was complete.

And then everything changed. In 1979, I was diagnosed with primary multiple sclerosis. I was thirty-three years old. Jamie was five and Andy was three. Of course, like any Jewish mother, my first thoughts were of the children. How would my diagnosis affect them and their lives?

A few days after the diagnosis, our rabbi's daughter celebrated her Bat Mitzvah. I cried during the entire service. I was glad the temple was packed so David and I could hide in the back of the sanctuary. Even though I knew MS was not a terminal illness, I couldn't contain my fears for the future and worries of not living to see my daughter reach this milestone.

Right from the start, David and I knew we had to tell the children something. Even though they were so young, they could see, hear, and feel that something "bad" had happened; Mom cried a lot, and Dad, Grandma, and Grandpa talked in hushed tones.

Jamie's behavior began to change. Our tiny, outgoing little dynamo with Shirley Temple curls didn't want to leave the house to play with her friends. We had to leave her bedroom door open at night because she told us she was afraid we'd leave the house in the middle of the night without her. And there were many nights when she'd wander into our room and climb in bed between us. At three, Andy was usually a happy-go-lucky child who loved to dress up and pretend. Now he began sucking his thumb and carrying his special blanket around the house, something he had stopped doing months before.

One night we told the kids that Mommy had an illness that the doctors didn't know much about, and there was no medicine to make Mommy better. Jamie's first question to me was, "Are you going to die?" Although only five years old, Jamie could ask serious, perceptive questions that went straight to the heart. Oh, how I wished I could have protected my beautiful little girl from the realities of life! That night I cried myself to sleep. Was my illness going to rob my children of the carefree childhood they deserved?

In the months after my diagnosis, I tried to act as though nothing had changed even though, in my heart, I knew it had. I wanted our lives to be as normal as possible. Denial is a wonderful coping mechanism. It anesthetizes you from the pain of reality. My denial manifested itself in my trying to pass as normal.

One of my earliest memories of my limitations was at a Chanukah party a few months after my diagnosis. My friends knew of my diagnosis, but I acted as if it was no big deal. It was relatively easy to do because no one could see the weakness in my right hand and in my legs. Nor could they feel the overwhelming fatigue I felt after doing a simple task like making lunch.

At the party, all the other mothers were bouncing around serving and cutting food for their children, wiping up spills, doing dishes, assembling toys, and acting as referees. I felt guilty for not having the energy to be an active participant and not doing what I perceived as my share. I was afraid to carry food because I was unsteady, and a slight bump or misstep might cause me to spill or drop what I was carrying. And with all the activity and commotion, I could feel my energy level dropping by the minute. I looked fine on the outside, but inside I felt awful.

That night after the kids were in bed, I cried in David's arms. I had always had unlimited energy—now I couldn't keep up. When would my children recognize that I wasn't like the other mothers?

The Jewish mothers I knew growing up wanted their children to have the things they didn't have when they were young. Likewise, I wanted to give my children experiences and opportunities I never had. Our kids loved their gymnastics and ice skating lessons. Thankfully these activities were offered close to our home. However, as time passed, I had trouble helping the kids dress for these activities, and I couldn't lace up their skates tight enough. Reminders of things I couldn't do for myself or for my children were everywhere.

After a few years, the doctor told me that I did not have remitting-relapsing MS, the most common form. I had the chronic progressive type, which meant steady deterioration. Sadly, even today there still is no effective treatment for this progressively disabling type of MS. No matter what I did or didn't do, every day I lost physical abilities.

As the years went by, David pitched in and tried to provide the additional help that was needed, but he worked all day, and he had already taken over many of the jobs I considered mine. The guilt I felt was enormous. I felt guilty because I couldn't be a room mother, Brownie leader, or class trip chaperone. I felt guilty asking other parents to drive my children, knowing that I couldn't reciprocate. I felt guilty that my children had more energy than I had and that at times they were left unsupervised because I was too weak and exhausted to get myself out of bed. I felt guilty because I'd tell them that I'd take them someplace with every intention of following through, and then I'd let them down because my strength and energy disappeared as if someone popped a balloon. I missed many of their soccer games, swim meets, recitals, plays, and other activities because the weather was too hot, or it required too much walking, or it wasn't in an accessible location. I wasn't there to cheer them on or console them when things went wrong. I began to feel as if I was a parent in name only. Other people were taking my place and doing things with my children that I felt I should be doing.

It was bad enough not being the parent that I wanted to be, but it was my inability to protect my children from pain and embarrassment that hurt the most. I remember a few incidents that directly affected Jamie. While she was in elementary school, one of her classmates saw me walking down the hall. My unsteady gait prompted her to ask Jamie if I was drunk. When I could no longer braid Jamie's beautiful blonde curls, we had her hair cut. Jamie was devastated. And, to add to her unhappiness, one of the girls at school told her that her haircut was ugly and asked, "Why did you cut your hair?" When I started to use a three-wheeled scooter wheelchair, Jamie told me how she hated people staring at us. Upon further questioning, she told me she was afraid the stares would make me feel bad and then I wouldn't want to leave the house and go places with the rest of the family.

Even though I had no control over my illness, I tried to remain positive about the future. But it was hard . . . *very hard*. I used great amounts of energy keeping the lid on my Pandora's box of worries. If I let myself begin to think about the future, a flood of dark and foreboding thoughts threatened to consume me.

I hadn't prayed much since I was a child saying my good-night prayers. But I began to pray, in the quiet hours of the night, that I would have the strength to deal with my increasing disability. It was comforting to feel that I was not alone. I didn't blame myself for the illness. I knew it wasn't a punishment for something I did wrong. I was not angry at God and, surprisingly, never asked "Why me?" Rather, my thoughts were always, "Thank God it's me and not one of the children." My "bargain" with God was, "Do whatever you want to me; just don't touch my kids."

I realize now that my Jewish values and upbringing taught me to be hopeful about life. My ancestors, despite all the odds, never gave up hope. They made the best of bad situations and continued to believe that life would and could get better. My journey was not nearly as desperate as that which my ancestors had survived. Surely I could hang on until a treatment or cure was discovered. As physically disabled as I was, I still had the power to control my attitude. There's an old Hasidic saying, "Let us not die while we are alive." I held on to that thought in my darkest hours. And for a few years, it worked for me.

But as MS continued to destroy my physical abilities and deplete my strength, it got harder to stay positive. Every day, Pandora's box of worries threatened to blow open like Old Faithful. My emotional instability permeated every aspect of our family life. If I was "up" things were manageable. If I was "down" nothing seemed to go right. I felt responsible for the climate in the family. It was a lot of pressure.

I'm not sure when the suicidal thoughts began. I do, however, remember two distinct events that affected me deeply. I think it was after these events that the dark thoughts began consuming my days and nights. When Jamie was eleven and Andy was nine, Andy wiped out on his bike and really hurt his leg. Some high school kids saw him and carried him home. Andy was crying and in pain. I was in bed having another bad MS day. I was unable to get up to help him. Jamie had Andy lie down on David's side of the bed next to me. She cleaned Andy's wounds and bandaged him up. I was so proud of my capable, responsible daughter. When she and Andy left the bedroom to go watch TV, I cried. It broke my heart that once again, my child had to be the responsible one and I couldn't be the mom I wanted to be.

In the months after the bike episode, I had trouble getting in and out of bed by myself. I also needed help in the bathroom. David had been helping me with those tasks, but when he wasn't home, the responsibility fell on the kids. They had to lift and transfer me. I hated my body and MS for what it was doing to my family and me. My children did more for me than I did for them. By this time, I had no use of my legs and dominant right arm and hand. I had only minimal use of my left hand. I was dying a little every day. And if that wasn't enough, I felt horribly guilty for not being able to do for my children. How would they ever learn about tzedakah if I didn't teach them?

The kids were too young to remember that I had been a nursery school volunteer and chaperone, that I was active in the temple, as well as an officer in the sisterhood. They never saw me work a temple rummage sale, bake for school activities, or build and run a booth at the July Fourth picnic in our community. I thought they'd have memories of me only as a taker, not a giver. That cold reality hurt me to the core.

I started thinking Jamie, Andy, and David would be better off without me. They could plan outings and know that they wouldn't be canceled because Mom wasn't up to it. Even on the best days, they wouldn't have to plan family activities around Mom's mandatory three-hour afternoon nap. They wouldn't be subjected to Mom's depression and sadness. Jamie and Andy would be spared from the mood swings and irrational, angry outbursts that occurred all too frequently. I remember when Jamie was twelve, she told me sternly one day, "Mom, stop yelling at me. You're not angry at me. You're angry at the MS. Go take a nap and you'll feel better when you're not so tired."

I thought about David, too. If I was dead, he could find himself a "real" wife and partner, someone who had the energy to keep up with him and the kids. He and the children would not be burdened with doing all my jobs. He wouldn't have to listen to me cry myself to sleep. Nor would he have to wake up in the middle of the night to take me to the bathroom or roll me over because I could no longer turn over in bed. If I was living a nightmare, he was too. I never questioned his love for me. He was magnificent beyond words. But I loved him enough that I was willing to disappear from his life so that he could have a second chance to love and be truly happy.

I was in the process of writing these thoughts in a letter. That's the letter Jamie found hidden in my desk. She was right! I was planning to take my life. I knew I had to do it soon or I would become too disabled to do what I had planned. I already had the pills I needed. I even talked with our rabbi. Today, I can't remember a word he said. However, I remember him listening patiently. We talked about David and the children and when he left, I felt peaceful.

When I walked in that day and saw Jamie holding the letter, I was horrified. Jamie never went into my desk. She had her own. But that day, she was looking for a paper clip.

The heart-to-heart talk that followed was a turning point in my life. I was honest and admitted to Jamie that I wanted to die. We held each other and sobbed until we had no more tears. Jamie wanted me to promise her that I wouldn't commit suicide. I knew that if I made that promise, I'd have to shelve my plan permanently. If I lied to her and took my life, it would scar her forever and she might never be able to trust another adult. It was a gut-wrenching decision. But no matter how strongly I felt about my plan, I couldn't stand seeing my child in so much pain. The thought of her crying at my funeral was more than I could bear. I had to put her first. Her arms around me told me heart and soul that my job on earth wasn't done. I was still needed no matter what my physical condition might be. If I hated what the MS did to me, by taking my life, MS would take part of Jamie's life too. I couldn't do that to my child.

In the end, I promised her I would not follow through with my plan.

EPILOGUE

That was eleven years ago. After that life-altering afternoon, avenues of communication with Jamie opened and have remained open to this day. Yet I worried that that afternoon had taken away part of my daughter's childhood and caused her unnecessary pain. I needn't have worried. Both Jamie and Andy remained emotionally and mentally normal. As teenagers, they tested the limits, challenged authority, and disappeared into their bedrooms for weeks at a time. Not surprisingly, their friends were more important than our family. Any embarrassment that we caused them did not seem particularly related to my physical condition. David and I were both treated as if we had not a brain in our head. As difficult as these teenage stages were to live through, I took heart that Jamie and Andy were doing what every other adolescent was doing. They were separating from us and trying to develop their own independent personalities.

However, the realities of my life continued to be challenging. As teenagers, the kids were not happy that I was always around. One day they told me, "Mother, get a life." I listened. They were right. I needed something of my own. If I was going to be here for the long haul, I had better figure out what I was going to do with the rest of my life. I sought ways to cope with the illness by reaching out. And I began a writing career.

The writing led to a self-syndicated column of Making Life Easier tips, which led to the writing of five books. I wrote a catalog resource book for finding helpful but often difficult-to-find aids for daily living. Then I wrote a book on dressing tips and clothing resources for people with disabilities. When I began speaking about my experiences as a person with a disability, audiences wanted more, so I compiled a book of essays chronicling my personal journey living with MS. The Arthritis Foundation commissioned a book of Making Life Easier tips for people with arthritis. Then Demos Medical Publishing hired me to write a book of Making Life Easier tips for people with multiple sclerosis.

My life began to turn around. My depression lifted and my MS stabilized. I still needed help with just about everything, but I had learned how to manage despite my limitations. I was happy that I had found another way to use my teaching skills. By using my professional training and personal experience, I found a new passion and purpose. There was a way I could help others. Instead of dreading each new day, I was now getting up with a sense of hope and anticipation. I began to feel like I *could* be a role model for living a Jewish life—like the wonderful women in my family with whom I had grown up.

Today, Jamie and I are closer than ever. That watershed event is something neither of us will ever forget. I've had the blessing of watching her grow up. I've kvelled with pride as she read from the Torah on her Bat Mitzvah. I've seen her go to the prom and receive awards. I watched her graduate with honors from high school and college. I've been to her first apartment and seen where she works. I've seen her offer thoughtful, heartfelt advice to friends and nurse sick roommates. I've seen her excel in jobs and read employers' outstanding letters of recommendation. I've seen how responsible, organized, dependable, intuitive, and perceptive she is. I understand why once you're a friend of Jamie's, you're *always* a friend.

She's a National Multiple Sclerosis Society volunteer in Chicago, where she now lives, and is taking young leadership classes through the Jewish National Fund. She has many Jewish friends who enjoy being together while doing things that make a difference. It makes me enormously happy to see that Jamie did learn about tzedakah. I know that giving to others will always be part of her life.

Three months ago, Jamie went through a rough time when her perfect twenty-five-year-old life seemed to be falling apart. We talked nightly on the phone. As mature and self-sufficient as she is, she still needed me to be her sounding board, cheerleader, confidant, and friend. After every phone call, I thanked God I was still here for her.

Last month, Jamie and I had lunch together. After lunch, we stopped in the rest room. As my beautiful daughter looked in the mirror, I caught her looking at my reflection. Quietly, as though giving voice to sacred thoughts, she said, "I can't imagine how I would have gotten through the last few months without you. Aren't you happy, too, that you're still here?" Yes, my darling daughter, I certainly am.

– 8 –

On Mourning
for Soldier-Sons in Israel

Amia Lieblich

Yesterday, April 12, 1999, another young Israeli soldier, Noam Barnea, was killed in Lebanon. I did not know him or his family. But in the daily paper I saw his snapshot—merely a boy, with trusting eyes. The paper says he was twenty-one and about to be released from active service in five days. For some strange reason this "very last moment casualty," which by a slightly different fate would not have happened, happens all too frequently here. I recall that when my nephew served in Lebanon last year, it was during the very last week of his service that my sister almost went out of her mind with sleeplessness and worry. Nothing is as painful and frightening as the death of a soldier in action, be it combat or accident. Such a repetitive event, a brief news item that no one in Israel ever gets used to, represents my worst fear as a mother, and I am sure that in saying this I voice the feelings of all Israeli mothers, and probably also mothers on the enemy side.

During the fifty years since the establishment of the state, more than 22,000 Israeli soldiers have been killed in military service. A vast proportion of these casualties are male. Bereft families are very common in Israeli society; everybody knows some. As psychologists usually comment, for parents, the death of their adult son or daughter is the hardest loss to recover from.

Readers are probably aware of the following basic facts: It is mandatory for all Israelis who reach the age of eighteen to serve in the Israeli Defense Force (IDF) for two years if they are women, or three years if they are men. Although some exemptions are legally possible, the majority of Israeli youngsters do serve in the army, and this has become a normal life stage for the draftees and their families (Lieblich, 1989). Women do not serve in combat duties, where their lives can be endangered; only male soldiers are assigned such roles.

I am a mother of two boys and a girl. I will not write about my daughter today, as the experience with girls in this area is so different. My first son, Yuval, served in the IDF as a combat soldier from 1982 to 1985. My second son, Eliav, has been enlisted since 1998, and is presently a combat soldier, too. Simply stated, my sensitivity to the imminent danger to my sons has never left me since the day they were born, and has colored my experience as a human being, a mother, and a female citizen of Israel, every single day. Questions come up again and again: For how long shall we sacrifice our sons, when it is our basic role as parents to protect them? What for? Is there no alternative way? And yet, along with these fears, these painful questions, I am proud of my sons, of their patriotism, their courage, and their no-nonsense attitude about all this. I am also thankful to them, because with their bodies, minds, and courage, they often protect me, their mother.

My literary and academic interests in the lives of individuals and families in Israel, in the shadow of war, stem from this personal pain and concern. Even when my firstborn was merely a schoolboy, being a psychologist and a Gestalt therapist in Jerusalem, I started to collect clinical and literary materials in hopes of shedding more light on how others cope with the ongoing threat to the lives of our sons (Lieblich, 1978, 1989, 1998). I found out that indeed this is a major topic in the lives and experiences of all mothers whose sons serve in the army; fathers, too, although I will concentrate on the mothers' voices here.

The birth of a boy in Israel always evokes slightly ambivalent reactions on the mother's part; with all the happiness of having a boy, the birth of every son is anxiety provoking because of the imminence of his military service. On the same grounds, many mothers accept daughters with great relief. This anxiety may be conscious or unconscious at different periods and stages of development. Immediately after a boy is born, I have heard many parents say something such as, "If this son will have to serve in the army, we are getting out of here"—a threat that rarely materializes later on. The most apparent expression of this anxiety is in the saying: "When you grow up, we will have peace, and you will not have to serve in the army"—a saying that has been contradicted so far by three generations of parents and sons serving in the military.

It is the most difficult moment in the Jewish Israeli mother's life, the one most frightening for all of us, when she finds out that her son has been killed in the army. How does she speak about her loss? How does she cope? How is it depicted in poetry and literature? In what way is this tragedy a social role as well as a personal experience?

I would like to look at these questions from a historical perspective, examining two instances of mothers' reactions, examples that represent two different generations in Israeli society: the founders, the fighters of the 1948 War of Independence, as compared to their children's generation, who are the parents of today's IDF soldiers. Today's soldiers, who fight and die in Lebanon, are the founders' grandchildren. Each of these generations is, naturally, heterogeneous in this respect, as well as in many others. However, I would like to demonstrate how the dominant contents of their reactions to bereavement have gone through a drastic generational transition in the fifty years of Israel's statehood, a transition that reflects deep ideological and political shifts in Israeli society.

Many languages use the term "motherland" to connote a special attachment between a person and his or her land. In Hebrew מולדת—homeland, and mother, the one who bears children—יולדת, have the same root, ילד, which actually means a child. Thus, even the old language creates a bond between mother, child, and the land. Not surprisingly, in public discourse, the mother frequently represents the nation as its symbol, and the individual loss of each son is also a collective, national loss. The famous quotation from Jeremiah the prophet, has come, for example, to represent a universal but also national situation of mourning:

קול ברמה נישמע, נהי, בכי תמרורים, רחל מבכה את בניה, מיאנה להינחם על בניה, כי איננו

"A voice is heard in Ramah, lamentation and bitter weeping, Rachel is weeping for her children, she refuses to be comforted for her children, because they are not." (Jeremiah, 31:15)

PAST REPRESENTATIONS
OF MOURNING MOTHERS

In Israel, in the past, the mother who lost her son in a "just war," "a survival war," defending the homeland, has been one of the most powerful images of the hegemonic Zionist culture. Like Mary and Jesus in the dyadic position of the pietà, so has the sorrow of bereaved Israeli mothers been depicted in pictures and poetry. Examining these images, several themes seem to emerge. A mother who has given life to her son is now presented as the tragic heroine facing his death. The primordial, biological mother-son relationship, which is aimed at giving life and protection from harm, is confronted with the national relationship between citizen and state, which—in two steps—has first taken the child from his mother, and than taken his life from him. Yet, in the founding generation, this tragedy was mostly accepted as justified, by the collective as well as the family, due to its significant contribution to the renewal of the state.

Most of these early ideas are presented in a five-part poem by a well-known male poet, Uri Zvi Grinberg (1948), known as the poet of the nationalist camp. The poem was written during the War of Independence, in November 1948, and titled "By Virtue of a Mother, Her Son, and Jerusalem" (בזכות אם ובנה וירושלים). It describes a mother whose son was killed in battle—in Hebrew we say "fell," a term used much less in English—trying to open up the blocked road to Jerusalem. The poem presents the narrative of a single mother whose whole world darkens and shatters as her son dies. At first she loses the will to live. Yet she copes with her tragedy and finds a way to accept her bereavement by integrating her private experience with the collective Jewish history of loss and redemption. This integration, says the poet, is the true victory, the spiritual-moral triumph of the mother. Even though the battle came to nothing, Jerusalem is worth the sacrifice of a son.

Miron (1992), in his analysis of this poem, points to the curious fact that the father is totally absent from this work, so that a complete love story unfolds between mother and son. The death of the son is conceived as the mother's defeat in a duel with her rival—another female lover, namely Jerusalem. But the woman loves Jerusalem, too, and at the end of the poem she invokes the people and the soldiers never to give up the שלמות of Jerusalem as a whole.

The words of the poem are much stronger than mine. I will look more carefully at some of the lines in Hebrew, followed by my translation. The poem starts as a lamentation:

אם על בנה מקוננת/ בני, בני, תשעה ירחי לידה/ ולילות לפני הריון, לילות כמיהה/ איך אבדת בשרי

ודמי...

A mother laments her son / my son, my son, nine months of labor / nights before pregnancy, nights of longing / how were you lost, my own flesh and blood . . .

In the second part, she frames her son as a hero, and Jerusalem as his other mother, a collective mother who takes his blood, instead of giving it:

בני נפל בגיבורים, בני היה גיבור/ בדרך ירושליימה השותת דם בצמא/ גם היא אמנו, ובני -בנה/

ושלה כולו הוא עכשיו

My son fell among the heroes, my son was a hero / on the way to Jerusalem, thirsty for blood / She, too, is our mother, and my son—her son / and he's all hers now.

And at the very end of the fifth part:

בזכות אם שנתנה את בנה כלפיד בלילך/ עוד יבקיע שחרך וידרוך בגבוה חילך

By virtue of a mother who donated her son as a torch for your night / your dawn will break and your army will soon march high.

While being public symbols, however, the voices of bereft mothers of the past were silenced by society, not to be heard. For both mothers and fathers, the highest level of valor was in carrying their pain in silence—in other words, according to the Western culture, in a masculine manner. In his recent book about the Sabra, the first generations of those born in Israel, Almog (1997) describes funerals and mourning practices in the first thirty years of the state. He characterizes the entire Israeli culture of that period as suppressing emotions, especially pain and sadness. Open emotional manifestation was considered a weakness as well as "primitive" behavior (see also Lieblich, 1978). In military funerals, no crying was heard in public from either men or women. Moreover, crying was interpreted as a protest against the need for and justness of fighting, something totally taboo at the time. From a feminist perspective, this norm is highly masculine, and probably harder to practice for mothers than fathers. Men, as fathers, were at least given the voice of the rituals of Jewish religious mourning, such as in saying Kaddish in public for their sons. The voices of mothers and other females were totally silenced, their natural tendency for emotional expression completely denied. Their self-control was considered to signify patriotism. It also conveyed the message, "I can take care of myself, I will not fall as a burden on others, who have more important, national duties to carry out."

A NEW TREND OF COPING AND PROTEST

The description in the previous section represents the cultural discourse in Israel until the beginning of the 1980s, when the atmosphere started to change. Until then, Israeli mothers of soldiers killed in action were presented, both in mass media and the arts, as state symbols, as heroes, and as victims. Today, the private sphere and normal individual needs are not dominated to the same extent by the public sphere and the needs of the collective. Following a general cultural trend, individualistic modes of discourse and experience have taken over this area as well. With the decline of nationalistic ideologies, the rise of the peace movements, the crumbling of consensus about the need for war, and the greater influence of Sephardic subculture, which has always been more emotional, there has also been a change in the way bereaved mothers are represented. Mothers' voices, women's voices, are heard more in mourning. Men, too, cry more—even young soldiers often cry in public at funerals, a phenomenon that is hard for many Israelis to accept. The practices of mourning and the discourse about the dead have been returned to the private, feminine realm (Gur, 1998; Hendle, 1991; Naveh, 1998).

There are many expressions of this trend. Women speak in public, in emotional and personal terms, about their sons. Many families resent the ready-made clichés of national language concerning the tragedy of their sons (Weiss, 1998). This was manifested, for example, in opposing the standard inscriptions on soldiers' tombstones, which used to be determined by the state and identical for all soldiers, and requesting the right for free expression in this context, which is not only individualized, but frequently subversive. In other words, women as mothers are taking their rightful place as mourners for their sons and, in so doing, change the entire discourse around their death in military action.

A recent interview with Manuella Deviri, a bereaved mother, is a strong demonstration of the new trend (Livneh, 1998, my translation of the quotes). I do not know how representative she is, although many letters were received by the newspaper *Ha-Aretz* in her support, several of them claiming that Deviri's interview signifies the end of the "cult of bereavement" in Israeli culture (Letters to the Editor, August 7, 1998, August 14, 1998). But even if hers is a lonely voice, I find it an important one to hear and amplify in counterdistinction with the heroic mother described in Grinberg's poem. Even if not all bereaved parents would agree with Deviri's sentiments, the mere fact that such sentiments can be openly expressed and supported in Israel today represents a tremendous transition toward freedom of expression and sanity—at least according to *my* judgment.

Deviri's youngest son, Yoni, was a soldier killed in Lebanon on February 26, 1998. Two generations down from Grinberg's fictional mother, Deviri, too, is not crying in public, yet she refuses to be politically silenced. In her interview, given to a female journalist, Neri Livneh, Deviri manifests both individuality and political awareness. She wants to appropriate her tragedy and act out her sorrow in her own individual manner. Furthermore, she mobilizes her emotions for political protest.

To begin with, she is openly against the "holy cows of bereavement," and especially the traditional image of the bereaved mother:

> To be a bereaved mother, אם שכולה, is such a big and meaningful title, that from this terrible moment of the night of the twenty-sixth of February, when I was informed that I earned this title, for many people I ceased to be Manuella Deviri the

> woman, the human being. . . . Even if for a moment I felt that
> okay, something terrible has happened to me, but I am still
> alive . . . nobody would let me. (Livneh, 1998, p. 36)

Deviri continues to describe the attitudes and public expectations
of her as a bereft mother. She is expected to cry all day and never
smile. If she does not look totally ruined, it means she does not love
her child as a mother should. She objects to this norm for several
reasons. First, she believes that Yoni's death is enough of a tragedy,
without the "need to ruin" his mother's life, too. Furthermore, from
her perspective, showing mothers crying on their sons' graves has
become banal, and signifies acceptance of this fate, rather than taking
action against it.

Her reaction to what she calls a "show of national grief" is both
personal and political. She does not believe in the slogans about the
whole nation as a big family in mourning. For her, the only proof of
deep care is stopping the ongoing bloodshed, and this belief has
driven her into antiwar political activism:

> You can fall easily into this narcissistic trap and adopt this stance
> of the bereaved mother. For me, the significance of Yoni's
> death is that I have discovered how meaningless I am, and that
> the only thing I can do is to be truthful. . . . I feel that Yoni's
> death has given me a great clarity of vision. Suddenly I have
> no more patience for nonsense. My first duty toward Yoni, the
> child who keeps living inside me, is . . . never to be silenced
> again. Not to let people forget for a moment that Israel must
> withdraw from Lebanon, must make peace with the Palestin-
> ians. Perhaps, if I had done something for these goals before,
> Yoni would not have been killed. (Livneh, 1998, p. 36)

When the journalist, impressed with her intensity, asked her why
her words carry more weight or validity than anyone else's, Deviri's
simple answer is "because I have already paid the price."

To me, her voice represents a new composition of private and
public languages, of the feminine and masculine voices and modes
of being, in today's Israeli discourse. The time has perhaps come for
mothers, a "new" kind of mother—individualist, feminist, and daring—to enter the public arena in Israel for their sons' sake, for their

own sake, and for the sake of the future. It is, after all, our essential role as mothers to protect our sons and daughters, and not to sacrifice them, but to look for an alternative to the ongoing bloodshed in the Middle East.

This is indeed manifested in a small but powerful women's organization for peace that emerged recently in Israel under the provocative name "Four Mothers," referring to the four matriarchs of the Jewish nation—Sarah, Rivka, Rachel, and Leah. Four women started the movement, all mothers of combat soldiers in active service, on the tragic night in 1997 in which two IDF helicopters, transporting soldiers to their duty in the South of Lebanon, collided and crashed, leading to the loss of seventy-three lives. The political activity of Four Mothers aims toward immediate, unilateral withdrawal from Lebanon, where most casualties of Israeli soldiers have occurred in the last few years. The movement's public activities started in August 1997. Since then, it has been able to mobilize a lot of action, interest, and identification, as well as vehement opposition. Although the core of activists consists of no more than ten women, more than 10,000 individuals signed petitions expressing their identification with their demands.

In their discourse through the mass media, spokeswomen for the movement said that as mothers of soldiers who might pay the highest price for the Israeli position in Lebanon, they have the moral right to evoke a public debate on, and support for, the withdrawal. They said that while their sons keep fighting, they do all they can for their sons. They advocate one supreme value, which is the holiness of life. In several interviews they said: "Enough with feminine helplessness and avoidance of political action," and "We gave birth to these sons, we raised them, and handed them to the army on a silver tray. It is now our duty to act for their survival."

Not surprisingly, public opponents to the movement, on various levels, claimed that these are "hysterical women" (although the movement includes men!), who have no experience in the army and absolutely no understanding of the complicated political situation in the Middle East. One can assume that their status as mothers of soldiers actually protects them from even more severe attempts to silence their voices. During the summer of 1997 a new movement, "Three Fathers" (referring to the three biblical patriarchs), was announced by fathers of soldiers in Kiryat Shmone—the northern town that suffers most from hostilities from Lebanon. This group argued that the Israeli Defense Force should remain in Lebanon and protect the north, and that "women who sit in coffee bars in Tel Aviv have no right to experiment on the safety of our babies in Kiryat Shmone." This movement ceased to exist immediately after its only public appearance, however, while the Four Mothers persists in its protest activities.

The following quote from Irit Letzter, a Four Mothers activist (Beker, 1998), succinctly expresses their credo, using the old myth of the binding of Itzchak:

> I am a mother of four. When my eldest son went to the army, and volunteered to the paratroopers, I had such a panic reaction that right away I got pregnant with another child—a girl this time, thank God. She is now a year and a half old. I know the association is terrible, it terrifies me, too, but that's a mother's instinct, there's nothing you can do. . . . When God told Abraham: "Go get your son, your only one, the one you love, Itzchak"—Abraham obeyed right away, he didn't argue with God. Had God asked Sarah for the same, she would have certainly said: "Go away; forget it. I will not sacrifice this child." (p. 5)

It is late in the evening in my house in Jerusalem when I finish writing this short paper. A helicopter is hovering over the sky of the city, breaking the quiet of the night. Is it, God forbid, another soldier on his way to the hospital, wounded or dead?

REFERENCES

Almog, Oz (1997). *The Sabra—A portrait.* Tel Aviv: Am Oved (Hebrew).
Beker, Avichai (1998). Mothers' war games. *Ha-Aretz,* January 2, p. 5 (Hebrew).
Grinberg, Uri Zvi (1948). By virtue of a mother, her son, and Jerusalem. *Herut,* November 26, p. 3 (Hebrew).
Gur, Batya (1998). *A stone for a stone.* Jerusalem: Keter (Hebrew).
Hendle, Jehudith (1991). *The mountain of the erring.* Tel Aviv: Kibbutz Ha-Meuchad (Hebrew).
Letters to the Editor (1998). *Ha-Aretz,* August 7, August 14 (Hebrew).

Lieblich, Amia (1978). *Tin soldiers on Jerusalem beach.* New York: Pantheon.

Lieblich, Amia (1989). *Transitions to adulthood during military service.* New York: State University of New York Press.

Lieblich, Amia (1997). *Conversations with Dvora—An experimental biography of the first modern Hebrew woman writer.* Berkeley, California: The University of California Press.

Lieblich, Amia (1998). Mother-son relationship in the shadow of war. Paper delivered at the Conference on Mothers and Sons, Toronto, York University.

Livneh, Neri (1998). The holy cows of bereavement. *Ha-Aretz,* July 31, pp. 32-38 (Hebrew).

Miron, Dan (1992). *Facing the silent brother: Studies in the poetry of the War of Independence.* Jerusalem: Keter (Hebrew).

Naveh, Chana (1998). On loss, bereavement and mourning in Israeli experience. *Alpaiim,* No. 16, 85-120 (Hebrew).

Weiss, Meira (1998). "We are all one bereaved family": Personal loss and collective mourning in Israeli society. *Studies in Contemporary Jewry, An Annual,* 14, 178-192.

– 9 –

On My Son's Induction into the Israeli Armed Forces: A Feminist Mother's Prayer

Naomi Graetz

You were a miracle child, discovered one month old in utero when I had a cyst removed. Eight months and eight days later you were inducted into the Jewish faith, with a cut, a knife, blood, and wine on a Shabbat morning during the month of Kislev while I huddled in the bedroom waiting for your cry. When you were thirteen, we said, "Baruch she-petaranu mi-onsho shel zeh," (Blessed be the One who absolves us of this one's punishment). We laughed, because you weren't a punishment, and thirteen was too young an age for us to be getting rid of you.

You are eighteen now and I feel that I am being punished in your going off: not only will I have to start doing laundry on Shabbat,[1] but I will be expected to send you and your friends the unhealthy candy and cookies of which you were previously "deprived." No more trips abroad together for us. The long-awaited sabbatical will have to be delayed. My newly found need to focus on finding myself as a woman clashes with your needs.

I've been dialoguing with Palestinian women and now have to shift my empathy from them to you, the Israeli soldier, who is their enemy. It gets to be too much; the dialogue group disbands.[2]

The rethinking I undergo is minor compared to my newly churned up feelings of pride and dread. Every article in the newspaper about a soldier's suicide, Russian roulette, and training accidents causes introspection and guilt. Did I raise him strong enough to withstand basic training?

I revisit the story of the Akedah, the Sacrifice of Isaac, and identify with Sarah, Isaac's mother. I wonder if Sarah, like me, questioned why she allowed herself to be dragged on aliyah.[3] I never thought of myself as a self-sacrificing Jewish mother—certainly not sacrificing one who is part of my self, flesh of my flesh, my only son. But I have chosen. I identify too with Joshua's mother. Is any land so important that I must teach my son to be a good soldier? Giving birth to a son in the state of Israel means to me:

> The knife, the Agony.
> The pain, again to Choose. . . . my son, the live one.
> I am he. Or am I the dead one—
> Lost, abandoned, On the altar,
> On the way to the knife . . .
>
> Send him off if you can.[4]

I write this and realize that not only do I have the strength to send you off, but that I must. Whatever pacifist thoughts *I* have about war, they will have to be put on a back burner for now. The enemies out there that want to destroy us are real, not abstract. Peace is not on the horizon yet. It is important that you learn to be on your own with a support system backing you up. Eighteen is young to become your own man—if not now, when? This is your test and mine. You will be told to shoot first—and I will hope that you will not have to; that you will not witness battles and death at first hand; but that if you do, you will be able to draw sustenance from our tradition.

How do I, a feminist with pacifist leanings, send you off? With ambivalence, with love, with fear, with pride, with support, with the knowledge that whatever you do we will be there for you. Lech-lecha b'shalom; Hazor b'shalom. Go in peace. Come back safely.

NOTES

1. The Israeli army sends its soldiers home every other Shabbat; the trade-off for this is that the army is not responsible for laundering its soldiers' clothing. Guess who is expected to wash the grimy uniforms? The religious Israeli family

with a soldier in its midst has to figure out how to get the laundry washed, dried, and ironed from erev Shabbat, the time the soldier walks in, until motzae Shabbat, when he goes back to the base.

2. Reading this almost ten years later, prior to its publication, I wish to remark that I am now newly involved with the Palestinian women who were very politically engaged during the Intifada and are now active in feminist causes and raising money through traditional channels such as the New Israel Fund.

3. The word aliyah literally means "going up" and is used to describe people who immigrate to Israel. Aliyah is opposed to the word yeridah, which means "going down." The latter term is used to describe those who leave Israel. Olim and Yordim (immigrants and emigrants) are charged words—they don't merely describe migrants, but are used in approval or disapproval. Thus even today a yored or yoredet, someone who leaves Israel, is looked down upon by some, as if he or she couldn't stick to what God has decreed to be the destiny of our people.

4. This is an excerpt from a poem I wrote titled "Akedah Revisited" (*Judaism,* Summer, 1991) reprinted in my collection of aggadot, *S/He Created Them: Feminist Retellings of Biblical Stories* (Chapel Hill, NC: Professional Press, 1993).

10

Jewish Mother and Son:
The Feminist Version

Phyllis Chesler

I am a Jewish mother because I am the daughter of a Jewish mother. My mother, Lillian Chesler (of blessed memory), died on February 24, 1998. Only now that she is gone do I really begin to know her. I think about her more now than when she was alive. She is more present, closer. I hear her more clearly—I know just what she would say in any given circumstance. I have learned her lines. I know them well. Although I fled from the family madness, violence, secrecy, and denial, I have also come to understand that my mother is the one person I have most tried to please, the one person whom I could never please—and she might say the very same thing about me.

My mother was—is?—very smart, energetic, and ambitious. I used to say (even to her) that she could run a small country, but that's exactly what she thought she was doing as she presided over our family of five. My mother was the youngest of five sisters, of whom three survived. She was born seventeen years after her next eldest sister, the only one to be born in America. My mother functioned as an interpreter for her Yiddish-speaking parents in an English-speaking world. She was the baby, the family's last hope for a son. My mother was the domestic servant, first to her eldest sister, then to her parents. She quit school to support her ailing, aging parents. This never bothered her; it was her greatest mitzvah, good deed. My mother spoke of her parents in a hushed, obedient, slightly frightened, or rather awestruck tone. "Ma," I would ask, "how could you stand it that they didn't let you go to college and they wouldn't let you study ballet either?" "What do you know?" she'd say. "There was no choice; they needed me. You don't ask questions; you just help out."

And while she berated me bitterly for my "wild" ways, she actually never forced me to help her with the ever-returning housework; she allowed me to do my nonstop reading and writing and drawing and thinking. . . .

From time to time, my mother visits me wearing either her pink or her aqua pastel chiffon dress, beaming. She is, finally, becoming my fairy-book Guardian Angel.

*   *   *

Before I became a mother, my ego knew no bounds. I thought I could overcome all obstacles through force of will, not by bending to circumstance or trusting in forces larger than myself. For me, motherhood was something of a reverse Zen experience. In the beginning, I had no responsibilities other than to my ideas. Having a child was a passage from detachment to attachment.

I learned that life does not stand still, that it is always changing, growing, dying, being renewed. For years, when I had looked in the mirror, I always looked the "same" to myself. Time became real for me when I began to measure it by my son's obvious, visible growth. Time became more finite.

I comprehended, in my body, that I would die.

Upon becoming a newborn mother—oh, how the earth pulled me down, grounded me, deepened my imaginative reach. Becoming a mother changed my life. It humbled and empowered me, slowed me down, made me kinder and infinitely more vulnerable to cruelty. Having a son, not a daughter, was a challenge to my passionate, woman-centered feminism. I used to joke that if I'd had a daughter, she would probably have rebelled against my Warrior Program for Girls by marrying young and embracing a traditional life. I was unprepared for a son; thus, I accepted him as he was. I had no program to impose upon him.

I lie. How I lived my life, the ideas I held most dear, were, for my son Ariel, his earliest knowledge of Eden, the site of origin, memory, safety, familiarity, the place from which he was "sent forth." In Beresheet (Genesis) 3:23, God does not "banish" or "exile" us from Paradise. Like a mother, God "vayishalchahoo," sent us forth, released us, into History, to confront mortality, pain, danger, destiny, and covenental glory.

In my thirty-seventh year, I quietly and deliberately chose to become a biological mother. At the time, I had been a feminist activist for a decade, and a university professor and therapist for eight years. I had already published two books and was working on a third. My husband was an Israeli, born after the Jews had a sovereign state of our own; through his mother, he was also among the ninth generation of descendants of the Baal Shem Tov. Obviously, this all mattered to me, as did his promise to co-*mother* our child.

More than twenty-two years have passed since I was first pregnant with Ariel. In the beginning, we were raw, strangers to each other, mere possibilities; as he aged, we grew, miraculously, closer. We continue to defy the so-called normal course of "development," in which young boys, girls too, are supposed to reject the world of their mothers, in order to receive their fathers' or the world's blessing.

Now, in his twenty-first year, Ariel towers over me—not fair, I jest: I should be taller since I've read more books than he has. I am, of course, proud of his height, in every sense. He's not merely pro-mother but pro his own mother! He is a writer and a poet. He is also an ardent feminist. Quietly, he's changed his name to mine.

How have I managed to wrest a feminist son from this world? Was this destined, was it something I did, or something my son brought with him—his gift to me? Is he "mine," because his father abandoned him—and I was all Ariel had? I doubt it; too often, this scenario leads other, similarly father-wounded sons and daughters into overly prizing the absent father, taking the omnipresent mother for granted.

Mothering a child can be an incomparable rite of passage. However, I certainly do not romanticize mothers or motherhood. The working conditions are inhumane, the choice to mother more forced than free. The Forced Motherhood Experience does not transform every woman into a saint. Some blossom; others, martyred, shrivel.

Perhaps I was more conscious than most women that I did, indeed, have a choice about whether "to be or not to be . . ." a mother. Perhaps, like most women, I, too, yearned for my mother's love and approval—and in its perceived absence, gravitated toward having a child—as if only a child could meet a grown woman's longings for union and intimacy, and satisfy a Jewish daughter's obligation to become a Jewish mother.

However, I did not sign on to be a single mother.

Even with household and child care assistance, being the sole female breadwinner and primary caretaker of a young child is the hardest job on earth. For me, it meant working twelve to eighteen hours a day, seven days a week, enduring escalating expenses, a decline in both income and "prospects," and little time to squander on adult-only social or sexual diversions. On the other hand, the children of single mothers often tend to develop a more balanced, human Self; they often embody both "masculine" and "feminine" traits. Sons cook, do the family laundry; daughters repair toilets. Sons (but daughters too) sometimes go into their mothers' businesses.

In a beautiful introduction to a 1998 edition of *With Child: A Diary of Motherhood* (Chesler, 1998), Ariel writes:

> This is [my mother's] warrior's tale and she is an ancient bard. She sings a prayer that is her *Shema*—her motherly prayer, the most important prayer in Judaism. She writes, "Hear, O Israel, I am one. Mother and Child. Male and Female. Past and Future." I can also hear a fairytale-like sound to her story. "In colors of blood and air I spin without stopping: colon, foot, eye. By day, by night, for nine months, I weave you: precisely. Faithfully." This is so witch-like, her spinning me into gold, into body.

And: "I love my name, what it means, and how it sounds. I am glad to be a Shakespearean spirit, a lion of God, a secret nickname for the city of Jerusalem, a small city in Israel, and even a little mermaid if people must insist on it."

I am blessed by my son. I was very lucky in other ways too.

"Mother-writers" (the phrase is Tillie Olsen's) have, in the past, often been condemned to long periods of "silence." Instead of writing, they did the washing, darned socks, mended dresses, grew vegetables, cooked, preserved, baby-tended, child-tended, husband-tended, entertained, attended church. Harriet Beecher Stowe had no room of her own. She lived for others: six children and an extended family. Thus, Stowe could only write sporadically, in between her endless other tasks. Like Charlotte Perkins Gilman and Rebecca Harding Davis, Stowe, too, finally had a "breakdown." I would too—wouldn't you?—if you wanted to write a book that would "make this whole nation feel what an accursed thing slavery is," but your domestic duties would not allow you to get to *Uncle Tom's Cabin* for nearly fifteen years?

As others (Sappho, Adrienne Rich, Toni Morrison, Mary Gordon) have said: a child is a woman's greatest love. On its behalf, she must sleep less, accept no social engagements, write quickly, and for only a few precious hours at a time: while her child is sleeping or in school. Above all, she must be able and willing to put her work aside when her young child needs her.

I was not this kind of mother-writer. I wrote at home, but my door was absolutely shut when I was writing. True, I always paid someone to be "on duty" in my place. Often, that woman judged me harshly for turning my back on my own child. Sometimes, my son did too.

Ariel writes:

> My mother's office door is shut, but that means nothing to me . . . I knock calmly on her door and enter before she can reply. Her books surround her as usual and she sits with a pen in hand. "I'm off-duty!" she informs me. I do not comprehend that phrase and reply "You are not a taxi Mom, I need to talk to you."

Touché.

In my time, few divorced mothers and children were invited to be part of coupled, married social life. Single mothers each drowned alone; we didn't live collectively. There was, as yet, no lesbian baby boom or single-parent adoption movement, nor did pro-child, feminist utopian communities exist in New York City.

Ariel's Israeli grandparents, aunts, and cousins all lived in Tel Aviv and rarely saw him. My mother definitely "helped"—but her help was always accompanied by blaming-and-shaming, not only me, but Ariel too. As Ariel grew older, he did not want to visit *my* mother without *his* mother there to protect him from the nonstop barrage of criticism. Ariel's two uncles, my brothers, are fiercely misogynistic. Both have hair-trigger tempers. One was a wife beater and child abuser, the other routinely cursed and threatened each of his girlfriends (I know; the wives and girlfriends usually turned to me for help—and then, predictably, turned on me for actually daring to offer any). I did not want to expose Ariel to them, but even on those rare occasions that found us all together, my brothers rarely paid any attention to Ariel. Once, one of my brothers terrified Ariel by holding him down and keeping him in a choke hold long after a then-five-year-old Ariel began sobbing.

"Think," said I, "of what you have been spared by not being forced to grow up with cruel or rivalrous older men." But in my heart, I felt guilty that I had not been able to provide Ariel with good male role models who also loved him.

In my time, (single) mothers who did not wish to mother in utter isolation had to work hard to create and maintain the extended family they did not already have. Most of the women I knew had either rejected marriage and motherhood or had already "sacrificed" themselves for their children and husbands long ago; they had no time to waste. When I became a mother, I was surrounded by women who lived for careers, art, revolutionary activism. I often had to keep my motherhood "in the closet" to be accepted among them. (But then, I had to keep my revolutionary feminism in the closet to be accepted among more traditional women.)

To my surprise, the men at my university (The College of Staten Island, City University of New York), were more—not less—angry at me when I became pregnant. I understood that my feminism, pro-student positions, and public visibility had offended and threatened them. I was not prepared for the viciousness that my pregnancy unleashed. For example, once I knew I was pregnant, I tried to have my next-semester teaching schedule changed so that I would not have to continue teaching a late afternoon to late evening schedule. The male administrators refused to allow me to make this change. One male dean accosted me in the cafeteria and snarled at me, "Why don't you just quit and become a 'real' mother? Decide what you want: To be a mother or to remain on staff. You can't do both."

This kind of thing, and far worse things, had happened to many other female professors at every branch of City University. I know; I interviewed them.

I had begged the publisher of my third book to bring it out while I was pregnant, not after I gave birth. The publisher refused—then insisted that I go 'round the country to hawk the merchandise. I had no choice. I was the sole support of my family. I weaned Ariel, against my will, and did so. When I decided I had to write *With Child: A Diary of Motherhood,* a female editor at this same house said, "What is this bullshit? You can write a 'real' book. Why waste your time on this nonsubject?" A male editor at another publishing house, whom I'd never met, told my agent: "What could she possibly write about pregnancy or motherhood? She's not a 'normal' woman and she won't be a 'normal' mother."

My own mother (may she rest in peace) did not approve of me any more now that I was finally a mother. She would still greet me this way: "What, another book against the men?" Only after she died did one of her friends happen to tell me that, on a bus ride across America they took together, my mother would literally run to the library in each city to see if they had any of my books. My mother never stopped criticizing me because I was not a full-time stay-at-home mother. It hurt more, not less, each time she did so.

But surely I found support among the "sisterhood," you say. Not exactly. Both heterosexual and lesbian feminists were, at least in my experience, without mercy on the subject and reality of motherhood. Some feminists were so angry at what motherhood had done to their own mothers (or the pain their mothers had passed along to them) that they remained hostile to biological motherhood in general, and to the mothers of boys in particular. Actually, I also believe that many accomplished women were so mother wounded that they kept looking for that maternal resource everywhere, and behaved rivalrously or, at best, indifferently, toward another woman in the act of "mothering" someone else.

Once, I did a benefit for a group of academic feminists. I took a mainly sleeping Ariel (and a baby-sitter) along. Some women kept their distance. One woman looked at me with deep distaste; another remarked that I was "parading my biological narcissism all over the place."

Understand: I was being treated like a "star." I had heard horror stories about some radical lesbian feminist groups who had physically and psychologically attacked the mothers of young sons when they tried to bring them along to an all-female conference/music festival/academic meeting. Each year, I asked to bring Ariel along to the Famous Feminist all-female Passover Seder in New York, which I co-founded and co-led. The leaders of this group included two heterosexual married mothers, two formerly married, later-in-life lesbian mothers, and two divorced women, one heterosexual, one a later-in-life lesbian, neither of whom were biological or adoptive mothers. All wanted their third seder night to be "male-free." "But how," I asked, "will the men of tomorrow ever be different if we do not expose them to feminist Judaism, if they have no memories of women as both spiritually authoritative and tender?"

On the other hand, the *anti*-feminists were even worse. Most felt (and still feel), that a "good" mother must marry both husbands and houses, and bury themselves alive, full-time, "for the sake of the children." Being told that God wants (married) women to procreate and that all who refuse His commandment are evil or crazy elicits naught but a fine fury in me.

In the beginning, I was supported, totally and only, by Ariel's father, my co-mother. At the time, I would have told you that men could do the work of mothering/parenting too, that like women, men, too, could go far beyond the obligations of economic support. (Some do. More don't.)

For a year and a half, Ariel's father refused to return to school or to find any gainful employment. Instead, he took excellent, maternal care of our son. Actually, he kept the serial live-in housekeepers (whom I found and paid) excellent company, took Ariel to his doctor appointments and to the park, daily, changed Ariel's diapers far more expertly than I ever could, and was always calm in an emergency. The stay-at-home neighborhood mothers confused him with Dustin Hoffman in *Kramer vs. Kramer*, and they thought I was Mrs. Kramer, the "career monster." And then my husband began to fall apart. Friends told him I was "using him," that being a co-mother was not a "man's" job. Friends encouraged him to threaten to kidnap Ariel and take him to Israel (he did make this threat), in order to get me to give him money (which I did do). I had already embarked on the research and interviews for what would become *Mothers on Trial: The Battle for Children and Custody;* I knew enough to take his threat seriously.

My husband told me he was having an affair—and then he walked out. I was certain that he would not divorce our son, too.

I was wrong.

He walked out and never looked back. I, the Amazon warrior, found I could not walk away. I could not drop the baby. Whether gender differences are innate or conditioned, I began to note, and rue, some of the differences. However, I learned that even a pro-mother, pro-collective child-rearing Israeli kibbutz can have fairly rigid, punitive views of what a "good" mother can and cannot do.

Once, in 1980, after working at the United Nations and attending an international, profoundly anti-Zionist/anti-Semitic conference in Copenhagen, I flew to Israel with Ariel and a baby-sitter. My mission: to convince the Israeli government to hold a radical feminist conference. I also wanted to live on a kibbutz for a while. For years, many kibbutzim were reluctant to allow single women, including Yom Kippur War widows to join, lest they "steal" the married men. I, too, was perceived as such a dangerous single woman. Eventually, with the assistance of Israeli writer Yoram Kiniuk, I found a Hashomer Hatzair kibbutz that housed all its children in a Children's House (I had been a member of the Hashomer Hatzair kibbutz movement from the ages of eight to eleven).

I had to stay over in Jerusalem for some back-to-back meetings for one night. When I called the kibbutz, the woman on the phone insisted that I come back, that my baby-sitter (with whom I was sharing a small cottage), had fallen ill working in the orchard, and a two-year-old needed his mother. "I can't come back," said I. "Why not put Ariel in the Children's House for one night?" "Oh no, we can't do that." "All right, then. Put him out in the road for the night if you must." Of course, they did no such thing. Ariel spent an uneventful night with all the other children. And I got naught but glares and stares upon my return.

Who helped me bring Ariel up? Women, sweet women. My mother, in her way. Paid housekeepers and nannies and, in 1983, my first live-in female lover. In 1992, my second female lover, a lawyer, fought very hard (and successfully) for more than six years to obtain child support. She had to put Ariel's father in jail for this to happen, but that's a tale for another day. The court battle rages on.

Ariel's feminist education continues. Last year, a neighborhood magazine, *Brooklyn Bridge*, asked Ariel to "Brooklynize" his introduction to *With Child*. Ariel worked hard on draft number one, and sent it in. Time passed. Finally, his editor, a woman, apologized and explained that her boss kept changing her mind about what she wanted from a piece, that it wasn't just Ariel's piece. Ariel worked on draft number two and sent it over. Again, a long time passed. I finally called on his behalf, then encouraged Ariel to call one more time. There was a new editor. Maybe things would now work out. Finally, Ariel went over and sat down with a male editor who, in no uncertain terms, said the following: "Your piece is very good but, frankly, it is not at all what we had in mind. None of us believes that any son could have such a positive relationship with a feminist mother. We know you have a *Mommie Dearest* to write. We also understand that if you are still living at home or financially dependent upon your mother, you are probably afraid to tell the truth. So, look us up in the future when you are ready to tell that truth."

REFERENCES

Chesler, Phyllis (1991). *Mothers on trial: The battle for children and custody.* New York/San Diego: Harcourt Brace & Co.

Chesler, Phyllis (1998). *With child: A diary of motherhood.* Introduction by Ariel Chesler. New York: Four Walls Eight Windows Press.

11

If I Can't Tear the Toilet Paper, Why Can I Flush the Toilet?

Barbara Green

My oldest son, Daniel, is a ba'al teshuvah, a secular Jew who embraced Orthodox Judaism. One day while visiting him in Jerusalem I brewed him a cup of tea. We sat and talked but after half an hour I saw that he wasn't drinking his tea. "Has it gotten cold?" I asked eagerly. "I can heat it up for you." "Oh, no," he said. "Perhaps it's still too hot? I can add cold water," I added reassuringly. "No, really," he said. Still the level of tea didn't decline. "Then what is it?" I asked in bewilderment.

After a few moments of intense concentration, Daniel began to laugh. For a moment I forgot he was wearing a black hat and suit, the unmistakable hallmarks of an ultra-Orthodox Jew. Gone were the profound differences in our lifestyles, mine militantly secular and his totally observant. In that instant, we inhabited our old life together with moments of strife punctuated by warm laughter. Finally Daniel explained his dilemma.

"I don't know how to deal with this situation," he said. "As you know, Jewish law requires respect for one's parents and forbids humiliating or embarrassing anyone. Because you are my mother, I don't know how to tell you . . . " (very long pause here) " . . . that you put salt in the tea instead of sugar!"

When I tell people that my son is a ba'al teshuvah, I brace for the predictable response. Usually there is a sharp intake of breath, accompanied by a barely audible, "Oh, my God!" "How did it happen?" they ask. "What made him do it? How do you deal with it?"

I replay the tape in my head, rewinding to the fateful day when it all began. After so much self-examination, the inescapable conclusion remains: In some ironic twist of fate, it was MY doing. Or was it the inscrutable workings of the God in whom I don't believe? Or something else? Still, there's no denying that I started the proceeding. Here is how it began, innocently enough, to be sure.

Like so many young Jewish men of the 1970s and 1980s, Danny had lost his moorings. Drugs, a hitchhiking trip across the country, a brief flirtation with a cult all characterized this period of his life. In reality he was searching for meaning and purpose and something to hang his life on. He was in and out of the university, doing brilliantly while there but finding the experience without significance. We watched, helpless to counter his aimlessness. We also feared he was about to give up on Judaism. He complained that religions divided people rather than uniting them. I was afraid he was walking away from something he knew little about.

One day I read about a weekend of learning for Jewish college students sponsored by the local university Hillel Association. Hoping that Danny would learn something about Judaism before he decided to renounce it, I urged him to attend the seminar. He was reluctant. For the first time I could remember, I asked him " . . . to do it for me." Again, the response was tepid. Finally he gave in and signed up.

But on the opening Friday night he had a bad cold and announced he would go to the seminar the next day. I pushed hard, arguing that the opening session would likely set the stage for the rest of the weekend. I suggested that he could come home after a few minutes if he didn't feel well. Reluctantly he left for the Hillel building, returning at midnight. The next morning he left the house before the rest of us awakened and again didn't return until very late.

On Sunday morning when we finally caught up with each other, he was eager to describe what had happened. He began with the sentence, "I felt as though I had been touched by God." These were not words he had learned at home; it was his own unique response. We didn't know what to say.

In Danny's search for meaning and purpose in life, he had discovered . . . Orthodox Judaism! Now, fifteen years later, he spends his days studying Torah in a yeshiva in Jerusalem, is married and the father of five, and lives in a religious town. In almost all ways, he is more like my shtetl grandfather for whom he was named than like my husband and me.

His transformation was slow but steady. He began weekly study with a rabbi. Next came the decision to wear a yarmulke, which his co-workers called "his little hat." He scrupulously followed the injunction to "put things straight" with people he had wronged, going to each one and asking forgiveness. Soon he took on the commandment of strict Shabbat observance. We watched with increasing incomprehension, still secretly hoping this was a stage. Finally, the issue was joined when Danny asked us to make the kitchen kosher. Suddenly, religious observances that he had taken on for himself threatened to engulf all of us. We refused.

Once I met a woman whose son had given up a brilliant career as a physicist to become "haredi," ultra-Orthodox. "Rena" was so dismayed that she cut off all contact with her son. By the time I met her she was the grandmother of seven children whom she had never seen. One day she asked herself, "Who am I punishing?" She reconciled with her new family soon afterward.

I couldn't imagine cutting off contact with Danny, but the first few years after his "conversion" were very difficult for all of us. Like all new converts, he carried everything to extremes. The prohibition against carrying anything on Shabbat meant he wouldn't wear gloves in the winter in case he dropped one and couldn't pick it up. In the spring he refused to smell the flowers lest he be tempted to pick one, another forbidden Shabbat activity. He permanently abandoned his on-again-off-again university career, insisting that everything one needed to know was in the Torah. We listened with heavy hearts as he frequently phoned a rabbi in a distant city for advice, clearly signaling our inability to advise and counsel him. He replaced old friends with new "religious" ones.

After eight months of being an Orthodox Jew in a little town in the Midwest, Danny decided he needed a more supportive environment. He moved to Monsey, New York, a town of ultra-Orthodox Jews where he studied the arcane laws of Judaism in a yeshiva with other newly religious young men. Strange as it may seem, I shall forever be indebted to that institution, for it was there that the basic rules of our new relationship were laid down. Here he was taught that the family is the central unit of Jewish life. Young men students, called yeshiva bochers, were asked to examine their relations with their families. If the basic ties were strong, they were urged to pay attention to those ties to ensure they didn't fray. If the relationship had been damaged by the son's "conversion" to ultra-Orthodoxy, it was imperative to create a new, positive relationship. Thus it became a required duty, not merely desirable behavior.

I read everything I could about his new world: fictionalized accounts of "conversions" to fundamentalist Judaism, sociology, anything that rendered intelligible this strange new territory. It helped me to understand the underpinnings of Danny's universe, so unlike mine. Yet, in the early years, I must confess I hoped it would all go away. The differences between us were almost too great to be navigated. The hole in the fabric of our family could never be repaired. No more beach vacations together—ultra-Orthodox men mustn't see women in bathing suits. The likelihood of Danny attending his brothers' weddings seemed remote—unless we provided glatt kosher food and asked all the women to dress modestly.

And then he himself was married, and with the arrival of grandchildren everything changed for me. Danny's wife, Naima, is a seventh-generation Jerusalemite, ultra-Orthodox, of course. Her warm and loving persona captured my heart from the first. And she seems to have responded to me with an open heart as well. Our differences are made easier because she and her entire family have dovish views on making peace with the Palestinians, something that is quite important for me. They also deplore violence and coercion on religious matters. Some of them even believe in separating religion from state in Israel. Because of these "enlightened attitudes," it's fairly easy for me to move among them. More so than it used to be.

At Danny and Naima's wedding, her grandmother admired my dress. Seeing me hatless, she offered a head scarf that she said just matched my outfit. I declined politely. Soon she returned, this time telling me how lovely I would look in the scarf. Not comprehending her hidden message, again I declined. Finally she explained that the men present would feel more comfortable if I covered my head. I donned the scarf.

Today I know the rules. Now I wear dresses with sleeves below the elbows whenever I visit Danny. My skirts are long. I don't wear slacks. On the street I wear a hat, though once inside it comes off. I do these things I don't believe in so that I won't embarrass my grandchildren in front of their friends or neighbors. Even the laws of kashrut are easier for me to observe, though I still don't understand many of the fine points.

A few years ago Danny brought his two oldest children to visit us. To make the kitchen kosher, I sought guidance from the local Lubavitcher rebbetzin. Among other requirements, she explained that I needed to take new pots and pans and knives and all metal utensils to the mikveh to make them kosher. As I was about to leave for the mikveh, two important problems arose. I called the rebbetzin and asked: "When I go in the mikveh, am I naked or do I wear a bathing suit? And do I jump in holding the pots and pans, or do I get in first and then retrieve them from the side of the pool?"

She was too polite to laugh but she must have stifled a giggle as she patiently explained that there were two mikvehs: one for ritual bathing and another, quite separate, for koshering utensils. The latter, filled with water, was shaped like a supermarket ice cream case complete with sliding door on the top. One didn't actually go inside it.

Danny and Naima and I laugh about this story. Yes, I can tell them about these funny misunderstandings. Danny's sense of humor has never deserted him and so he appreciates these gaffes. He says we should write a book together about the misunderstandings that occur. He wants to begin with my naive though serious question about toilet behavior on Shabbat: I did once seriously ask, since we're forbidden to tear toilet paper on Shabbat, whether I'm allowed to flush the toilet. They reassured me that the latter was permissible. (And for the curious: one tears a daylong supply of toilet paper before Shabbat begins.)

Humor acts as a salve for our fractured relationship—but it can never fully heal the breach. In moments of total honesty I readily admit this is not the life I would have chosen for my son. But then who among us can choose our children's lives? If I look at Danny's life through his eyes and not mine, he is a happy, fulfilled man. And I choose to concentrate on all the lovely things about his life: the beauty of the Shabbat meal; the glowing eyes of the children as they repeat the familiar rituals every Friday night; Danny's head bent over each child as he gives them the customary weekly blessing; the joy with which the entire family welcomes each new baby as though it were the first child in the family. His core values aren't so very different from mine after all.

And there is more. In the world of the ultra-Orthodox, the sense of community runs high. People help one another in fundamental ways. My daughter-in-law, with five young children and no household help of any kind, manages to run a free clothing exchange in her tiny apartment. A neighbor has basic medical equipment for anyone who gets sick in the middle of the night. My grandchildren automatically ask their parents for a coin when they see a beggar on the street. The commandment to give charity is stressed from an early age, so this behavior is natural and normal, even for a two-year-old. What a contrast to my friends and acquaintances in the States who rationalize not giving a quarter to a homeless person because ". . . he'll just buy booze with it."

On Danny's part, his concern for my welfare and respect for my values follow naturally from the commandment to honor one's parents. Those attitudes go a long way toward smoothing our common path. Naima is a loving daughter-in-law. But if truth be told, it's the sight of my five darling grandchildren that binds me to the family forever. It would take a harder heart than mine to resist them when they ask on the phone, though I am 7,000 miles away, "Are you coming for Shabbos?" And each week I have the same feeling: I wish I could.

SECTION III:
JEWISH VALUES

12

On the Other Hand

Sandra Butler

I have three children now. The eldest, now an eighty-nine-year-old woman, leans against my body, hair flattened against her skull, the water of the shower spilling over both of us. She looks up into my face with gratitude and whispers, "You're my best mother." I rest my palm on her cheek and say nothing.

Janaea, my firstborn daughter, is a forty-one-year-old entrepreneur and artist. No longer a dancer and choreographer in New York, she has become a brand-new wife in a small country town. Now, instead of crowded classes and rehearsals in either overheated or damp studios at less-expensive off-hours, she teaches in the local YMCA and is developing a communitywide school for dancers and musicians. Her weekly calls describe all this activity with exhausted delight. They are trying to become pregnant and she assures me that when she does, the baby will need close contact with her "grandma."

Alison, my youngest daughter, is a professor of economics and keeps her life scaled down as she struggles with fibromyalgia. Students, faculty meetings, her own research, a new partner, and their life together take all her time, energy, and passion. Both my girls work hard, and live with care and attention. Now I am a mother to my own mother and to both of them. But here, in these pages, I want to return to the earlier years, when I was a child raising children, excavating the meanings of a complex Jewish tradition while identifying my own values, stumbling and righting myself over and over again.

I was a good girl, enacting the precisely circumscribed roles designed expressly for middle-class Jews of the 1950s. At eighteen,

I thought that I had chosen to become a wife and a mother. I knew with unexamined certainty that mothering would bring a sense of connection, satisfaction, and adulthood. I would have children who would unequivocally love me and be, without hesitation or ambivalence, cherished in return. I believed that love was enough to create happy endings.

Within the first years of my marriage, I found myself trapped in a too-small world of husband and children. Home and garden. Errands and entertaining. My home bulged with furniture, rugs, china, toys, clothes, dwarfing me, taking on a life of its own. I began to move in smaller and smaller circles. From the stove to the table. From the car pool to the market. Shepherding my daughters to friends' houses to play in their well-equipped backyards. Fueled by amphetamines, then easily available, and necessary to maintain the requisite thinness that defined elegance and sophistication to me, I grew more and more restless.

An inevitable divorce became final when I was twenty-five years old and my two daughters were four and six. The three of us moved from a sprawling suburban home to a very small apartment in New York City, which was quickly inhabited with my worries. Worries about getting a job, about stretching the food budget, guilt about the possibility I had made a terrible mistake and was ruining my daughters' lives. My parents protested that my ex-husband had been a good man. A "catch." What was wrong with me? I was a divorced woman with two children who had no one to look after them when I went to work. Little girls who wore house keys around their necks had selfish and bad mothers. In 1963 Jewish women didn't neglect their children by putting their own lives first.

I took a job, my first, as a medical office manager, and the three of us settled into our new routine. We left together each morning, the girls on their way to school and me to work. Both carried door keys so they could let themselves into the apartment after school to begin their homework and await me, rushing through the door carrying groceries for our dinner several hours later. We perched at the butcher-block counter for our meal, and then they had their shared bath as I reviewed their completed homework. After I read bedtime stories and tucked them into their bunk beds by eight o'clock, I whispered the final good night, rinsed out my nurse's uniform and white stockings, polished my white shoes to prepare for the morning rush, and fell across the bed exhausted. When the alarm rang at 6:30, I arose to repeat it all again.

The weekend was consumed with cleaning, a week's worth of laundry, and inexpensive adventures for my two little girls. We attended story time at the museum, rented rowboats in Central Park, and watched bread rise in neighborhood bakeries. I never wanted them to know how little money we had and created adventures that masked my constant struggle to survive. At the end of the month, one daughter would be selected to choose a color for Sunday dinner. They never noticed that the meal was potatoes, rice, or spaghetti masked with food coloring. Often I would steal a candle to make my offering more festive.

Our lives were not mirrored anywhere in the Jewish world in which I had been raised. There, wives stayed at home to care for their husbands and raise several children, much as my mother, and her mother before her, had done. I had never known a woman who went to work outside the home. Yet now, I was surrounded by very different Jewish mothers, women who sat together on the benches in Washington Square Park as our children played together. These women talked about everything. Some were working at outside jobs, others were raising children at home, but all were involved in political activism. Women like these were unfamiliar to me. Men talked about politics. Some, such as my grandfather, even organized to fight the bosses and what he described as "the crooks who ran everything." But I had never been exposed to women who were involved in politics except to have a carefully stated opinion. Saturday night dinner parties allowed married women to agree or disagree with the most recent Walter Lippman or James Reston column in *The New York Times*. That was politics. Now, I found myself drawn to these eager women and listened carefully to their conversations.

Within months, our lives became intertwined as I became more involved in the school PTA. Each meeting was filled with heated and often bitter arguments about the merits of busing black children out of their neighborhood schools into primarily white communities. Feelings ran high, divided almost evenly along racial lines, and the city grew polarized. I, along with my new friends, joined the

Harlem Parents Committee in an attempt to support the painful, complex, and ultimately unsuccessful effort to integrate our neighborhood school system. We marched. We picketed. We held press conferences. We tried to counteract the public perception that pro-busing parents were all black. I was one of the few nonblack mothers on the picket lines that ringed the school. All of the white women, it turned out, were Jewish.

The political momentum accelerated when my daughters and I joined the first demonstration against the war in Vietnam. As we marched down Fifth Avenue, 300 strong, my daughters kept their eyes straight ahead, pretending to be oblivious to the eggs, red paint, and jeers flung at them. They were both proud and frightened, the former all I noticed. I tucked my daughters under my arm or into strollers for the political demonstrations that were a growing part of our lives. When Janaea was eight years old, she sold Vietnam moratorium buttons in Washington Square Park, her jaw thrust forward with the urgency and importance of her task. Within weeks, Alison announced that she would no longer salute the flag during homeroom period since the pledge was not true. There was no freedom and justice, she insisted, and until there was, she would not participate. Her teacher tried to persuade this stubborn child to change her mind, but she would only agree to stand silently along with her class and insisted upon keeping her hands at her sides. Freedom and justice were daily words in our lives—daily Jewish words.

In third grade, Janaea's best friend had become the teacher's scapegoat. She returned home one afternoon to angrily and tearfully announce that the teacher was mean to Celie and that it wasn't fair.

"You're right," I agreed. "It isn't fair at all to do that to anybody, especially when you are in charge, like a teacher."

My daughter's eyes widened, and after a pause she asked, "So what should we do?"

Hers was the natural question since she had already learned that if something was wrong we must do something. We had, in her short life, already marched, demonstrated, picketed, and written postcards to our legislators, always addressed and stacked up beside the hall table. Doing something wasn't new to her, but doing something about her own life was.

We sat down at the kitchen table, just as my grandfather and I had done when I took a problem or question to him. We looked at the situation first "on the one hand," then "on the other hand" as he led me gently to new ways of thinking. I had always felt respected, very nearly like a grown-up, as he helped me solve the problems I brought to him by introducing me to the ideas of complexity and multiple points of view. When we finished talking about my concerns, he would lean back, clicking the sugar cube against his teeth as he sipped his glass of tea, and carefully explain the unjust world of bosses and their treatment of workers—of which we must always remember we were a part—and the need for the workers to get together to get rid of the crooks who ran everything. I had learned his deeply Jewish lessons about the workings of power, the pain of injustice, and the necessity of fairness well. Now, I would teach them to my own daughter.

"What do you think you could do to help Celie?" I began.

"Maybe I could tell the teacher she's being mean and unfair?" my daughter offered tentatively.

My grandfather's words faded and I refocused on the uncertain face of my child.

"That might work, but what if she gets angry at you?" I asked, trying to push her thinking forward.

"Then I'll tell the principal?" she whispered, chin beginning to quiver.

"What do you think Celie would want you to do?"

"I don't know. She pretends she doesn't care, but I saw her crying once in the bathroom."

We strategized together, examining ideas and possibilities, looking at the pros and cons of each. We finally concluded that she would talk first with Celie, then with Celie's mother and me. Days later, Celie's mother and I sat on a bench along the back wall of the principal's office while the girls carefully lowered themselves within the big armchairs in front of his massive walnut desk. He was bewildered by this unpredictable shift in his expectations, and attempted repeatedly to talk past his pupils directly to us across the large room. We kept referring him back to the girls sitting in front of him, and finally he grudgingly spoke to them. They explained what was going on in the classroom, why it wasn't fair or just, and what he should do to make the teacher stop. The teacher was indeed chastised, and for both girls, their first experience in righting their own wrongs and making their own justice was a success.

In what little time was left of my evenings and weekends, I volunteered at the Urban League to act the part of a wife in a white couple pretending to look for an apartment, one that would be abruptly off the market when, within hours, a black couple tried to rent it. More meetings followed, with demonstrations and picket lines increasingly the outcome. Several nights a week, my daughters fell asleep on hard folding chairs in church basements or across piles of coats thrown over the beds of crowded apartments. More and more often they did their homework on the kitchen table of a stranger's apartment, trying to concentrate over the din of heated debate in the next room.

I had become a Jewish mother who sat at oilcloth-covered kitchen tables, talking excitedly about the next demonstration, meeting, newsletter. I was learning that to be a good Jewish mother meant to speak up and to open up a big mouth. A good Jewish mother taught her daughters to fight back.

In 1971, when Janaea was fourteen, she returned from the library with a flier announcing a women's consciousness-raising meeting the following week.

"Go ahead, Mom. It'll be interesting and maybe you'll make some new friends," she encouraged.

That evening, I sat in a circle on a faded shag carpet and discovered, as my daughter had years before when she "stuck up" for Celie, that I could and must act in the service of my own struggles, my own diminishment as a woman. I had found women's liberation. Within weeks, I was a founding member of the newly developed Women's Studies Collective. I read, studied, argued, and listened as I examined the ways I had been socially constructed as a female. I was unlearning a painstaking education that had trained me to enter a mute and muted life filled with rules, admonitions, and endlessly appropriate behaviors. I was developing a political vocabulary to define myself and my own history.

I enrolled in a degree program designed for working adults the following fall. Now I was becoming not only a Jew who acted in the world, a Jew like my grandfather, but the kind of Jew who studied, a Jew like my grandfather had been before he came to America. I was working full time, participating in meetings and organizing most evenings, and had stuffed small bits of time to study into the late night and early morning hours. My mothering filled the few available moments that remained. Our mealtimes were random and often forgotten in the demands of term papers and deadlines. My daughters were neglected in the service of my studies, lost in the shuffle of meetings and demonstrations. There was not enough time to read, to talk, to play. There was not enough time for me to have both my own life and to help them toward theirs. Yet, they witnessed a mother living with passion, purpose, vision, and commitment. Those lessons have not been lost on them, even though I know they paid a price for my divided attention.

Now, decades later, when I ask my girls what was particularly Jewish about my mothering, they both single out the rituals that shaped their childhood. We celebrated Chanukah each year, and there were always eight presents for each daughter. I prepared Seder and invited all those who were strangers. The international students, the ex-cons, the lost souls. The three of us participated in the steady stream of demonstrations and rallies in the service of righteous struggle, long before I had even heard the phrase "tikkun olam." Alison reminds me, "In San Francisco when I was growing up, if you were a Jew you went to EST, to the Zen Center, not to temple. Jews looking for meaning and community went outside." She's right. We too went outside. To political activism.

My daughters and I sit together drinking iced tea for long hours as they regather their childhood memories. Janaea's stories begin when, at six years old, she performed as a bumblebee in the all-white, primarily Jewish suburban pageant. Then, several years and a lifetime later, she sang and danced as the only white member of the Soulettes in a New York inner-city junior high school, witnessed by the uncomprehending and horrified faces of the rest of our family. As an adolescent, she swept into the romantic dancer's life and legacy of Isadora Duncan and shaped a future that incorporated my powerful enthusiasms and allowed her to design her own. I see my younger body in hers. I see my attention to detail, my passion, and my discipline. This child of mine loves unreservedly and engages our conversation as she does everything: no hedging or construction of safe places. I listen carefully to the ways my long-ago words rest upon her tongue. I see the ways I filled her heart with my uneven legacy.

"The values of fairness and justice for people continue to be central to my life and I live them in my own way now," she assures me.

Alison continues with firm certainty. "Being a Jew and having had you as my mother is all just like breathing. I wear a Jewish star, and identify myself as a Jew in my work life, which is mostly Christian and male. But you taught me that I had to find my way through the contradictory teachings and choices."

During her adolescence, she attended a prosperous synagogue in San Francisco, where the dominant theme of Sunday school classes revolved around watching Holocaust films every day for one hour in order to teach the students their responsibility to personally re-populate the destroyed Jewish world.

She explains, "You were trying to keep balance between femi-nist studies and activism on the one hand and mothering and a full-time job on the other—trying to make it all fit. I, too, was trying to contain fundamentally contradictory struggles in my adoles-cence. I didn't quite fit in the secular world as a Jewish kid but didn't fit in the Jewish world either. That in-between place is prob-ably the best description of my growing up. You weren't like other mothers, and I wanted you to be. But I was also proud of you and felt you were so brave in trying to find your own way. The contra-dictions resulted in both a sense of consistent alienation and a powerful lesson in holding on to my own path. I wanted to go to Israel as a kid and eventually traveled there three times. A kind of touchstone perhaps. A place in the world that bridged both my deep identification with the Holocaust and the secular aspects of my political upbringing."

The next morning I call my mother to tell her what her grand-daughters and I are talking about and ask her, "If Grandpa had let you study at Talmud Torah when you wanted to, and Grandma had let you go to normal school after high school to become a teacher, how would it have changed how you lived and were a mother?"

A moment passes, a moment when I realize I am holding my breath. "If my parents had let me study the Jewish things I wanted to learn about, or if I had been able to have a profession, I wouldn't have had children. I would have gone to business," she replies immediately without need for thought.

"That's all I wanted for you," she continues brusquely. "To be a student, to have a profession so you could be independent, be able to travel. Go where you want, do work you like. Not be trapped."

I remember the faded snapshot of my mother in her twenties perched on a stool in a cafe in Cuba, smiling delightedly into the camera. She, too, had wanted more. She hungered to see the world beyond Newark, New Jersey. Beyond the early marriage her sister had made, beyond the babies, the repetition, the limitations. How she wanted her hungers to be mine. How she wanted me to complete her interrupted dreams. How I longed for my daughters to share and further my own.

My mother urged me toward a world that she had been denied by her own mother, a world of work and study, a world of financial success and status. She frightened me with her burning urgency and was not able to listen to my own tentative young words and ideas. As a girl, I didn't know there were other lifelong voices within her drowning out my own. My Jewish mother was ferocious for me and terrified for herself. We never spoke of any of this. I fled at eighteen into a marriage with a mild and undemanding man. I fled into my mother's worst fears.

Once, when I was eight years old, I returned home from school where my mother awaited me, milk and cookies already on the kitchen table.

"How was school?" she would always ask. "What did you learn today?"

I didn't understand then that she had no one to talk to. I couldn't have known how hard she was trying to fit herself into a world that had always been a compromise. I still see her crumpled face one spring afternoon when, wishing I could come home to an empty house, eat ice cream, and read a romance novel, I yelled, "How come you don't play cards or go to meetings like the other mothers? How come you're always home?"

She didn't answer, just turned and walked down the dim hallway and into her room. Now I am flooded with memories of how many afternoons my daughters came home to a casserole in the oven, a hasty note on the hall table. Did they long for a traditional Jewish mother who would greet them with a warm smile and the reassuring tradition of milk and cookies? They never said.

Now I understand some of the inevitability of forgiveness, the patience required to disentangle the unfinished dreams that propel us all forward. I know now that it was not easy for my daughters to have a hungry, ambitious, powerful, often inattentive Jewish mother. They were often frightened, sometimes lonely, and didn't have enough time to be children.

My daughters, my mother, and I have begun to talk together, our words binding us to one another like tightly grasped hands. Alison has an advanced degree and a professional career. Education: my grandfather's, my mother's, and my own deepest hunger. She teaches students, helps them to think critically. Janaea has created a company of dancers and musicians. She lives in a community embedded in meaningful artistic work. Relationship and generativity, my old longings. She, too, has found her own translation of my mothering. Now I understand that I gave my daughters what my mother gave me and her mother before her and then as far back as there is memory. The truth of my life as I lived it was my legacy. It is, finally, all there is. I wanted them to fill their days with activism, study, friendship, and passion. They have.

– 13 –

Old Clothes and Food from Afar

Michele Clark

My younger daughter, eighteen years old, wears mostly second-hand clothes. When I was her age I dressed mainly in black—black turtlenecks, black tights, black sneakers. So this choice of hers shouldn't bother me, should it? But it does. Despite my own history, or perhaps because of it, I long for her to go for something a little glittery, something new. I know it's useless when I beg her to shop at an ordinary retail store. Amused, she replies, "But isn't this a good thing? Think of all the money I save you." I ponder the meaning of her choice and my own reaction but I come away with no conclusions. Although trained as a psychotherapist, here I am singularly without insight.

Instead I return to the meaning of my own clothes choices of the 1960s when I spent many of my nights and weekends hanging around the streets of Greenwich Village, staying out late with strangely bearded young men. These behaviors were much bemoaned by my parents, grandparents, my numerous aunts and uncles. What's to become of the girl? Why is she so unhappy? They did not know, nor did I, that I was looking for a way out of the modern choices I saw before me. They didn't know, nor did I, it wasn't obvious, that I was really looking for a way to have a clear identity, like my grandmothers who were women of valor as described in Proverbs 31:

> A woman of valor, who can find her?
> . . . She is like the merchant ships
> She brings her food from afar.

My grandmothers were immigrants from Eastern Europe who helped build small family businesses. One minded the warehouse while her sons went out selling paper and twine to small retailers. The other baked knishes, cholent, and other meat delicacies that sold on the counter of her husband's kosher market. They were often in aprons, and they wore no makeup. Their goals were clear: No Cossacks at the door, a prosperity that might ensure security and traditional observance. My grandmothers didn't care about becoming real Americans. They lived in the United States as they would have lived in Europe, had Europe permitted them to live and prosper.

> She considers a field and buys it . . .
> She girds herself with strength,
> And makes her arms strong.
>
> (Proverbs 31:16-17, trans. 1993)

And I wanted that—not, of course, the ancient limitations, not the helping out in the store, no no no—I wanted the clear goals, the absence of doubt and anxiety.

Their English-speaking children, my parents, uncles, and aunts, moved to the suburbs. They did want to become real Americans, though they also wanted to remain Jews. This combination of identities was not so easy to do. Hence the anxious criticism that pervaded their homes, our childhoods.

To me, the artists in Greenwich Village and the Beats who dressed in black believed in a combination of high ideals and simple living. They despised consumer culture and social competition; they didn't care about clothes or looks. Now, many decades later, the role of women in the Beat Generation has been much chronicled and criticized. But I'm not talking here about how it really was, but how it seemed to me then.

Now, the Jewish mother I try to be is an amended, modern, woman of valor, though I am not kindly as she is described, and only occasionally wise. Like her, I work for a living. Like her, I help to make my family prosper. Unlike her, I have a public life and a public voice. I can be "known in the gates . . . among the elders," along with my husband. My house is modest and handmade, built by my husband and some friends, and I specialize in cooking hearty rather than fancy foods—roast chickens, stews and polentas, lentil and bean soups. My younger daughter doesn't tell her friends at college that her mother is the best psychotherapist—which, in any case, I'm not. She says she tells her friends, "My mother makes the best broccoli." And I am touched and satisfied, although I wouldn't be if I wasn't also a pretty good psychotherapist, if I didn't also have a place in the public world.

When I asked my older daughter to define a Jewish mother, she said it was "someone who loves her children more than anything, someone who has dark curly hair, someone who's smaller than me . . . who just loves her children so much and worries on their behalf. Someone who worries . . . noisily. . . ."

I was pleased that she said this because I can't say it of myself. And yet I think it's so. I put my children first. This doesn't mean I am self-effacing. I am not. I hope I have taught them to listen to and take care of the self. But it does mean, as my older daughter said: "You were very emotionally and physically in my space . . . emotionally in the same exact space that we were standing on—and that was very important to me . . . for me it was a good thing—not always—when I was a teenager, but all the other times . . ."

My mother put her children first, as well. She loved and loves her husband, but her children always come first. Often this was difficult, for us and for her—the intensity of it. But it was also a gift. As my mother catered to her daughters as well as her son, we, my sister and I, came to expect others to give us their attention. We were not self-effacing; we were not supposed to be. We were important, sometimes too important. But, still, significant turns out to be better than insignificant; no need for meek or mild in our family.

The feminist Bible scholar Tikva Frymer-Kensky says that in the Bible " . . . mothers are always supportive of their children and loyal to them. . . . Biblical women often perform dangerous acts to save the life of their child . . . when children were at stake, women defied improper commands and were not intimidated by authority" (1993, p. 121). These children are all sons. My mother extended that protection and passion to her daughters, as well. And I have tried to do the same.

My mother wasn't always sure of what she had to offer, and neither am I. Perhaps parents never are. Years ago I began to discard the asceticism of Goodwill furniture and black apparel. My younger daughter did not even know me in that phase. So what statement is she making when she scours the thrift shops for good deals? Some gift I didn't mean to offer, whose meaning I look forward to some day understanding. Or maybe it just has nothing to do with me at all.

REFERENCES

Frymer-Kensky, Tikva (1993). *In the wake of the goddesses*. New York: Fawcett.
Translation Hebrew Study Bible (1993). New York: HarperCollins.

– 14 –

My Journey
Toward Jewish Identification

Linda Stone Fish

My brother called me last night from New York. He recently visited our home with his new wife, who is not Jewish. He called to tell me how hurt they were by a few incidents that happened during their stay with my family. During a dinner conversation, my fifteen-year-old son Isaac said something about shiksas (non-Jewish women) and we all laughed. Another incident involved my twelve-year-old son Aarlo, who made a mention of an M-O-T (member of our tribe) and looked at his new aunt and said, "not M-Y-T (member of your tribe)." Both incidents were so insulting to my brother and his wife that he threatened not to return to our home. I am embarrassed by this form of Jewish attitude and behavior and continue to struggle against it. I am beginning to replace this separatist identification with a positive identification, and I have learned many important lessons along the way.

As I struggle with the ways that Judaism informs my life and the life of my current family, I am convinced that the development of Jewish identity is both an emotional journey and a response to lived experiences. When I entered motherhood my Jewish identification was unexamined, then it was based on fears of anti-Semitism, and now it is moving toward the positive. Throughout my journey, I have traveled with an internal compass that directs my mission, is influenced by experiences along the way, and is internally driven toward understanding and fullness. As I map the journey I recognize and appreciate the constant and dramatic individual, familial, cultural, and historic forces that are involved.

UNEXAMINED IDENTIFICATION

I grew up in Newton, Massachusetts, a close suburb of Boston. I did not know a single non-Jewish person until I went to high school. At least I did not know that I knew any non-Jewish people. I thought President Kennedy was Jewish because everyone in Boston thought he was part of the family. I also grew up in a large extended family. My mother was raised in Newton, her sister, her brother, and their children all lived in Newton, and her mother and father were there as well. Everyone was Jewish. All my friends were Jewish, all my camp mates were Jewish, all my neighbors were Jewish, all my friends' friends were Jewish—this was our world.

We went to Hebrew School three times a week and we were all Bar and Bat Mitzvahed. We went to temple on the High Holy Days, spent Chanukah at my aunt's house with a dreidel filled with toys. We celebrated Passover and did not celebrate Christmas. No one celebrated Christmas, so it was no big deal. We did not discuss Christianity, or the fact that Jews are a small minority in a Christian country, nor did we compare ourselves to Christians. We compared ourselves only to my mother's brother's family: they were the real Jews. They kept kosher and had Sabbath dinners. They were a bit strange, a bit too Jewish. Over the years, they stopped inviting us to Passover dinners because we were not religious enough.

I never thought about being Jewish, what it meant, or how it fit into my life. We did not practice any Jewish rituals in our home. We did not celebrate the Sabbath, my father never went to temple, except when we were Bar and Bat Mitzvahed, and I was never told I could not do something because I was Jewish. There were many things I could not do because I was a girl, but not because I was Jewish. My brothers had grand Bar Mitzvah parties at hotels with bands and photographers. My sister and I each had a pizza party in our basement. My mother used to say that the boys got Bar Mitzvah parties and the girls got weddings.

The only thing I remember learning in Hebrew School, other than the language itself, was that God gave us certain gifts and we had to use them. I remember one teacher who showed us the numbers on her arm and told us that we better keep our religion so that America won't finish what Hitler started. I once asked my father whether he believed in Adam and Eve or in evolution and he looked at me as if I was beneath a reply. Of course I believe in evolution, he seemed to imply. Only really stupid people believe in anything else.

IDENTIFICATION BASED ON FEAR
OF ANTI-SEMITISM

I did not question my identification as a Jew until I was sixteen years old and a foreign exchange student. Before this experience, I do not remember being confronted with how non-Jews perceived Jews, nor how their reactions influenced the way I thought about myself. I was living with a family in the south of France, crying myself to sleep every night because I could not understand enough of the language to communicate in a way that made me less lonely. One day, while picking wild mushrooms, one of the girls in the family asked me what religion I was and I answered, "I am Jewish." She dropped her basket of mushrooms and ran down the hill to tell her mother. That night at dinner, there was silence and discomfort, which lasted for three to four days.

When I came home from France, I told my family about this incident. My parents told me that the French were anti-Semites and that I should be careful about whom I tell about my religion. This is the only conversation about Judaism that I remember having with my parents, other than fights about going to Hebrew School.

My maternal grandfather went to temple every Saturday morning. He sat in the same seat at the back of the temple. Recognizing the danger of being a Jew in prewar Austria, he and many members of his family came to the United States, earning enough money by the late 1930s to send for their relatives. One sister had polio and was detained at Ellis Island for a year. Immigration officials would not let her enter the country and she was sent back to Austria, never to be heard from again. Like the discussion of Jewish identity, Holocaust memories permeated our home and our community, and were not discussed. It was better if you just kept things like this quiet.

I went to college and dated a Catholic boy. I did not know the impact it had on my parents until I later started dating my future husband. My mother told so many friends that I was dating a man named "Ron, Jewish" that some of her friends actually thought his last name was "Jewish." I do not ever remember having a conversation with my parents about the religion of my future mate. I remember my paternal grandfather, a judge, commenting on divorces. He said that people should marry people similar to themselves because so many things go wrong in marriage that the stronger the base of similarity, the easier it would be to stay married. This was the extent of my education about marrying outside my faith. Similar to never having a conversation about whether I would have children, it was simply accepted that I would marry someone who was Jewish. This unspoken acceptance instilled a form of identification in me similar to that which I had with my skin color. I felt a familiarity with those like me, a lack of awareness of others, and an absence of any critical consciousness about how being Jewish informed my worldview and me.

Ron and I were married with a traditional Jewish ceremony in the cold and unfriendly temple in which I had had my Bat Mitzvah. We lived together for eight years before we had children. We led an unexamined Jewish life, practiced no Jewish rituals in our home, and did not discuss much about Judaism until the children were born.

Ron and I have four sons. Isaac is fifteen, Aarlo is twelve, Hugh is ten, and Avery is five. Isaac was born in Lafayette, Indiana, while I was writing my dissertation. During our first visit to Lafayette, driving around town with a realtor, he wanted to show us an apartment above a church. He asked us what denomination we were and we unashamedly answered, "We're Jewish." He responded, "We don't have any blacks or Jews in Lafayette, so we have no trouble from either group. We're just a nice, middle-American happy family." This was a poignant reminder of the message my parents had given me when I told them about the incident in France, a reminder to be careful about telling others that I was Jewish, and it furthered my fear of anti-Semitic attacks.

Lafayette was not accustomed to Jewish families. When we wanted a bris, no one knew what to do. I asked my obstetrician whether he would be willing to perform a circumcision in front of my family. He had never performed one before an audience, but he was a flexible young physician, willing to accommodate our family.

Needless to say, it was not a religious ceremony and did nothing to further our Jewish identity.

When Isaac was a year old, we moved away from Lafayette. As we thought about where to relocate, I was very clear that it had to be a place that was friendly to Jews. I knew I wanted to live in a Jewish community and I knew I wanted my children to grow up with people who did not find them alien because of their religious orientation. I did not think about finding a good synagogue or involvement in the Jewish community, I just wanted to be comfortable. I had images of calling Isaac's name at a playground and people staring at me because we were different. I knew, in order for me to feel pride as a human being, I needed to be connected to people who felt connected to me because I was Jewish, not people who saw me as "the other."

This fear of anti-Semitism became the basis of my Jewish identification as our young family grew. While I have always believed in a power higher and more encompassing than human beings, I did not grow up with any home-based religious rituals, and did not practice any in my own home. Instead, my Jewish identification was primarily with Jewish people and not with any formalized religious practices.

My fear of anti-Semitism slowly turned into a self-isolating, separatist, ethnocentric, and reactive position. This form of Jewish identification guided me through the early years of parenting. I now see it as a mentality that breeds great pride and tremendous alienation from those whom you fear. For example, when Isaac was five and I was commenting on his burgeoning intelligence, he asked me why he was so smart. I told him he was smart because he was Jewish. This type of comment suggests that his intelligence is based on being Jewish, and that those who are not Jewish must be less intelligent.

SEPARATIST IDENTIFICATION

We moved to Syracuse, New York, and immediately bought a house in a Jewish neighborhood. I enrolled my children in the Jewish Community Center's (JCC) Early Childhood Education Program. As a faculty member in the Department of Child and Family

Studies, surrounded by great wisdom about all child care options in the community, I asked no one's advice, nor did I shop around for preschool options. The minute I walked into the JCC, perhaps in the parking lot, I made the decision to enroll my children.

While the JCC happens to have an excellent day care program, that was not the primary reason I chose it for my children. I selected it because I felt accepted there as a Jewish mother and knew that my children would be accepted as Jewish children. If I had a concern about certain practices or worries about my children, I did not have to think that I would be misperceived as a nagging, overbearing Jewish mother. If my children cried when I left, I did not have to worry that anyone would treat them like whining Jewish children. When I engaged myself in conversation with other mothers dropping their children off at school, there was a familiarity that was comfortable and nonthreatening.

Raising young children is a bonding experience. Exchanging stories about diaper rash, ear infections, separation anxiety, exhaustion, confusion, and developmental milestones are all ways to be in connection. This is the way young families find and engage in social support systems. We immerse ourselves in relationships with people who are different enough to provide stimulation, suggestions, challenges, and learning opportunities, but similar enough to provide comfort, acceptance, understanding, and empathy.

The downside, however, is that the fear of anti-Semitism can breed separation and alienation from the "non-Jewish world" because we do not engage in relationships with people outside of our own group. When we do not feel accepted and safe in the larger community, we may shy away from relationships with others. Those who are too different, who are not in our social radar, become strangers. We may even begin to question whether other people experience the same things that we are experiencing.

This separatist attitude, which begins as a response to the outside world, can also seep into relationships within our own community, where the unspoken tensions between stay-at-home moms and working mothers are profound and divisive. My mother, like most American Jewish mothers in the 1950s and 1960s, was a stay-at-home mother. There was never any doubt that I would be a mother who worked outside the home. My mother used to worry about who would take care of my children. When Isaac was about five months old, we went out to lunch with my mother. I went to the bathroom and when I returned, Isaac saw me, smiled, and put his arms up for me to hold him. My mother looked at me and said, "Oh, my God, he knows you." My mother had assumed that he would not bond with me, an aimless child without his Jewish mother, because I left him in other-than-mother care for about fifteen hours a week. To her credit, she now thinks we have done a wonderful job raising our children, tells all her friends that we have a truly remarkable coparenting relationship, and that we have the greatest boys on the planet.

My interactions with stay-at-home mothers are tense as well. I resent the forced patronizing smiles of the room mothers when I rush out the door on the way to work. They resent me when they are left doing all the volunteering and being pivotal in keeping our community thriving and vibrant. I have a grand social support system in the Jewish community. When baby-sitters don't show up, schools are on vacation, or my husband and I both have to work late, there are many, many families I could call to help me out. But I do call only the two families who have two full-time working parents, and they are the only ones who call me. I never call the stay-at-home mothers to take my children even though many have offered to do so. Again, this identification organized by fear of others encourages engagement with those who are similar and alienation from those who are not.

TOWARD A POSITIVE IDENTIFICATION AS A JEWISH MOTHER

A number of experiences and emotional shifts have occurred that have redirected my internal compass toward a positive and life-sustaining Jewish identification that is focused on understanding how Judaism informs my life as a woman and a mother. For me, changing direction is not something that happens all at once. It is a gradual process. It is not like suddenly leaving the old direction and becoming a different person, it is more like waking up one morning and realizing that I have been focusing in a new direction and had not been aware of it. There is no date I can label as the start of my shift, nor can I tell you how comprehensive it is; there are some lived experiences that inform my journey.

My father died when my second son, Aarlo, was six months old. We sat shivah for a week in Boston. Friends and family came from across the country to sit with us. Sitting shivah was my first positive Jewish experience. It made sense. Staying home for a whole week with my family made sense. Being with family and friends made sense. The way we buried my father made sense. Coming back to work wearing a torn black piece of cloth made sense. The mourners' Kaddish made sense. For the very first time, Judaism gave my experience some meaning. It provided a ritual that actually helped me.

When I went home to Syracuse, I looked in my library, filled with Jewish books I had never opened. Curious about how Jews think about death, I was hungry for Jewish teachings for the very first time.

Two years later, when my third son, Hugh, named after my father, was six months old, we went to the bris of our very dear friend's son. The child's father, Steven Kepnes, who teaches Judaic studies at Colgate University, spoke after the circumcision. He talked about our covenant with God and the reason behind the ritual. Steven explained Judaism in a simple, articulate, and passionate way that I understood. He explained that a mitzvah is a commandment, a covenant, and a blessing. I felt a flutter of spiritual awakening. At the time I chalked it up to emotions associated with breast-feeding. But it did not go away. It pulled at my heart like a toddler's hand pulls at yours to move you in a certain direction. And like a good Jewish mother, I obeyed.

I began to read about Judaism. I am an avid reader of novels and feel particularly drawn to Jewish writers, whether they identify as Jewish or not. But I had never voluntarily read anything about Judaism. As I began to read the Tanach, Jewish commentary, books about Jewish rituals and Jewish law, I began to think more about social justice issues from a Jewish perspective. As a feminist, I was drawn as well to women's critique of patriarchal Judaism, and also drawn to the history of the Jewish people. As I began to read about Judaism, I also began to talk about Judaism. I started to become profoundly disappointed with those Jewish scholars, artists, writers, and performers who were not acting in ways I thought Jews should act. Woody Allen married his stepdaughter and I boycotted all Woody Allen movies. I had many heated discussions with my friends and family members who could not understand how I could take a moral position about an artist. I began developing a positive identification with Judaism and could not understand why others were not doing the same.

IDENTIFICATION AS A JEWISH FAMILY

We sent our sons to the Syracuse Hebrew Day School because it had a full-day kindergarten. We grew to love the school. While religiously based, it did not in any way make us feel bad about not being "proper Jews." I felt chastised once by a mother when I held a birthday party for my son on a Saturday, but she was right and I never did it again. I felt embarrassed when I sent valentines to my first son's kindergarten class, but soon thereafter, I began to take an interest in the meaning behind Jewish rituals and practice.

By the time I decided it was time to start practicing Jewish rituals in the home, my older children were old enough to notice a difference. Observing the Sabbath was the first gradual shift in our house that went unnoticed until it affected them. First, we just lit the candles and said a blessing over the wine and challah every Friday night. Then we had dinner in the dining room. Then we added our own rituals to the Friday night dinner. But when I decided that we should hang out as a family on Friday nights and not watch TV, play Nintendo, or turn on computers, this did not go unchallenged. We have a rule in our house forbidding those activities during the week. The boys insisted that they relaxed with media in the same way that I relaxed with quiet family time. We spent many Friday night dinners talking about this shift in our new family ritual. "Why is it that your burgeoning interest in observing Jewish practice has to affect us?" they asked. "Isn't Shabbat about doing what *we* want to do, too? We want to relax and enjoy the Sabbath just like you do." For now, we compromise. My husband and I relax, and they can watch TV, but they can't watch it in my room, where they like to cuddle up, and we do not organize Shabbat dinner around electronic media.

We do not keep kosher yet, but I do not allow any pork products into my house. The boys have not had pork products at home for years, but for every birthday dinner they want pork chops. Avery, our youngest, who has never had pork, hates meat, and doesn't even know what pork is, asked for pork chops for his fifth birthday meal. The other day, Aarlo told me that I was depriving him of an educational experience because he might have a test at some point that asks about pork products, and he won't know the answer. Then, of course, if he doesn't know the answer, he will fail the test and not get into an Ivy League school. I will blame him, he says, but it will be my fault entirely.

My children also appreciate my Judaism in a way that makes me profoundly happy as a mother. This year for Chanukah, Isaac bought me the videotape of *Schindler's List*. Aarlo helped me clean the house for Passover, taught me the ritual about burning the last crumb of leavened bread, and did it with me. Hugh is very careful on Shabbat, making sure he is home in time to light the candles and getting Avery to participate. They don't want to go to temple with me, but this is not something I push. Jewish observance for me, at present, is more home-based than synagogue centered.

As a positive Jewish identification has begun to direct my life, opportunities to learn more about Judaism continue to come my way. I realize that I feel the same passionate hunger to understand Judaism in all of its aspects that I had felt trying to understand family therapy. It has become all I want to read. I have read many books on the Holocaust, and visited the Holocaust Museum in Washington. I am doing research now with Maureen Semans, interviewing Jewish families about their own ethnic identity. As my passion grows, I see ways in which it also has a positive impact on my husband and my children.

My husband, Ron, has decided to look at Jewish meditation as a practice rather than Eastern meditation. He also reads my copies of *Lilith*, a Jewish-feminist magazine, as diligently as I do. My positive Jewish identification has informed him in ways that forty-five years of forced identification as a Jewish man has not.

I am a Jewish mother. My mothering is informed more by Judaism than by anything else. I am also a practicing family therapist who has been teaching family therapy principles since before I had children, but I parent like a Jew and not like a family therapist. What is the difference? A family therapy colleague talks about

Jewish parenting as ethnic parenting: "Jews parent like other ethnic groups who have been oppressed. They are hypervigilant. They worry too much and are overinvolved." I do not think of myself as an overinvolved parent, and I believe my children and husband would agree. Unlike my colleagues, when I talk about Jewish parenting, I do not question my level or style of parental involvement; instead, I speak of a deep directional space that guides my mothering. There is a hypervigilance that comes from centuries of oppression, but this does not define my parenting. Instead, it is defined by centuries of cherishing life and a commitment to privileging that which is precious.

Cooper (1997) retranslates the thirteenth-century Jewish sage Abraham Abalufia's definition of spiritual connection:

> Now we are no longer separated from our source, and behold we are the source and the source is us. We are so intimately united with It, we cannot by any means be separated from It, for we are It. (p. xi)

This statement speaks to how Judaism affects my mothering. While it is indescribable, the force that has been directing my compass comes closest to being a spiritual source.

The fear of anti-Semitism is externally driven and organized by actual or perceived threats and experiences, which may cause a high level of hypervigilance and overinvolvement in some Jewish mothers. The world is not a safe place, and we need to protect our children from violating experiences. If this fear is all we give our children of Judaism, however, it may leave them alienated from the richness that positive identification has to offer. The separateness and exclusivity, which linger out of fear, are what my brother and his wife are fighting against in their effort to educate us. Slowly but surely, I lead less often with that part of myself.

As a positively identified Jewish mother, I give my children a heritage of remarkable ancestors and a legacy of social justice. I give them the knowledge that, if one is oppressed, we are all oppressed. I show them the importance of community and ritual, and I teach them the value of tikkun olam, healing the world. As a Jewish mother, I take my children very seriously. They are cherished human beings who know more about themselves and about how the world works for them than I will ever know. I also give my children the model that life is to be taken seriously, but not too seriously. Some of the greatest moments in our family have been moments when we have laughed at ourselves.

When I suggest that my parenting is informed by Judaism, I do not intend to imply that non-Jewish mothers do not give their children the same things, nor do I intend to imply that all Jewish mothers give their children these same values. I suggest instead that I identify these aspects of my mothering as coming from a Jewish source that guides me. My own experiences and my desire for spirituality have affected this internal direction toward understanding and fullness. While my children may laugh at my dedication, be embarrassed by my strong and personal identification, and mock my desire for ritual, they are marvelous, curious, loving, kind, generous, and open spirits. This is the gift that Judaism has given them.

REFERENCE

Cooper, D.A. (1997). *God is a verb: Kabbalah and the practice of mystical Judaism.* New York: Riverhead Books.

– 15 –

Am I a Jewish Mother?

Liz Cordonnier

When I think of Jewish mothers, I think of my great-grandmother. An integral part of my life until she died when I was eight, my images of her are still vivid. Heavy, Russian bones, thick Yiddish accent, she was perpetually dispensing love and food to the several generations of offspring that continually surrounded her. My mother, her first grandchild, was born on the heels of her giving birth to her ninth child, and I appeared even while the many other grandchildren were still being born. I was the one who first called her "Bubbymommy," which became the name all the children used. She was, after all, my Bubby's mommy. Despite the legion of children in her kitchen, on her lap, or in her arms, there always seemed to be an ample supply of potato latkes and applesauce at dinnertime, made from scratch, of course.

Bubbymommy could read no English, so we children fought for the honor of reading to her any words that appeared on the television screen. There were many Bubbymommies such as her in my neighborhood. Virtually everyone I knew over the age of fifty had been born a Russian Jew, and until I was about ten I was convinced that a Yiddish accent was a condition of growing old, like wrinkles.

When I think of Jewish mothers, I think of my Bubbies, both of whom lived within bike-riding distance of my home, both of whom provided a haven of care, support, and unconditional understanding during my turbulent adolescence. I think of warm kugel fresh from the oven, the feel of wet matzo balls in my hands before we plunked them into redolent chicken soup, and the comfort of loving, strong arms around me. Being called shaina punim. I got over the fact that neither grandmother ever acquired a Yiddish accent.

When I think of Jewish mothers, I also imagine my own mother, as all-American as she is. Although far removed from the old world, she still kvetched when I disappointed her, kvelled when I did something right, but was careful never to give me a keinanhora. She carried her emotions on a short fuse, and we laughed hard and cried hard, with little in between. She sent me to Hebrew school, but let me drop out when I got bored. She served frozen dinners, but could whip up the best fried matzo in the family at Passover. She believed, like the generations before her, that assimilation was the Jews' worst enemy, and that it was the duty of Jewish women to raise Jewish children.

Where does this leave me?

At first, perhaps I would have said that I was a Jewish mother of a non-Jewish child, my son coming into the world looking so much like his Anglo-Irish father, reminding me so much of him with his smile, his playfulness, and eventually his interests. We gave him a strong Irish first name to go with his last name, but gave him the middle name of my deceased grandfather in the Jewish tradition.

I remember the pride that shone in my Bubby's eyes when she held her great-grandson for the first time. He was barely twenty-four hours old, a raisined slip of a person in a diaper and a hospital bracelet. "Will there be a . . . bris?" my grandmother whispered to me hesitantly, cautiously. "It's done, Bub," I replied, shaking off a pang of guilt. "They already did it here at the hospital." She nodded, undoubtedly disappointed, yet probably relieved that at least he was circumcised, even if not under God and her family's watchful eyes.

When my daughter was born, another Irish name, which to me was so exotic and unique, was already picked out. But as the months went by and she would gaze at me with deep, mahogany eyes so much like my own, with a face so much like mine, I had a crisis of identity. It was only then, after having been fortunate enough to be lulled into contentment by a loving marriage and happy life, that I considered the possibility that I was denying my children their Jewish heritage. I was suddenly seized with uncertainty. Where did my babies belong? In my attempt to meld together my husband's world and my own, had I forgotten that my children were half Jewish? Living in a town where Jews were rare, would they reach adulthood with no connection to their Jewish side? Four months after my daughter was born, amid Christmas and Hanukkah celebrations, I asked my husband if we could change her name.

I have given up much for the man I love, the man I chose because of the caliber of man he is, and the kind of a husband and father that I was confident he'd make. He is that, and more. When we fell in love, we agreed that no organized religion could keep us apart. We dissected our beliefs and discovered that our values and visions were one and the same. We could remain who we were and share in each other's cultural differences.

Rather than practicing one religion, we agreed to introduce our children to the good in both our faiths. Even though my husband was open to exploring it, I made the difficult decision not to raise my children as Jewish. The husband I cherished was shaped by his Christian background, and half of his blood was theirs. How could I make their devoted father the outsider?

My friend's Christian husband converted to Judaism before their children were born, so the whole family could practice one religion. When he walked into our house one December, I remember the wistful look he gave the Christmas tree under which his son and mine played. How happy I was that I had not asked my husband to surrender his upbringing.

Yet I think, being the Jewish partner of an interfaith marriage, I bear the brunt of the guilt. After all, we are the persecuted ones, the minority. I worried: had I reneged on my duty to pass on my faith? We all give up a piece of ourselves when we join in marriage. I would never give up my morals, nor the fiber of who I am. Yet how much of my heritage would I have to forsake? Did I still qualify as a Jewish mother?

Our children do not go to religious school. But while we teach them the richness of both of our religions, we teach them tolerance of all beliefs. Decorating the Christmas tree is a joyous family project in our home. Our children know that Dad is the authority in this area, and that he is sharing with them a favorite tradition of his childhood. We also light the Hanukkah menorah and sing the blessing; my husband knows it as well as the rest of us, but it is my domain. Together we celebrate Yom Kippur after I have fasted, and discuss how we can better ourselves in the coming year. And together we cried at the Holocaust Museum, as we witnessed the unfathomable prejudice that people can direct at one another.

As my children grew, I began to realize that our lives constantly exposed them to Jewish traditions and ways of life. I have taken care to use opportunities such as Holy Days and weddings to teach them the significance of important Jewish events.

Detractors will argue that our children are growing up without a sense of identity, and that the issues will become more complex as they get older. Now, after a dozen years of motherhood, I say not so, on either count. They are growing up open-minded, knowing that it's all right to have loved ones who think differently, worship differently. I consider my children blessed, feeling at home at the Easter egg hunt at Grandma's as well as the Seder at Bubby's. As my children, now approaching the teenage years, grow older, it has become easier to explain the differences between their grandparents.

Their upbringing may not be as cut-and-dried as that of other children, but it may help them understand that there are not always simple answers to the complex questions of the world. I see no sign of lack of identity on their parts. On the contrary, if my children were asked where they fit in, I think they would proudly declare, "Everywhere!"

Is this what a real Jewish mother teaches her children? I asked my Bubby, whom God has still kept with us, if she considered me to be a Jewish mother. "Certainly," she replied. "And what else would you be?" Although we live a secular life, I never stray far from the lessons my faith has taught me. I make sure that my children understand the rituals of the Bar Mitzvahs they attend, understanding that they will never have one of their own. I must admit that they possess a better tolerance for others' views than I did when I was growing up. They are unafraid to learn, listen, and question the beliefs of all people. To them, it's normal and natural for different people to believe different things. No one in their lives is loved any differently because of their faith. And when they choose their own paths, they know that no one will love them any less, whatever life they decide to lead.

Have I done my duty as a Jewish mother in carrying on my faith? I am not certain of the answer, but I know that my children have brought Judaism into a family that otherwise would have had little exposure to it. They are Ambassadors of Love.

What do I wish for my children in the future? That they grow up with strong Judeo-Christian values, high morals and standards for themselves and those who are to be a part of their lives, and that they demonstrate kindness, understanding, and compassion to those around them. That they will be better people for their broad theological exposure.

As my son approaches thirteen, I feel regret that we will not be celebrating his coming of age. Yet I believe that what I hope for him can be accomplished without a Bar Mitzvah. When he recently told me that he felt lucky to be a part of both the Christian and Jewish world, I kvelled: I am doing something right!

With love and commitment, we have made it work. Despite my doubts and fears, I have not given up who I am or what I am about. I have not neglected to give my children a heritage. Contemplating this article has brought to the surface what was there all along: I *am* a Jewish mother. *I* am a Jewish mother! How lucky my children are to have one!

Conversion:
The Mother of Invention

Laurie Davis

When distance from family members and Jewish community and the lack of a Jewish partner and coparent might be expected to make Jewish mothering a trial, why do I find it a boon? Why is it that I, who stopped believing in God before I quite gave up hope in the Tooth Fairy, and who was once bodily removed from the offices of the *Canadian Jewish News* for trying to place a paid advertisement condemning Israel's invasion of Lebanon, find myself determined to raise daughters who will call themselves Jews? How did I become the woman who placed a "Jews Wanted" classified ad in the local paper some years back?

Why do I, the feminist daughter of a woman who converted to Judaism and a man who was as much an atheist and a socialist as a Jew, even care about this business of my daughters' Jewishness? How is it that, highly critical of organized religions generally, and deeply disturbed by the routine exclusion of women from the religious rituals of the nearest city's only synagogue, I have become a mother who, each December, can be spotted in the classrooms of my daughters' rural school talking about Hanukkah and Jewishness?

* * *

I am descended from a long line of not-very-Jewish mothers, yet I find myself the increasingly Jewish mother of two daughters. Still, to be frank, my Jewish mothering is something of an improv act, and I entertain long-standing doubts about my own legitimacy as a Jew and a Jewish mother.

My Jewishness, and that of my sister, my daughters, and my niece, hangs suspended from the fragile thread of my mother's conversion. We sway precariously close to the what-might-have-been fate of being not-Jewish.

This fragile thread, my mother's conversion, upon which so much depends, was not very much discussed in our family. Referred to, yes; it was important to my parents that we did not see ourselves as half Jewish, that we understood that my mother's conversion had spared us that fate.

Perhaps we did not discuss her conversion because the fact of her acceptance and involvement in the small Jewish community of our town was what really mattered. But perhaps we did not discuss her conversion for other, more superstitious, reasons—as if by fingering the one delicate thread that connected us to the longer-than-imaginable fabric of Jewish history, we might fray it with our worrying.

I knew that she had traveled across the Canadian-U.S. border to Buffalo, New York, for her conversion, and this troubled me. The Buffalo of my childhood was the place where women went to buy bargain-priced clothes, smuggling them back across the border by layering them under the clothes they had left home in. It seemed an inauspicious place for a conversion. Although my parents explained this cross-border journey—conversions weren't available any closer to home—I could never really shake the notion that my mother's conversion had been a kind of take-out, bargain-basement conversion and not, perhaps, The Real Thing.

This nagging doubt about my mother's—and hence my own—authenticity as a Jew, is also rooted in uncertainty about whether a conversion to Judaism *can* constitute The Real Thing. Despite my mother's apparent acceptance by the Jewish community and my father's family, I suspect that as a child I intuited and internalized the long-standing Jewish suspicion of the convert, and the convert-bride in particular.

My father, whose childhood was fractured by the early death of his mother, and who spent much of his young life in places with few, if any, Jews, would not likely have been of much use to my mother had she needed assistance in things Jewish. Since my father's sisters lived far away, she improvised.

Each night of Hanukkah, when we were small, my mother brought out the "Hanukkah bag." This was a cleaned and pressed white cotton bag in which she had sewn up sixteen gifts, one each for my sister and me for eight nights. The gifts were individually sewn into self-contained compartments, so that the ones we chose each night could be cut away without exposing the others.

For years I believed that Hanukkah bags were as much a part of conventional Hanukkah celebrations as lighting the candles, eating latkes, and playing dreidel. It is possible that my mother had learned about this practice from someone, or read about it, but as I have never found another Jew who has heard of it, I feel pretty certain that she invented it. My mother was a creative woman—a painter, a seamstress, and later, a teacher. The Hanukkah bag was an inspired thing, and we loved it. If I could sew properly I might have considered more seriously the notion of using a Hanukkah bag with my own children, but my lack of needle skills saved me from having to weigh the value of perpetuating my mother's improvisation against a lurking, somewhat shamefaced desire to try to do it "right."

More than that, I was spared having to confront my growing realization that my mother's improvisations were the direct consequence of her conversion. In retrospect, I wonder if I might have been more willing to adopt her improvisations had she been born Jewish.

This sneaking sense of not being a sufficiently authentic Jew has possibly both constrained and inspired my Jewish mothering. My daughters and I don't prepare or cook pork in our home. Each Friday night we light the candles and say the blessing. At Yom Kippur and Rosh Hashanah I try to arrange a special dinner with my sister and her daughter. On Hanukkah I give the girls a gift each night, we light candles, and play dreidel. We eat a lot of latkes. For the past few years we have tried to attend the Hanukkah party at the synagogue about an hour away. My older daughter participates in an outreach program for Jewish teens from small communities. Recently, we started learning Hebrew together as a family. But my doubt persists: If the Jewish community employed quality-control inspectors I fear I'd be put out of business.

Each year, as Passover approaches, I go into crisis. Will I or won't I? The thought of making a Seder for our small family alone seems all wrong. For a few happy years a young couple lived nearby. As she was Jewish and he was easygoing, they were easily conscripted to join us for Jewish holidays. While it lasted, I had a brief sense of how it could be: natural, not contrived. During this period, we managed to have a proper Seder with twenty guests, most of them Jewish. After the couple moved away from our area, I returned to my previous bumbling approach, calling family members, who all live hours away from us, offering what were, I suspect, half-hearted invitations: I have never felt at all sure about what kind of Seder to do.

One Passover, I succeeded in luring another family, along with my sister and her daughter, to spend a night of Passover with us, with the intention of holding a proper Seder. I didn't then have any Haggadot but I must have anticipated that either my guests or sister would bring some. But the day arrived and we were Haggadot-less. My Jewish guest, as it turned out, was no more sure of the script than my sister and I. Her partner, who was not Jewish, had been looking forward to a "real" Seder.

My memory of that dinner is tinged with a queer mixture of embarrassment and defiance: my sister and I, with our mother's gift for improvisation, took turns reading aloud whatever pertinent passages we could find in my mother's old cookbook, *A Treasure for My Daughter.* This book, given to my mother by my Aunt Sarah, was our family passport to Jewish food. My mother, a capable and creative cook, followed the recipes in this book more religiously than was her usual style. In some ways, this was the most Jewish book in the house.

The non-Jews looked on, bemused and appalled. And, although rather proud of my improvisational skills, I had managed, nevertheless, to get it not quite right.

If forced to articulate the "grounds" on which my Jewishness or Jewish mothering might be found wanting by the quality-control inspectors of my imagination, I anticipate failing grades for not having chosen a Jewish mate, not belonging to the shul, not sending my daughters to Hebrew school, not supporting Israel. But when I review this list, I realize that the areas in which I have "failed" are not ones that I see as particularly important to me as a person, a Jew, or a Jewish mother.

I think that my mother was primarily responsible for shaping my ideas of what it means to be a Jew. When I try to capture pertinent memories from my childhood, one incident stands out. When I was about eight years old my best friend lived across the street. I was also friendly with another girl, Linda Obermeir. The Obermeirs were German, and both Linda's parents had been in the German army. I do not recall being unwelcome in her house, though I was uncomfortable with the framed photos of her parents in uniform. Nor was Linda unwelcome in our house. Our parents, however, had little contact.

One day at school some sort of conflict between Linda and my best friend started to brew. It escalated after school and culminated in a gang of several girls chasing and taunting Linda on her way home. I was one of them, not actively participating perhaps, and trying, somewhat passively, to persuade my friend to stop her part in it. Linda managed to run back to the school and attract the attention of a teacher, who sent Linda on her way and gathered the rest of us together. She called us "catty." I remember being struck by the inadequacy of this word. Even then, I knew it had been a truly shameful event.

By the time I got home I was sick with remorse. I may have confessed to my mother because I was afraid she would learn of it some other way, but I think it more likely that I told her because I wanted to be absolved. I think I hoped she would tell me I had been good and brave because I had not said any mean things, or thrown any stones, and because I had asked my friend to stop. Instead, she ordered me to get my coat on and get in the car. We were going to the Obermeir's and I was going to apologize to Linda. I was horrified. I begged and cried. I may even have vomited. She was resolute. We would go now, before dinner, immediately.

When we arrived at the Obermeir's, Linda's mother came to the door. She was surprised to see me and stunned to see my mother. The family was seated at the dinner table. My mother had to prod me forward until I was in the room. Linda stood up and stepped toward me. I blurted out my apology. I remember how amazed

Linda seemed by what I was doing. I think I asked her forgiveness and she gave it. We left shortly afterward.

I don't remember exactly what words my mother used on the way there or on the way home. I know we both felt that this was the worst thing I'd ever done.

What I learned from my mother that day was that to be passive while something wicked was happening was to be complicit in that wickedness; that such passive complicity was precisely the key ingredient in Hitler's recipe for Jewish extinction. She helped me to know that being Jewish, being a member of a frequently victimized group, did not confer goodness or innocence, was never an excuse; it was, if anything, a responsibility to take positive action to prevent such wickedness. This remains the core of what it means, to me, to be a Jew.

Is it ironic then, or quite proper, that my mother, the woman who taught me what it is to be a Jew, was a convert to Judaism? The answer to this question, it seems to me, lies in each person's notion of what Jewishness is. My mother showed me that being a Jew, her kind of Jew and, for now, my kind of Jew, is an act of will, not a genetic inheritance.

It might add value and texture to my daily existence to be more observant, know more Hebrew, observe more Jewish holidays, have more Jewish friends, live closer to our Jewish family members. But none of these things are to me as important, as essentially Jewish, as raising my daughters to be this kind of "willful" Jew.

Who, then, do I imagine the quality-control inspectors to be? And why am I giving them office space? Are they, perhaps, the officials who demand documentation—proof—of my authenticity as a Jew? Do they, perhaps, suspect that, for me, the stigma of *being* a Jew has often been more manageable than the stigma of my mother not being *born* a Jew?

On reflection, I wonder if I feel caught between the quality-control inspectors, on one side, and a gallery of theater critics on the other. If being a Jew, my kind of Jew, is an act of will, it follows that my performance, my actions, will be evaluated. As I think back over my life I realize it is more likely that I have disappointed non-Jews, failed to seem Jewish enough.

My sister and I grew up outside of Toronto as the only Jews in both our elementary and high schools. We were different, but did not suffer unduly because of this difference. Being both a part of, and yet apart from, the larger community allowed me to stand back and look at my world. Forever being the only Jew in a group of friends, a classroom, a school, was forever to be a representative—a conscripted child diplomat for world Jewry. Strangely, I don't recall minding this (although it could, perhaps, have contributed to my performance anxiety). Possibly I relished this role and the insider-outsider status it conferred on me. If not, how to account for the fact that this is precisely the position in which I have placed my daughters?

I think that growing up Jewish, particularly in a non-Jewish community, helped me develop ethical and political muscles. I want my daughters to have such muscles. Is it, perhaps, through the alchemy of motherhood that I became drawn further into Jewishness? Being Jewish gives us a kind of bus pass to history.

If the improvisational nature of my Jewishness and Jewish mothering makes me something of an "exception" among Jewish mothers—and it may not—it places me firmly within my own family's tradition of "exceptional" characters. My mother, her own mother, and her grandmother all married outside of their religious upbringing. My paternal grandfather, with his wife and seven children in tow, tried his luck on a series of unsuccessful farms in rural Quebec. My grandfather's stubborn idealization of farming as a way of life meant that my father and his siblings were fostered by neighbors and sent to orphanages while their father joined the gold rush and did prison time for bootlegging between bursts of tailoring—all in aid of raising money for yet another farm. My father was variously a hard-rock miner, amateur boxer, union organizer, and soldier before he became the successful salesman of my childhood. Ours is not a family history peopled by rabbis and gentle scholars.

And the "exceptional" characters are not exclusively found on my side of the family. My partner's mother, a lifelong Anglican churchgoer, organist, and a widow of an Anglican minister, has spent her retirement years exploring and excavating her Christianity and its roots in Judaism. Another sort of mother might have been threatened by her son's common-law arrangement with a Jew and the subsequent appearance of Jewish grandchildren in a family that still closely identifies with the church. Instead, she warmly refers to me as her "daughter-out-law," sends me books she's reading about Jesus, the Jew, and greets the appearance of our Hanukkah menorah in her house at Christmastime with glee.

With such idiosyncratic ancestry, what kind of Jews are my daughters?

Neither one of them will likely have a Bat Mitzvah. I will not witness them reading from the Torah. Perhaps if I had had a Bat Mitzvah, or perhaps even if my father had had a Bar Mitzvah, it would mean more to me.

Instead, I picture other, actual, times: my youngest daughter's speech to her class on the Jewish holidays in grade five. My eldest daughter, in grade eight, standing before her classmates and telling them how, the previous day, they had upset her by their rowdy and insensitive behavior during a movie about Jews in hiding during the Second World War. I see my daughters' faces at the dinner table as we talk about the daily incidents of bullying, name-calling, discrimination, and just plain unfairness. I hear the questions they ask. I can see that they are beginning to lead examined and sometimes courageous lives, and I am enormously proud of them.

If being Jewish gives them a hook to hang their consciences and developing identities on, so much the better. I am grateful that this fragile thread, this connectedness to Jewishness that I offer them, is in such worthy, capable, and "exceptional" hands.

While I have sometimes worried about my ability to present a "true" picture of Jewishness, I suspect that I have begun to revel, anarchistically, in the freedom that a Jewless environment gives me to construct for my daughters a way of being Jewish in this time and place. Where once I felt abashed about reinventing Jewishness to suit my life and ideology, my recent explorations into Jewish history have led me to suspect that I am merely doing what many other Jews, in other times and places, have done before.

– 17 –

A Wandering Mother

Jane Ariel

If home provides an anchor for the soul, I have been searching for one since I was a small child. I was lonely in my house in Scarsdale, New York, the daughter of assimilated Jews who moved to a wealthy suburb to provide a good education for their children. We were somewhat out of place because we didn't have much money, nor were there Jews in the immediate neighborhood. My mother wanted us to have the best opportunities. Like many Jewish parents, she was very ambitious for us, often with a judgmental and critical edge. In response, I became a performing pianist at age nine, played basketball and baseball on school teams, and worked hard academically. In the midst of my quite public successes, my mother did not seem to notice that I was often isolated and restless, and I didn't know how to speak to her about my internal struggles. I also didn't share this part of myself with my two brothers, who were themselves grappling to relate to our mother's expectations. My father was only a shadowy presence, unassuming, in spite of his warmth and sense of humor. He went to work every day selling motor oil to garages around the state.

My mother had no background in traditional Judaism, but she identified ethnically as a Jew. We didn't belong to a temple, and we celebrated Christmas like our neighbors. There was no daily experience of Judaism or any religious education. In spite of this, I valued being Jewish without understanding why. Maybe this was partially because my father's family, immigrants from prewar Germany, had been active in the establishment of the Reform movement in the United States. My father cared about Judaism in his quiet way. We would dutifully travel to Manhattan each Rosh Hashanah. We would enter the temple, find my father's relatives in their usual pew, kiss them, and leave. On our way home, we would stop at my great aunt's apartment, where we were served chicken salad to mark the holiday.

My father died when I was eighteen, a year after my unplanned youngest brother was born. When I was twenty-five, this brother, very beloved by the whole family, died of a brain tumor at the age of seven. I needed to get away from the painful and exhausting trauma of his prolonged illness. It was just after the Six-Day War in Israel, and one day, after reading a newspaper article describing what was going on there, I suddenly decided to go, even though I had had no connection to Israel while growing up. Something compelled me. In retrospect, I might have been reaching out to my father, who had always wanted us to be more Jewish. I remember his chagrin many years earlier when I went to sing in a midnight Mass at the local Catholic church. He let me off three blocks away so that he wouldn't be seen taking his daughter to church.

Thus in the fall of 1967, still full of grief, I found myself in Israel. I had meant to go for the summer and come back to New York to my apartment and my very interesting job in the poverty program. From the moment I arrived, I loved the country. It immediately gave me a sense of belonging that I had never known before. I looked and dressed like many Israeli women. I could have been a kibbutznik in my tastes and manner. The hourly news seemed related to me. I loved the sparsely forested hills above the sea. The stone of ancient villages drew me in. I was moved by the songs, many connected to a vibrant, current history. It felt as if there were meaning in life just because I was there, a Jew in her own country. I believed that I had come home and could rest.

Because of a random encounter, I was offered an exciting job at an educational research institute just being established at the Hebrew University of Jerusalem. Although I spoke no Hebrew, everyone assured me that I would soon learn, and, in the meantime, I could have a bilingual secretary. I decided to stay. This was also influenced by another unexpected experience. On my way to Israel several months earlier, I had stopped in Naples, Italy. Boarding the boat to continue my trip, I noticed a handsome, suntanned man who was returning to Israel after a year abroad. After several halting conversations interspersed with French and English, our two common languages, we arranged to meet the following week in Haifa where he had a small apartment overlooking the sea.

Joseph was a Moroccan Jew, born in Fez, whose parents had immigrated to Israel when anti-Semitism had become unbearable in North Africa. When our paths crossed, he had been working for a commercial shipping line as an engine room mechanic. He subsequently decided to find a job that would keep him on land so that we could get to know each other. Each evening, from his balcony, we watched the brilliant red and gold colors of the sun setting over the Mediterranean. Six months later we agreed to marry in spite of the many cultural and class differences between us. His ties to his family were very strong, and they were the primary basis of his social life. I spent every Friday evening and most of Saturday with his family, because this was their custom. Although she couldn't read, Joe's mother was the granddaughter of a rabbi and was deeply religious. The food was prepared before Shabbat in a strictly kosher fashion, and the smells of garlic and spices always pervaded the house as we arrived. Then it was time for the blessings, dinner, and conversation around sweet mint tea. The family accepted me with an open heart, but over time I had trouble adjusting to what became for me a more constricted lifestyle. None of my husband's eight brothers and sisters had completed university, and he, because of being uprooted from Morocco as a young child, had never finished high school. It was hard to have the more reflective, deeper conversations I sometimes enjoyed in my connections with other people. Joe and I had to find different ways to build our relationship.

In 1971 we had our first son, Arik, and I began my journey as a Jewish mother. We were living in Jerusalem by that time, and I gave birth at Hadassah Hospital with a midwife in attendance. I remained in the hospital for seven days until the Brith Milah. Life was measured by Jewish time and rituals. We had a small apartment in Jerusalem, and I learned to hang diapers in the hallway during the three-month paid maternity leave that working Israeli women get. When we traveled to Haifa to visit my husband's family, I experienced a new way of relating to children. Maman, as we called Joe's mother, had a serenity about her that children always responded to, an unconditional love that emanated from her very being. There was no judgment. She was quietly present, as if she had nothing else to do. Children were sacred. I had never known this kind of mothering. I was in the presence of another kind of spirit, one that continually touched my heart.

In 1973, during the Yom Kippur War, our second son was born. This time we had to go to Hadassah Hospital in the early evening during a blackout. All the windows of our apartment were kept dark, and by night we lived in the shelter underneath the building. Driving without headlights took a long time, and I gave birth soon after arriving at the hospital. The corridors were lined with countless wounded soldiers and their families, and I was forgotten for five hours in the delivery room. My husband had returned home to be with our other son and to get some sleep. I was freezing cold but had been told not to move until a nurse arrived. Meanwhile the baby, born healthy, had been taken to the clinic. When I finally was discovered and wheeled to my room, there were no extra blankets to be found anywhere. I shivered for several hours in the dark. I remember thinking that if there were to be a next time, it would be better to give birth at home. In the following days in the hospital, I was continually reminded of and aghast at the horrors of war as I saw the suffering of the soldiers. In this atmosphere, we could not find a name for our newborn son. How could we reconcile all the visible pain and death with the beginning of his life? We waited seven days until it was time for the brith. Then we finally decided on Daniel, a name that would connect him to El, the sacred. It felt right.

Two weeks later, my husband was called into the reserves and didn't return for five months. It was a very tense time. I was alone with two small children, as many women were, so we tried to help one another with our daily lives. In our shikun, a small condominium, some of us shopped and cooked together and took care of the small children cooperatively when possible. We would gather in the evenings to talk and share any information that had been communicated from the front during the day.

Soon after the fighting stopped, I trained as an emergency ambulance driver to offset my pervasive sense of helplessness. Joe returned safely from Lebanon, badly shaken by all he had seen. It was his third war. After the first week at home, he didn't want to talk about it anymore.

As the years went by, Joe and I were involved in two worlds, one shaped by my life and work at the university, and the other by his life and family values. These two worlds could coexist, but we began to feel split between them. He often did not enjoy my friends or his sense of not being part of the university crowd, and I did not want to spend all of my free time with his relatives. Although it was very important for me to have our children ensconced in family, I was still quite "other" in the culture of his Moroccan, Sephardic world. Our intimacy was conflicted because of cultural differences: he had strong opinions about the way a husband and father should be, and I wanted more psychological understanding and less role rigidity. We were often angry at each other's desires. As Arik and Danny grew older, things that were important to me concerning their development were not important to Joe.

Our marriage became less and less viable, and I became more confused. My husband decided to leave for the United States in 1977 to try his luck there, a dream he had had for years. That separation was the virtual beginning of my becoming a single mother and led eventually to our divorce in 1979. Here I was in Israel, my children half Sephardic and half Ashkenazi. I was an American without a traditional Jewish background, and a single parent in a country where family is still a strong unifying force and a primary social unit. Sometimes I felt lonely and irreconcilably different. These feelings were not new.

Parts of me, however, were flourishing. I loved being a mother in a country that adored its children. I was surrounded by a different kind of parenting than I had ever known. In addition to my experience with Joe's mother, I observed that children in Israel were the center of life. No amount of attention or concern was too much, in spite of the considerable tensions and pressures of everyday life. Perhaps children were treated this way because of the tenuousness of life in Israel, because family love could offset the sense of being surrounded by hostile forces, or because children became bearers of hope after the Holocaust. It was a wonderful feeling to be able to send my five-year-old son to school alone on a public bus in the heart of Jerusalem, knowing that he would be protected. Teenagers were allowed to "own" the city where they lived, meeting one another everywhere at most hours, because of the freedom and respect they were given. Families sent endless packages to their young adult children who were serving at army bases throughout the country. I am not sure if this way of behaving is particularly Israeli or particularly Jewish because of the traditional reverence for families, or some combination of both.

My work at the university continued to be challenging and satisfying, and I had developed a community of friends with whom I socialized, played music, and shared political views. When I had difficult times, I was often buoyed by my sense of purpose in Israel. My children were sabras and, although they were half Sephardic, a group often oppressed in Israeli society, in their minds and in mine, they were simply Israelis. They had all the opportunities that being educated, middle-class, and Ashkenazi had opened up to me, and I felt my ambition for them moving generationally from my mother through me to them. The gap widened between them and the Moroccan side of their family, although this was not something we talked or even thought about then.

In the early 1970s, my mother moved to Israel after she divorced her second husband. She wanted to be closer to me and her grandchildren. When she came, I keenly felt the dissonance between the kind of mother she had been to me, and the mother I was learning to be. It was as if I were symbolically suspended between the children's two grandmothers. When they actually met at a Shabbat meal in Haifa, it brought the older generation of two cultures together, one a Smith College graduate, the other functionally illiterate. Maman welcomed my mother with generosity and an open heart. They found a way to talk and laugh without a shared literal or conceptual language as they ate wonderful Moroccan food together. My mother temporarily suspended her need to understand and analyze, responding wholeheartedly to the inclusive spirit around the table, while Maman made sure that everyone's immediate needs were taken care of.

I felt both of them in me. Neither was enough, and together their spirits created internal tension. Like my mother, I wanted my children to motivate themselves enough to become successful, and to contribute in some meaningful way to the world. I wanted them to have both the pleasure and the discomfort that comes from knowledge and the capacity to bring a critical mind to their experiences. On the other hand, I wanted to love them unconditionally like Maman and create an environment of complete acceptance. Maman loved all children simply because they were children, and she did not question the way she had been taught life was supposed to be lived. How was I to find a way to integrate both worlds for myself personally and for my sons? I so wanted it.

Living near us in Jerusalem, my mother became a very involved grandmother, and she and I had the opportunity to deal with some of our earlier difficulties. Arik was diagnosed at age five with Legg-Perthes disease, a degenerative hip disease that kept him from walking for more than a year. My mother was an extraordinary help during that period, and the two of them forged a strong and lasting bond. I couldn't have imagined a more supportive environment than we experienced in Israel; the hospital was full of kind caregivers and the school and community were very responsive to our special needs. At one point Arik was lying at home in a full body cast with a telephone connection to his classroom, arranged by the educational authorities so that his classmates could talk to him, and he could hear what was being taught. The whole school lined up outside to welcome him when he could walk again. It made me cry.

In 1980, when the children were nine and six, I was offered a grant to do my doctorate in family therapy. I accepted and decided to go to a graduate school in California. What would this mean for my children and how would I fare as a mother? They did not speak English, and I did not have a community to help me with them, although I did have two good friends in Berkeley, one Israeli and one American. Would it be too dislocating for them? Would they experience the same alienation I had felt during much of my life? The week before we left, I bought an apartment in Jerusalem to prepare for our return, using part of my grant money for a down payment. I needed to know that we had a home, even though it meant that we arrived in the United States with very little to our names.

In California we were all in severe culture shock. The attitudes toward family and children were so different. Hospitality is a very important element of Israeli society, but my busy acquaintances in

Berkeley did not seem to have time for us. I sought out Israelis to help us make the transition. Arik and Danny were in a school where the majority of students were African American, and my sons had had little experience with very dark-skinned people. They didn't know how to adjust to this different world. In Israel they had been with their friends in the same classrooms and neighborhood for years. Now they were without any history and few common experiences with their schoolmates. I spoke English with a slight accent and was often asked where I came from. I once again felt like a stranger, a foreigner in my own country. Time was no longer measured by the Jewish calendar; the Jewish holidays were hidden behind Christmas and Easter instead of shaping the rhythms of the year.

Arik's Bar Mitzvah was held in the Chabad temple, not because orthodoxy held any appeal for me, but because the rabbi was warm and eager. I didn't realize how profoundly the service would alienate me. I found myself behind the mehitza, as I had in Orthodox synagogues in Israel, while Arik was brought to Jewish "maturity" by the men on the bima. This was not my Judaism. I couldn't find any institutional expression that moved me, nor did I have enough traditional background to create a meaningful Jewish context for the children to grow in. Also, for years Arik thought he was black, as were most of his friends, and, since his Jewish identity was not helpful to him in joining his peer group, he slowly let it go. Three years later, still searching for a way to maintain our Judaism, I arranged for Danny's Bar Mitzvah to be shared with a friend whose family had become part of ours. It was led by a progressive rabbi who ministered to a Jewish Renewal synagogue without walls. This time, men and women shared equally in the ceremony. Although still feeling somewhat apart, I fully participated in this ceremony, surrounded by our new community.

Soon after our arrival in the United States, I had an experience that made it hard to continue being part of any conventional lifestyle. I fell in love with a woman and came out as a lesbian. I had been with women before, but had, in spite of this, always considered myself heterosexual. I was upset at this point that the children had to deal with my coming out without having a choice, but it was where my heart led me. They were continually exposed to the usual derogatory "you're a faggot" comments in the schoolyard and did not talk about my lesbianism with their friends for many years. Their father, who saw them rarely although he had moved to the States, believed that their association with me would encourage them to be gay and told them that it was not a normal way of behaving. As younger children, it was hard not to be influenced by his comments, but in spite of being surrounded by homophobia, they were very accepting of my relationship. My partner became an involved stepparent, even though it was complicated by the children's longing to have a more supportive father.

It took me five years to complete my doctorate, and I had to start developing my private practice in order to have enough money to live. Although it had never occurred to me that we might stay in California and not return to Israel, slowly life was shaping itself in such a way that that was becoming a real possibility. My partner was not Jewish and had her own children, which kept her tied to the States. Arik and Danny were losing their Hebrew and becoming socialized as Americans. I felt tormented. Every time I went back to visit Israel, I was taken over by a desire to be back to what felt like home. I could touch the soft-hued Jerusalem stone and taste the pita and hummus. I could hike in the rocky hills of the desert so beloved to me, and lie in the hot sun on the beach. I was welcomed by my dear friends who endlessly asked when we would be coming back.

When Israel invaded Lebanon, I felt even more conflicted. If we returned, I would have two sons who might be sent to the front lines in the army to fight a war in which I didn't believe. Before, when we lived in Israel, I had known that they would serve in the military; it was woven into the fabric of the society. Now, the thought that one or both of them could die for what I considered misguided political reasons was intolerable.

We stayed in the United States. The boys didn't want to go back and readjust to a different social reality, or relearn a language already foreign to them. Life was economically easier in California, and it would have been harder to be public about my lesbianism in Israel. We had good friends. Those were the arguments I continually had with myself. I didn't feel at home in California, and yet the image of "home" in Israel was tarnished with the evolving social and political realities there. Maybe I would never feel at rest anywhere. Maybe the world, with its complex intersections of different cultures and classes, global corporations, struggling economies, and incessant brutal battles for power and possession can never be a restful place.

The kids were growing away from daily contact with Judaism. We identified culturally as Israelis and Jews, but as it was in my childhood, Jewish practice had little effect on our daily lives. Even today on high holidays, I go to several different services in search of an experience that touches me. Arik and Danny don't mark these rituals unless they are visiting, and then sometimes they join me. I have not become affiliated institutionally, mainly because most synagogues focus on heterosexual family life and lesbianism is marginalized, as in the broader society.

Today my sons and I live in different parts of California. They have graduated from college and are building independent lives. Our emotional bond maintains our nuclear family, encircled by significant relatives and friends. Each of us continues to struggle with the notion of belonging and sometimes with the meaning of life. Our identities are not easily defined because we have often been outsiders, and we have wandered from place to place. I remain straddled between two worlds and still believe, in some muted secret place, that I will live in Israel someday. Each time my children have visited, I hoped that they would become passionately connected, and we would all return. After Danny spent a year studying in Jerusalem, he knew definitively that he wanted to return to the States. Arik never seriously considered moving. I have not yet sold my apartment in Jerusalem, but I do not think that I would live there if my children were not with me. What, after all, is most important?

If I have been looking for a home forever, perhaps the most important place I have found it is in mothering. Schooled in Israel, I learned something I hadn't known about giving and receiving. My love for my children has been single-minded, although, like every mother, I feel very sad and disappointed about what I couldn't provide because of what I lacked myself. I know that each of my children has suffered in his own way, but I can only hope that they have more of an anchor than I had.

In other aspects of my life, I have moved back and forth from feelings of belonging to feelings of alienation: as an American, an Israeli, a foreigner, a married and unmarried heterosexual, a partnered or single lesbian, a single mother, a Jew. As an older person, I have slowly come to understand that I need to turn more inward, and, were I at home there, I might wander anywhere in the world with some tranquility. In search of that, I have been drawn in recent years to the developing realm of Jewish spirituality. At a meditation retreat in the mountains of Colorado, I found myself alone in the woods with instructions to call out in Hebrew to that which is sacred. As my voice echoed among the trees toward the blue sky, I sensed a profound connection, a place to rest, which, for that moment at least, I did not question.

SECTION IV:
JEWISH IDENTITY—
DISCOVERED AND REDISCOVERED

– 18 –

Jewish Mother "from Scratch"

Béatrice Steinberg

I was born in the early 1960s in a suburb of Paris, France. As a young Catholic, I was baptized, went to Sunday school, and did my confirmation. I attended Catholic schools and chose to attend a Jesuit college. As a teenager and young adult, I was fortunate to meet and interact with exceptional spiritual leaders. In college, I volunteered as the class religious coordinator, which had the title, strangely enough, of Rabbi. I felt a strong connection to God, praying alone in my bed or isolated in a log cabin on a spiritual retreat.

When I met my husband, Rob, religion became an important topic right away in our relationship. Although Rob was not religious, it was very important to him to pass his Jewish heritage on to his future children. My relationship to God was very important to me. But I loved Rob very much, and after eight years of reflections, inner struggles, and learning experiences about Judaism, I agreed to raise our children within the Jewish religion. Religions differ as points of view but they are all looking at the same reality: "Don't we have all the same father?" (Malachi 2:10). I cared more about this spiritual reality than any particular theology.

I moved to the United States, embraced Judaism, and over the years became more and more familiar with Jewish customs and practices. Judaism grew on me as my two daughters were growing up Jewish. First, we made Friday night a special family dinner night and lit the Shabbat candles. Slowly, we added Shabbat songs, dances, special readings, and bedtime prayers. We started going more frequently to services, we wrote our own family Haggadah for Passover, built and decorated our own Sukkah, made Purim baskets for our friends and family and had our first family Shavuoth celebration last year!

I enjoy living with the rhythm of the Jewish holiday cycle. Each holiday ritual brings practical, educational, and fun opportunities to connect our daughters to God, to teach them the Jewish traditions, and to help them understand their role as human beings in this world. To help us create a Jewish environment at home we joined a vibrant Reform congregation. The experiences and friendships we have shared through the life of our temple have supported and inspired our family life. In addition, I have also gathered an impressive collection of Jewish children's books, videos, and audiotapes! I learned the aleph bet, blessings, prayers, and songs from the liturgy with my kids by listening to tapes in the car over and over again. This year I went as far as combining French and Jewish learning by acquiring French Jewish tapes!

Our children do not question that the rituals we are sharing with them are so new to me. With them, we only need to do something twice to call it a tradition. Together, day by day, we are building our own Jewish family traditions and my own Jewish traditions as well. I am so grateful that Jewish family life so naturally induces the spiritual connection to God that I have always wanted to share with my children. Tears came to my eyes when my five-year-old suggested that we sing Shema Israel to pray for a schoolmate whose grandfather had passed away. She chose these words because we sing them together every night, because these words have now become part of our lines of connection to God.

What had been a decision from the mind when I got married became, eight years later, a decision from the heart when I decided in 1996 to convert to Judaism. I was ready, and it felt so wonderful to make such an important decision in my adult life. I discovered in Judaism something I did not know I was looking for, diversity and intellectual challenge. None of my questions were answered by one single and simple dogmatic response, but by several opinions from various scholars of all the ages. And there is still so much I have not read and learned! In November 1998, I celebrated my adult Bat Mitzvah with four other women. In Hebrew we read from the Torah and chanted the Haftorah. For this special occasion, I asked my daughters if they could be the ones to present me with the gift of a tallit. Usually parents or grandparents present a tallit to their Bat or Bar Mitzvah child or grandchild to symbolize the beautiful meaning of passing the Jewish heritage onto the next generation. It seemed only natural that my daughters would be the ones to perform this meaningful act, as over the past ten years, they have been passing the Jewish heritage onto me.

I chose to write my Bat Mitzvah report on a subject that had been haunting me for a long time: on the one hand, I am strongly attached to my French culture and heritage, and on the other hand, my religious identity is rooted in American Reform Judaism. How can I reconcile these two identities? I reread my home country's history with the eyes of a Jew. This was a powerful and emotional experience as I had learned and witnessed so little in my youth about French Judaism. I discovered that Judaism in France is mostly Orthodox. I realized that if I had been born Jewish in France, my life and my religious practices as an Orthodox and most likely Sephardic Jewish mother would have been much different. I feel very fortunate that my children and I have discovered Judaism through Reform Judaism. I was welcomed as a non-Jew with no questions asked. I have been able to choose and add rituals as I and my family could handle them. I have been able to fully participate as a woman and as a non-Jew. These were essential factors in my growing into becoming a Jewish woman and a Jewish mother.

Without any Jewish background, I became a Jewish mother: I had to start from scratch! I had little knowledge but an open and determined mind to learn. As a Jewish mother, I have found in Judaism the creative resources to teach my children about God and expose them to spirituality in fun and stimulating ways. Only the future will tell how my daughters will feel about their own Jewish identity and education!

19

How Modern-Day Austria Made Me a Modern Jewish Mother

Karen Engel

It was finally the Austrian school system that turned me into a Jewish mother. Before I gave birth to two girls in Austria, I was probably like many other well-traveled, progressively minded Americans living with a European. But what challenged my previous identity as an assimilated, nonreligious Californian of Jewish origin, here in the southern Austrian town of Graz, were not fears of anti-Semitism or neofascism, but the fact that religious education is an integral part of the Austrian public school system. My daughters are faced with the choice of attending courses in Catholicism along with most of the other kids in their class, or being branded a "non-Catholic" and sitting the classes out with the "outsiders."

It is a situation that scares me. I am haunted by stories from my father and other relatives of how they felt being singled out at school as young boys in Germany and Poland after they had been identified as Jews. My father grew up in what was then the German/Polish "free city" of Danzig/Gdansk. The shock of being assimilated, one-of-the-crowd, popular members of the class and after-school clubs one day, and being cast out as hated, despised dregs the next, are childhood memories that continue to hurt him more than sixty-five years later. Of all the abominations, discrimination, and prohibitions that he endured before being able to emigrate, it is the relatively minor experience of being ejected from his school community which still brings tears to my father's eyes.

Sadly, our children and those of other non-Catholics are still being "singled out" in Austria—although in a benevolent, tolerant way, not with the hatred of the Nazi period. Around 80 percent of the population in Austria is at least nominally Catholic, and religion is taught in the public schools by special teachers provided by the Church. Children either attend Catholic religion classes with the majority of their classmates, or they attend the much smaller Protestant class, or they sit out the religious hour with the one or two other Muslems or "nondenominational" children. Whether we like it or not, this system has forced me and my non-Jewish husband to address the issue of our religious identity. Sending our children to Catholic or Protestant religion classes is out of the question for us as a matter of principle. Although we both agree that the children should be exposed to the main ideas of Christianity as part of understanding Western civilization and culture, attending catechism courses is going too far. I am simply not willing to turn my back on a family history that I cherish and respect. I was not raised religiously. But much of my Jewish identity comes from growing up with extended family members who identified strongly with the cultured, assimilated German Jewish environment of late nineteenth- and early twentieth-century Germany and with the assimilated, upper-class Jewish families of Poland.

My children, however, are growing up without any Jewish relatives close by. I'm afraid it would be very confusing to them if we identified them as outsiders, as Jews, and yet had nothing Jewish about our day-to-day life. Unless we can embody that Jewishness with positive experiences and meaning, I think there is a real danger that our children will reject being different and resent their identity as Jews. Choosing the "nondenominational" route like many of our like-minded, nonreligious friends is not really a choice with which we feel comfortable. Religious references and ethics permeate so much of Austrian secular life that, although general society is quite liberal (legal abortion, common-law marriage provisions, etc.), you cannot escape the constant influence of the Catholic Church.

When my Janina started coming home from kindergarten with stories about St. Martin who helped the poor, and with confused references to the child Jesus who "died for all the little children," we realized that Jesus was a presence with which to be reckoned. To this day, Janina insists that Jesus died in the very church near our home, and she sees him everywhere—crucified on a lonely cross in a city park, immortalized in the innumerable shrines that dot even the most desolate country roads, and remembered by the crosses that mark the summit of practically every Austrian alpine peak. I realized I needed to find a way to explain at a preschool level who Jesus was and why the Christkind (the Christ child) does not come to our house at Christmas. I also began to realize that religion is attractive to children because it conveys social ethics through stories and examples that children can easily understand. St. Martin, by the sound of it, wasn't such a bad guy, but I thought it would be better if I could find a Jewish parallel. And so our religious quest began.

The quest began in a different way around the time that Uwe and I decided to get married. After more than seventeen years of friendship, separation, and togetherness, we decided finally to confirm officially what had long existed personally between us—a committed, stable, and loving relationship that had long ago learned to accommodate our differences. The wedding also became a celebration of our decision to incorporate Jewish ethics and traditions into our family life as best we could, in accordance with our genuine feelings and values. True to ourselves, the wedding contained both traditional and unconventional elements unique by Austrian, American, and Jewish standards.

We decided to hold the wedding in Carinthia, a province in southern Austria, because we had already planned a week-long family reunion there at the same time. My sister-in-law, a Protestant religion teacher, introduced us to Chriss Fiebig. She is the head of the Jewish community in Bamberg, Germany, and lives part-time in Carinthia, where she gives workshops in Jewish religious traditions to an interfaith public. Chriss had been trained but not ordained as a rabbi, and a warm friendship quickly evolved between the three of us. As a German Jew who survived the Holocaust thanks to a Christian family who hid her during the war, Chriss understood and appreciated the diversity of our backgrounds as well as our multicultural family identity. Uwe and I could relate to her combination of holding progressive religious views while still cherishing Jewish traditions and ethics. So Chriss became our Baal Kiddushin, and although we revised it in many ways, Uwe and I probably had the most traditional Jewish wedding that the province of Carinthia had ever seen.

We met under a red and blue velvet chupah with gold fringe that was graciously, but unofficially, loaned to us by the tiny Graz Jewish community. It had been saved from the destruction of the Graz Synagogue and had been locked up among old Torah scroll coverings, collecting dust during the previous sixty years, in a drawer of the community prayer room. The secretary of the community office told me it was probably the first time the chupah was used since the Shoah. The wine benedictions were made over kosher wine made in Austria and certified by an Orthodox Viennese rabbi; music was a guitar and flute duo performed by the local parish priest and his wife—they had both learned Hebrew in seminary school and certainly knew more Yiddish and Hebrew than I did. After the meal, a non-Jewish engineer from the nearby town of Klagenfurt led us all in Israeli folk dancing. The ceremony took place outdoors in the inner courtyard of a fifteenth-century castle lodged in an alpine peak overlooking the Carinthian valley, a province renowned for its clear, sweet water lakes and mountain pastures, and notorious for harboring persistent unreformable Nazi sympathies. What better place could there be to declare oneself?

Although we both eschew religious dogmas and extremes of any kind, both Uwe and I believe that Jewish history, philosophy, cultural traditions, and religious rituals can help us to take note of time passing, to appreciate the diverse nature of human relationships, and to think about the ethical issues in everyday life. We are trying to incorporate more Jewish practices into our day-to-day life, and we want to give our children a Jewish education. This is no small task for a nonbelieving Austrian and a religiously ignorant Californian living in a city where there are barely 180 Jews in a total population of 300,000.

The Jewish community in Graz is frankly too small, too aged, too divisive, and too traumatized from the Shoah to provide our young family with much support or feeling of community—which is normally essential to Jewish life. It is a community of contradictions. Although many members of the community live in mixed marriages, we who do are made to feel that our spouses are not welcome. Sometimes I think the Jews here in Graz are more interested in preserving graveyards than in building a thriving living community. Last year during Purim services—on Purim of all days!—one of the men of the congregation asked me to leave the room because the baby had started to cry. "This is a religious service," he whispered to me indignantly. I was the only one present with children.

Everyone on the Board is male and over sixty. The older people who live here have understandably ambivalent feelings toward Austria and Graz, which are mixed up with paranoia, guilt, and a very insecure spiritual foundation. Services are Orthodox, with the sexes separated, and all in Hebrew, which only a few understand and follow. Yet no one is Orthodox. The most religious person I know, and the only one I know who keeps somewhat kosher (e.g., no separate kitchen or dishes, but generally separates meat meals from dairy), is an Israeli who lives with a Catholic Austrian woman in an unmarried relationship with five children. The community cannot get ten men together for a minyan for Sabbath services, and meets only for holidays. This makes it very difficult for many of us to find any meaning or even enjoyment in attending community services or events. Yet the community itself seems to be made up of a quite diverse mix of people—several mixed marriages, fairly unreligious practices, young families—and others who feel ill at ease at services and totally turned off by some of the practices and pronouncements of the Board. We don't have a rabbi. Services are usually led by a retired American tenor who used to sing in the opera and who, as the community's cantor, would probably be more than willing to liberalize the services if the Board would only let him.

But things are slowly improving. Over time, we have met a few other young families, all in mixed marriages, and we have celebrated Sabbath together. I helped organize the first children's Chanukah party that Graz had seen in decades. Some of the old-timers were surprised that there were so many Jewish children in Graz and that more people, around fifty, came to that event than even to the High Holiday services. Uwe grated five kilos of potatoes and fried latkes (potato pancakes) for everyone. Even more people turned out for this year's Purim services. This time, I called up a few families I knew to make sure they'd come. We baked dozens and dozens of hamantaschen. We dressed the kids in costumes, painted their faces, and provided every child with a noisemaker. The book of Esther may have been read in Hebrew, but none of those kids missed a chance to create havoc at the mention of Haman, and this year, no one threw me out of the room. On the way home, Janina told me that was the best party she had ever attended. She certainly exaggerated, but I basked in her exuberance.

Nevertheless, the activities of the Jewish community in Graz play only a small role in our lives. The main reason we remain active, despite all, is that I want my children to meet other Jewish children, to help my children feel that they are not totally alone in being different. To be a Jewish mother in Graz means, above all, embracing and dealing with difference. I'm still wrestling with this issue. Part of me needs to have an "insurance policy"—the ability to go underground if necessary. Another part of me fears that my religious beliefs alone are too shaky to provide my children with a powerful and solid bulwark against the temptations of total assimilation. It would be easier if I had no theological doubts, but I do. Moreover, I think that if my children suffer too much from being different, Judaism will become for them nothing more than a painful burden, a wedge driven between them and their friends for no apparent reason. Intellectually, difference is exciting, thought provoking, and creative. Emotionally, it's tough. Finding a balance between the two is part of my responsibility as a Jewish mother in Austria.

I have felt the need at times to be more up front with my Jewish identity in Austria than in California, simply to discourage the view of Jews as "exotic." Many Austrians have never met a modern Jew and are quite interested in learning more about contemporary Jewish culture. Yet I miss the normalcy of the American Jewish community. Although it is necessary, of course, to continue to address the Holocaust, I do get sick of the fact that the Shoah overshadows and dominates Jewish issues in this country. Most Jewish events deal with memorial projects, endless discussions on the roots of Austrian anti-Semitism, painstaking studies in minute details of prewar Austrian-Jewish relations, Austrian complicity in National Socialism, and wartime experiences. I am well read on the subject, but sometimes I simply cannot hear another word about it. There is more to life than mourning. Isaac Deutscher (1968) was absolutely correct when he said, "it is a tragic and macabre truth that the greatest 'redefiner' of the Jewish identity has been Hitler; and this is one of his minor posthumous triumphs" (p. 50). I can't attend another lecture on "Dealing with the Holocaust." What I want to know are things such as "Dealing with Being Jewish in Primary School: The Pros and Cons of Addressing Your Daughter's First Grade Class" (i.e., encouraging multicultural awareness versus embarrassing your child to hell), or "How to Build a Sukkoth Booth in the Snow," or "How to Find a Hebrew Teacher for One Class of Ten Students Ages 6-12," or "What If You Prepare for Bar Mitzvah and Nobody Comes!"

Sometimes I feel as though we are the blind leading the blind. Lacking any religious education as a child, I have learned to incorporate Jewish rituals into our family life by literally "going by the book." One day I was browsing in an English bookstore in Vienna when a particular book caught my eye, Blu Greenberg's (1983) *How to Run a Traditional Jewish Household.* Since we had just gotten married, I read the chapter on weddings, wishing I had read this book earlier, and annoyed, of course, to find out that we had apparently done everything "wrong." "I'm not Orthodox so I don't need this book," I told myself, and walked out of the bookstore. But it kept nagging at me as I walked down the narrow alleys and cobblestone streets of Vienna's old city center. At St. Stephen's Cathedral I turned around, walked back to the bookstore, and bought the book. For the next week, I sat outside on the kitchen steps of our small second home in the country reading Greenberg's book in the eastern Austrian morning sun before the kids woke up.

It was as suspenseful as reading a mystery novel. I had never known a Jewish Orthodox family as a child, nor did I know much about Orthodox practices. Reading this book was like taking a basic course in Judaism. I appreciated Greenberg's straightforward style, her clarity on the philosophical or religious meanings behind certain rituals, her down-to-earth humor, her honest doubts about certain traditions, and her attempts to reconcile feminist convictions with age-old male-dominated practices. Sometimes, while reading this book, I yearned to move to a Jewish neighborhood in New York where the Jewish structure of life was all there—the mikvehs, mohels, and rabbis, the kosher grocery stores and shuls, and where to be a Jew you only had to be like everybody else. I longed to be embraced by a community with whom to celebrate Pesach and Chanukah, to exchange schaloch manos, where my children could attend Purim plays, and where *everyone* stopped working on the Sabbath and on the High Holidays. I know that in real life I would rebel against the dogma and the restrictions, but for a moment it looked tempting, and a whole lot easier than having to plan and ponder every step we take to make Judaism a part of our everyday lives.

But we are trying. Much to the amazement of my family back in California, we have started celebrating the Sabbath and lighting the candles on Friday night. I feel simply like a proud Jewish mother when five-year-old Janina, with two-year-old Milena mimicking every word, recites the Sabbath blessing in perfect Hebrew, which I only learned when I was thirty-nine. Often I will bake a challah with the children. We also have started to celebrate the main Jewish holidays—perhaps not in an Orthodox manner, but at least in small ways that mark the specialness of the event, special foods and dinners, small celebrations with friends, special games and bedtime stories. The easiest thing about being Jewish in Austria is the food. Much of central European Jewry lived in the Hapsburg Empire, and much of typical Jewish food is today equally typically Austrian. Potato noodles with melted butter and poppy seeds, for example, a traditional Ashkenazi treat for Rosh Hashanah, is also a popular Austrian dish, Mohnnudeln. Latkes are known here as Kartoffelpuffer (or Erdapfelpuffer). Another typical dish for Chanukah is fried doughnuts, which Austrians love and know as Krapfen. The list goes on and on. At least my children will know they are Jewish and Austrian by their stomachs.

Living in Austria has forced me and my husband to learn more about Judaism. We've started reading the Torah, religious commentaries, and other texts, as well as subscribing to Jewish magazines. I have been asked to address interfaith audiences here in Graz on Jewish issues. That means that I've also had to study up fervently beforehand on specific issues, like researching the historical background of Chanukah, or taking a crash self-learning course on women and midrash. Although I may question much of traditional Jewish dogma, I am trying to make Judaism a framework from which to begin, a structure in which to consider universal ideas, values, and ethics. Much to my surprise, I am finding that I can relate to the essential meaning of many Jewish traditions, such as marking the end of the week on the Sabbath, taking time out to rest and to reflect and to appreciate our family. It's an excellent and much-needed practice in our stressed-out world.

I feel part of the modern Diaspora, modern in the sense of a different kind of Diaspora, one that has existed *since* the founding of Israel. Jews who live in the Diaspora play a revitalizing role in Judaism in that we are constantly having to define Judaism vis-à-vis a dominant, non-Jewish society. I have discovered how closely intertwined religious practices are with cultural Jewish traditions and how religious practices play an essential role in keeping the Jewish community together. I must ask myself constantly how much I am willing to assimilate into the dominant society, and how much I am willing to stick my nose out and be different, subjecting my children to the rigors of difference. In Israel, such questions would never be an issue. I could live as an atheist in Israel and still be a Jew. In the United States, American Jews are, by and large, so much an accepted part of American society, another segment of the American tapestry, that there simply is no inherent anomaly. In contrast, I could live in Austria till my days' end, adopt a Styrian dialect, and wear a dirndl, but I would never feel Austrian because Austrian history and culture are simply not part of my heritage. Nor do Austrians totally embrace their foreign-born as one of their own. There will always be a part of me that remains on the outside. My children, born and raised in Austria, may grow up to feel differently. I still have to get used to the idea that they could become emotionally attached to yodeling.

It has been important for us to adapt, to a certain degree, to the dominant culture around us as well. For one thing, we have to consider the needs of my teenage stepdaughter, Hannah, who is often with us and who has celebrated Christmas with us ever since she was a little girl. So our children, like their friends and their non-Jewish cousins, set out their shoes on the doorstep on the eve of December sixth, hoping St. Nicholas will have left them some candy, nuts, apples, and tangerines by morning. We bake Christmas cookies and make decorations out of salzteig (salt dough) like scores of other families in Austria, and we put up a Christmas tree on Christmas

Eve. My children don't associate these activities with a religious meaning, but rather join in the general fun and merrymaking that is part of this season. And why not? I don't think depriving my children of the fun their friends are having, without being able to give them much in exchange, will make them better Jews. Why should I exclude them from certain social activities when there is no Jewish community to include them in an equally warm and embracing way? Let's face it: Chanukah candles in Graz (which are almost impossible to find) burn weak and lonely in comparison to the genuinely charming Christmas atmosphere here with roasted chestnut vendors on snow-bedecked sidewalks, sleigh rides around the main city squares, bustling Christmas markets offering handmade arts and crafts, live folk music and Christmas caroling in alpine huts warmed by wood-burning stoves, and so on. Yet we do light the menorah, play dreidel, and eat latkes for Chanukah. It has become a family tradition to invite close non-Jewish friends as well to partake in our yearly Seder for Pesach, a holiday that Hannah especially enjoys. It's more important to reduce the exclusions where morally possible and stress the inclusions—such as sharing stories and traditions, inviting friends to big, sumptuous meals, and encouraging conversation and communication. It is more important that my children learn basic ethics and feel comfortable with their Jewish heritage in a non-Jewish society than to lead a strictly Jewish-only life.

To help my children feel that they are connected to this society, and to learn how Jews adapted to alpine culture in the past, I have become particularly interested in finding traces of Jewish life in the Alps. Vienna, of course, had a large, thriving, and cosmopolitan Jewish community before World War II, but not much is known about Jews who lived in rural areas. For centuries the Alps were not a welcoming terrain for Jews. Not only were Jews forbidden to own property, but alpine communities were generally unfriendly, prejudiced, and wary of strangers, not only Jews, but even people who came from villages a few hilltops and valleys away. In 1867 the Austrian government finally annulled the law banning Jewish land ownership in the Alps. Around the turn of the twentieth century, Jews did begin to settle in small alpine towns, even in the mountains of Styria. Their stories are finally starting to be publicized. The Shoah has failed to extinguish them completely.

An Israeli friend of ours has started a homestead in southeastern Styria with his Austrian wife and three bilingual children. Their children speak both modern Hebrew and German and go to the local school with the other farm kids. Their parents try to make a living by organic farming in cooperation with some other farms nearby. Their neighbors have been slow to accept them, not because they are Jewish, but because they are different. But by their very presence this family is doing more, I think, for the post-Shoah reconstruction of a Jewish presence in Central Europe than dozens of well-meaning lectures.

We are not the only Jewish family in Graz. There are several of us. We may be a small community, a quirky community, a difficult community. But we are here. As our cantor, Richard Ames, told me a few months ago: "Naturally, living here in these surroundings, your Judaism becomes something which is with you much more than virtually any other place, and perhaps that's good. Perhaps this feeling that one is not yet in an area of total acceptance makes us aware of our Judaism every day. It's much better to be aware of Judaism every day than to be in surroundings where you tend to forget."

POSTSCRIPT

This chapter was written before the extreme right-wing Freedom Party, led by Joerg Haider, came to power in February 2000. A thorough discussion of why the right-wing populist party has attracted voters is beyond the focus of this book. Although I am very concerned about the intolerance and xenophobia expressed by this party, I do not believe that it came to power due to latent anti-Semitism. However, as antiforeigner sentiment spreads, I think it is more important than ever to support cultural and ethnic diversity in Europe. More than ever, I feel committed to working for a strong, intellectually vibrant, socially visible Jewish presence here in Austria.

REFERENCES

Deutscher, Isaac (1968). *The non-Jewish Jew and other essays*. London: Oxford University Press.
Greenberg, Blu (1983). *How to run a traditional Jewish household*. New York: Simon & Schuster.

20

Learning to Speak German

Pamela Cravez

"Eins, zwei, drei." I listen to my son practice the harsh German consonants muttered low in his throat. Their clipped cadence disturbs me, his Jewish mother, arousing thoughts of Nazis and death camps, small children herded through sterile passageways, a maze of Holocaust images. I struggle to get above this visceral reaction and compliment my son on his diligence.

Only a few days earlier his fifth-grade teacher explained that—along with American history, science, and math—she intended to teach her students German, her native language, with the hope of taking them to Germany.

"Please let me know what you think of this plan," she asked the parents assembled in her classroom. She had just finished enthusiastically telling us how she'd like to take the children to Bavaria, and perhaps find a grade school there that would act as a sister school to my son's Anchorage, Alaska, class.

As she spoke I felt my discomfort. To the casual observer Bavaria may be flowers and castles, but I immediately think of it as the place where Hitler gained political strength, a place comfortable ridding itself of Jews. I looked around the classroom and realized I was the only Jewish parent. The man next to me raised his hand and asked if there were any tapes that he could get to help his child with German since he already knew the language and would like to help. I kept my mouth shut. Although I liked the idea of my son learning a foreign language, German was not the first language I would have chosen for him, nor was Germany the first European country I'd have planned for him to visit. But I felt paralyzed. I could not question this teacher in front of a group of people who did not seem to share my concerns. Not only would it single me out as the only Jewish person, it would single out my concern as a "Jewish concern," something I grew up keeping to myself.

I knew this sense of isolation, this reluctance to draw attention to my religion. It is deeply rooted within my family. My father, who grew up in the same small Midwestern town as I, is part of a large Jewish American family that spans four generations. His insular family limited its contact with the largely Christian community. I remember my mother pointing out my father's discomfort when he'd run into someone he knew from his school days. Only when pressed would he tell us children how he was beaten up as he walked to school because he was Jewish. Kids called him "kike" and "Jewboy." He acknowledged that one of the first German Bunds—an organization sympathetic to the Nazis—was formed in Sheboygan, his hometown.

While my father's family kept kosher and practiced Jewish customs within their cocoon, my mother's parents, in another small Wisconsin community, largely ignored their Jewish heritage. They didn't deny it; it just didn't seem all that important to them. When my mother moved to Sheboygan to live with my father, she found it difficult to find a group of friends at first. From the way she said this, I knew that part of the reason was because she was Jewish.

My own Jewish upbringing blended these small-town Midwestern strains. I regularly attended the Conservative temple, learned Hebrew, and celebrated my Bat Mitzvah. But outside the temple, we Jewish kids dissolved into the community. Of the 1,000 students in my high school, fewer than a dozen were Jewish and only one—the kosher butcher's daughter—clearly identified herself as Jewish and refused to participate in any events remotely connected to Christian holidays. This blending, for me, came at a price. As I stood in the stuffy basement room of the Masonic Lodge, singing with the high school Christmas chorus, I found myself mumbling the "Christ as King" lyrics, trying to figure out just what I should do when it comes to singing things I don't believe.

When I left Sheboygan I knew I would not return. That feeling of being part of a community that did not acknowledge or accept my differences—that encouraged a homogenous blending into the dominant culture—was damaging in ways I could not even identify for myself.

While my father felt the physical blows of anti-Semitism, a generation later I felt something different. I felt the need to accept my community for what it was so that it would accept me. I felt the pressure to show that although I may be Jewish, I was really no different from any of my Christian neighbors.

I've come to believe that my upbringing reflects my parents' best effort to give me both a Jewish identity and also a nonreligious identity. The Jewish identity lets me know who I am, where I come from. The nonreligious identity means that my religion is not used against me; that when people interact with me they don't think of me first as Jewish and therefore (insert whatever prejudice people may have about Jews).

I guess you could call this the "live and let live" policy: *Being Jewish is just fine as long as you don't tell us about it and it doesn't interfere with what we'd been planning to do anyway*—like putting a manger scene in the middle of my second grade classroom during the Christmas season.

Now, thirty-three years later, my hand stays down, my voice stays silent as my mind tries to evaluate the "live and let live" policy when it comes to providing German immersion and a trip to Germany in my own eldest son's class. Would my "Jewish concerns" interfere? Am I willing to let them interfere?

Since my children—one, now six years old and the other, eleven years old—entered day care, then preschool, and finally elementary school, I've had to grapple with when, and how often, to bring up the fact that we are Jewish. Do I let them receive gifts from Santa at day care? Do I make a fuss about doing a Hanukkah presentation for my child's elementary school class even though the teacher—who has the children making candy wreaths—doesn't think it's necessary? Learning German and having my eldest son's teacher plan a trip to Germany is just the latest crease in what seems a continuous unfolding of events that lend themselves to Jewish interpretation. How do I protect my children's Jewish identity and at the same time have them feel comfortable in their community?

When we moved to Anchorage in the early 1980s, before I had children, I found myself in a place that seemed to have an even smaller Jewish community than the one in which I'd grown up. The Reform congregation met in a small building that looked more like a house than a synagogue. The main room (living room?) barely held fifty people on folding chairs. I'd never been in a temple quite so informal.

During our first High Holiday services I found the Jewish community was much larger than the twenty families I'd seen on a full night at the temple. The services were held at the chapel on Fort Richardson and as I looked around the room it felt like a town meeting. People I'd seen at work, in passing, observed Rosh Hashanah and Yom Kippur. I found myself, once again, in a largely non-Jewish community where the Jews blended into the fabric of society.

But not every one blended in. A non-Jewish woman lawyer confided to me once—knowing that I was Jewish—that one of her colleagues, a particularly abrasive and outspoken lawyer, seemed to wear his Jewishness on his sleeve. Why was he so Jewish? Why did every issue have a Jewish angle?

"You're Jewish," she said as we walked down the street, "but you don't bring it up all the time."

I'd learned to mix into the community so well that a person could feel comfortable telling me when they thought someone was *too* Jewish. We don't talk about our religion all the time, she said to me, why should Jews talk about theirs? I understood her point of view completely. It was the point of view I grew up with—keep silent about my religion. But I was beginning to feel uncomfortable with this silence.

A decade later, by the time my eldest child began to attend Sunday school, the Jewish community in Anchorage had built a synagogue and attracted a rabbi dedicated to social causes. My son joined a class with a half dozen other Jewish children. By then, though, he already knew he was Jewish. Long before he was old enough to go to Sunday school, I found myself having to assess how I wanted to raise my child. I had to think about what it meant to be a Jewish mother in a relatively small city with a miniscule Jewish population.

Oddly enough, I began thinking about this as I made chocolate truffles one year to hand out to friends during the Christmas season.

That old "go along, get along" habit of being in the holiday mode without taking note of the holiday rolled over me in December, and I bought ten pounds of chocolate chips and whipping cream. My three-year-old son wandered around as I melted chocolate. And then I got a call from a journalist friend.

"You celebrate Hanukkah, don't you?" she asked.

"Yes," I said, licking my fingers.

"Can we take a picture of you and your son for the newspaper, lighting the candles?"

I ransacked the cupboard looking for candles for the menorah and found a few cracked and faded in an old box. I called a friend and got enough to fill out the menorah, so that by the time the photographer arrived it looked like we did this all the time.

Christmas truffles and lighting the menorah—I could feel the schizophrenia of the season close in on me. It didn't help that my husband had absolutely no tradition of going along and getting along. Raised in Miami, he knew only one set of holidays: the Jewish holidays. Every time we did something slightly non-Jewish, he questioned it. Why should we exchange Christmas gifts with our non-Jewish friends? I found myself questioning my own approach to the holidays.

Perhaps needing to make some sort of public statement, I turned my questions and deliberations into an essay for the newspaper. I figured sitting on Santa's lap was okay (if demanded by my toddler) and exchanging Christmas gifts was fine. But I decided to have no straddling in my own home. Potato latkes, a large supply of Hanukkah candles, an inflatable dreidel, and a shiny silver and blue Happy Hanukkah banner made the house more Jewish than anything in my youth. We invited non-Jewish friends over for Hanukkah meals. And soon my friends confessed that their children knew more about Hanukkah than some of their Christian holidays.

When my eldest child entered grade school he proudly proclaimed himself to be Jewish to his classmates. It was his special attribute. How else would people know he was a Jew if he didn't tell them? It wasn't as if they would be able to tell from the freckles splashed across his face, his light brown hair or blue eyes. He had to shout it out. And when he did, I cringed. Even though I publicly wrote about being Jewish, had gone to his preschool classrooms and kindergarten and talked about Jewish holidays as they came up during the year, somehow it didn't prepare me for my own child's response. Pride.

"Don't you like Jesus?" my youngest child asked the other day. I'd just pushed the button on the radio as the lyrics, "Jesus is just all right with me," faded.

"The song was over, a commercial was coming," I told him, knowing that's not what was really on his mind. He'd spent the past couple of years at a church preschool.

"You can decorate the cross with sprinkles, or just paint it," a teacher demonstrated as she held it up in front of the class. I could feel my cheeks turn bright red and the sweat pour out as I sat with my four-year-old child in my lap. I hadn't really paid close attention to all the eggs and bunnies coming home. Easter in its egg and bunny state is a fact of life in the spring. I don't think of bunnies and eggs as having a particularly religious significance. Crosses are another matter.

I told my son's teacher that he was Jewish and that making crosses would be inappropriate for him. Then I spoke with the principal. "How much religion is taught at New Horizons?" I asked.

"We are church-based," she responded. "We believe God is an important thing to teach children."

And so I felt myself tiptoeing. I didn't want to say anything that would offend anyone; at the same time I needed to make it perfectly clear that our religion did not include Jesus Christ, and I didn't want my son confused.

We talked and talked. Each time I felt as if I was learning a new language of communication between religious beliefs, some way to assert my own beliefs, my son's heritage, in the midst of a dominant religion. I learned to listen openly when teachers approached me with stories of how they knew other Jewish people. And I came to realize that there is a difference between anti-Semitism and just plain lack of knowledge about Judaism. In communities where there are few Jews, there are many people—well-educated people, open-minded people—who don't know about Jewish customs. My deep-seated reserve could do more harm than good. It could prevent a dialogue, prevent a sharing of information.

My son stayed at the preschool and I spoke about his Jewish holidays, bringing in matzo at Passover and the menorah and dreidel at Hanukkah. We skipped the Christmas program. And when projects had a religious slant the teachers spoke with me, and we decided together how to deal with it.

I could have pulled him out of the preschool and driven across town to the Jewish preschool. But I didn't want to do that. Inconvenience was a big factor but so also was this challenge to coexist. New Horizons was a fine school—though our religious orientations were different, our values were not. Children came first.

And so, again, the dominant culture blended into our lives, but this time I spoke up. From my child's question in the car I realized he picked up on the fact that he was different and it had to do with Jesus. So, we spoke again about Jesus, that he was a good man. Some people believe he was the Son of God, but we don't believe that, I said. We believe in just one God. We're Jewish.

"I know, I know, Mom," my impatient five-year-old barely lets me finish.

I still remember asking my parents about God. And my mother responding that God is a part of you. I envisioned this little space in the corner of my body as being reserved for God. As I got older the explanation my mother gave me ceased to have such a literal meaning. With the passing years I've struggled to understand what God is, what the idea of God is about. I've struggled with everything having to do with the structures and forms of my religion. But I have never failed to feel Jewish. That is my identity. And it is an identity that I wholeheartedly pass on to my children. I want them to know as much as they can about being Jewish. I want them to have the chance to value that part of themselves and their heritage. And I want them to feel free to say they are Jewish whenever and wherever they like. While I feel this on an intellectual level, it is still very difficult for me to watch it happen.

But it is getting easier. Although my children are just learning about their religion, they embrace it without reserve. They talk about God all the time. *He* does this. *He* does that. I find myself compelled to correct them. *God is not necessarily a man or a person,* I tell them. As I say this I realize I have to think about what God is. As they discover their religion, I rediscover my religion. I really don't find I have all that much choice, because as my children grow they are growing beyond my own understanding of what it is to be a Jew. I feel like I have to catch up to them.

And sometimes I have to lead, knowing they are already ahead of me. When a teacher teaches them something not realizing there is a "Jewish perspective"—such as planning a trip to Germany—I become, again, a mother searching for my child's path. Because my son is Jewish, he is a minority in this population and he is mine.

After parents' night in my eldest son's fifth-grade class, I spoke to another Jewish mother whose child is not in my son's class. She immediately recognized my concerns. Her mother-in-law is a Holocaust survivor. She'd gone to the same talk as I during High Holiday services and listened to the descendant of a Holocaust survivor talk about returning to her grandfather's former home in Germany: the emotional toll, the fact that Germans have not come to grips with their history, that there are no longer Jews living in her grandparents' town. Even more ominous was her story of meeting a person who'd been taught in school about all the good that Nazis had accomplished. It was only when he went to college that he learned of the extermination of the Jews.

My friend suggested I speak to the principal about the Germany trip. She offered to come along, then withdrew. We both instinctively knew that if we both went it would become a *Jewish issue.* And that is not what we wanted.

"This is your chance," my friend said.

I know she meant this was my chance to say what I felt, even if I thought it might single me out as the squeaky wheel, the one Jewish voice.

Although I'd heard my father's stories about anti-Semitism, I lived in their shadow, not feeling the direct blows. I turned away from "kike" spray painted on the sidewalk. It did not apply to me. I fit in. I sang in the Christmas chorus. My friends, the Schroeders, Sachses, Fuhrmans, Krauses, Bachausens, and Schneiders, might have German surnames, but they were not anti-Semitic. We worked on the school newspaper, the yearbook, and French club together. It's only since I left Sheboygan, since I've had children, that I've begun to recognize the subtle feelings of anti-Semitism that I've stored from my youth. It's only since I've stopped trying so hard to fit in that I can see things more clearly, that I've taken some time to understand and question the feeling of being surrounded by people who might not accept me if they knew I am really *different* from them.

We were standing outside on the street talking with our neighbors a few years ago. Their daughter routinely baby-sits for us. We have dinner together once a year. The sun was setting over the mountains and we felt the coolness of the coming fall. The talk turned to some person trying to sell something at the lowest possible price.

"They tried to Jew him down," my neighbor said. She looked at us, suddenly remembering we are Jewish, and we all fell silent.

My inclination is to apologize and explain away her gaffe, that she never thought about that expression before, and now that she socializes with Jews she will probably never use it again. But it is an expression used in society. It reflects a built-in supposition, a prejudice, that a Jewish person will try to get something for an unfair price. She learned that expression probably never having personal contact with Jewish people.

I went to see the principal and spoke with her briefly about the proposed trip to Germany. I told her of my concerns and she said she understood and would talk to the teacher. I felt like a coward going to the principal. I should have gone to the teacher. I took the easy way out.

The next day I called the teacher.

"I know this is just me and how I feel personally, but I am uncomfortable with the idea of my son going to Germany. I have a friend who just got back and there are still many disturbing things there. I think there needs to be some study of World War II." I blurted all of this out quickly.

The principal had already told her of my concerns. She felt bad. She'd been reading books on the Holocaust and on German Jews. In fact, she'd translated letters written during the war to Holocaust survivors from their families in Germany begging for help in getting out. Although she'd been born after the war, she felt the weight of German extermination of Jews. She did plan to teach the children about the Holocaust before the trip.

What she didn't tell me, but what I'd learned from a friend, was that her father had been a Nazi.

"We haven't told Aaron that his teacher's father was a Nazi," I told my running partner as we jogged down the trail. "I doubt he could separate that from her." And I wonder, can I?

"I had asked that he have this teacher. She is very much like my son, strong in math and geography, and drives her students to excel. They are a good match intellectually. She will stimulate him and he will get a lot out of her class."

"I'm German—my maiden name is Ritz," my running partner says. "You sound prejudiced against Germans."

And I think she may be right. When I talk about my son learning German and going to Germany I realize that I sound prejudiced against Germans.

"My favorite teacher was my sixth-grade teacher."

"You told me this already, Mom," my eleven-year-old son says.

"She loved South America. She traveled there all the time and brought back pictures. We learned a lot," I add. And then I remember. She was German.

When my great-grandparents traveled to this country from Eastern Europe, they landed in Baltimore and took the train headed for the Midwest. They first settled in Michigan but didn't like it very well. So they crossed over to Wisconsin and settled in Sheboygan, where they found a group of people who spoke their language. German.

I know a lot of Germans; even my family was originally German-speaking. I don't have anything against Germans, I find myself saying to Aaron's teacher. Where do these prejudices begin and end?

I feel like I've made his teacher feel terrible, that I've been insensitive. We talk. We talk again. And yet again. We agree to work together to do a unit on the Holocaust for the students.

I am still uncomfortable. It doesn't lessen at all. I know that my perspective is different from that of my son's teacher. But I've spoken; I've opened another dialogue. In some ways it reminds me of the dialogue about decorating crosses. Things don't become resolved necessarily, but they get talked about. In the process I have to reevaluate how I feel about a subject and about talking about a subject. I have to wonder about my own prejudices, those things

I've carried with me over the years, kept to myself, and never aired. Did my silence while growing up in a predominantly German town lead to my own prejudice?

"Am Freitag bin ich ins Kino gegangen." (On Friday I went to the movies.) The words come trippingly off my son's lips as he practices. They don't sound nearly so harsh as the first time I heard them. I hear instead my *son's* voice, its innocence as he searches for just the right pronunciation.

21

Washing Down the Chalk

Gayle Brandeis

A few weeks ago, a swastika appeared in chalk on the street in front of our house. Near it was written "Die!!!" in a childish hand. I have no way of knowing whether this message was directed toward me and my family. I am a Jewish woman, just starting to explore what my heritage means to me. Even if those scrawlings of hatred had nothing to do with me directly, they still chilled me right to the bone.

When my mother was a girl, her family moved from a predominantly Jewish neighborhood to a very gentile one. Their second day there, my mother woke up to a message chalked in large letters on their sidewalk: "KIKES, GO HOME!"

Chalk can be washed away. It is impermanent, nothing like the numbers burned into the arm of an Auschwitz survivor. Chalk is blunt; it cannot kill. In Russia, my grandfather watched a Cossack slice open the pregnant belly of his mother. I will probably—hopefully—never experience or witness such horrific persecution in my lifetime. I can barely even imagine it. But the chalked message has dealt a blow, the chalk dust working its way into my lungs, making it difficult for me to breathe freely.

I can remember a time when I was ashamed of my heritage. I was thirteen when we moved from a multicultural town to a very exclusive suburb. In the suburb next to ours Jews used to be prohibited from buying property. It was hard enough being the new girl in school, and then, worse, it seemed like anyone who even made the effort to talk to me inevitably asked: "Has your family joined a church yet?" I would sheepishly shake my head, not letting the word "Jewish" pass my lips.

I denied my Russian blood as well. My father had changed his name from Bransky to Brandeis during the McCarthy era because of job problems. The name stuck, although his commitment to his family history never waned. I, however, used the name to mask my true identity. In eighth grade, my new friend's mother, a strict Lutheran, asked me in a snide voice, "So what kind of a name is *Brandeis*?" "German," I piped up, creating a new past for myself, a mythical history of sauerbraten and lederhosen. "But what *else* is it?" she goaded, waiting for me to say "Jewish" and plunge myself into her category of the damned. I didn't give her the satisfaction. I also didn't give myself the satisfaction of feeling proud of where I came from.

Recently, my eight-year-old son was invited to a friend's house after school. The friend's mother told me how glad she is that her son is meeting a diverse group of kids after spending years in a private, homogeneous, Lutheran school, how happy she is that her son has a Jewish friend. I felt the strange inclination to deny my Judaism, to say, "Well, I am Jewish by heritage, but. . . . " Perhaps the fact that their family is also Lutheran, plus the strange fact that their house smells exactly like my friend's house did in eighth grade, made me feel the need to cover up my identity. I don't know. I'm so thrilled that my son is able to proudly tell people he is Jewish, without giving it a second thought. His Judaism is very important to him, even though he, like myself, doesn't understand fully what it means yet. For the last few months, we have been attending the family Shabbat services at the local temple, and my son is so into it—he has memorized almost all of the songs and sings them with great fervor. My four-year-old daughter loves attending temple, too, but more for the oneg treats at the end than for the actual services.

When I grew up, my family casually acknowledged a few of the Jewish holidays, though we practiced more in the spirit of family celebration than as an act of faith. We celebrated Christmas and Easter too, even though we have no Christian roots. Everything kind of blended together for me as secular family holidays, as excuses to exchange gifts and eat delicious stuff. I was never given any Jewish education as a girl, and never felt any spiritual connection to my religious roots, never knew what it really meant to be

Jewish. My knowledge of Jewish ritual is still quite vague, but I love it, especially when it involves food. The more I learn now, the more I am moved by the beauty, the earthiness of Jewish blessings and rites. I am amazed by how deeply they resonate within me, and am excited to incorporate more of them into my family's life in a deep, real way.

I recently read of five women in Ohio who decided to be Bat Mitzvahed. They spent their free time away from work and family studying Hebrew and practicing chanting. They all performed the ritual on the same day, then had a huge celebration together afterward. This definitely intrigues me. My younger sister chose to be Bat Mitzvahed, and I was deeply impressed by the commitment she gave to the whole process. I sometimes wish I had done the same. Even now, as a mother, I often have difficulty perceiving myself as an adult, and I wonder if the lack of a coming-of-age ceremony is in some way responsible. I don't know if I will ever go through with a Bat Mitzvah, but I hope that I can find some personal ritual to help me feel more connected to my ancestry, and to myself as a Jewish woman. I want to know more about my blood than the fact that it is O positive.

I am finding, happily, that my Judaism is creeping into my writing. I have pieces coming out in two Jewish-themed anthologies and was recently invited to participate in an upcoming Jewish poetry festival. I am thrilled to be drawn into the fold of the Jewish literary community, as well as the broader community of Jews, but in some ways I feel like an imposter. I don't feel yet that I deserve to be called a "Jewish woman writer" even though that is technically what I am. I feel that I am still just dabbling, as if I don't really "have it" quite yet.

If I knew more about my heritage, I don't think the chalk dust would still rattle so maddeningly in my lungs. If my sense of Jewishness was stronger, I think my anger would be stronger, sharper, than the uneasy, nonspecific anger I feel now. I would have been able to hose the chalk from the street, stand up straight, and take a deep, clean breath. My rage would be an integral part of my heartbeat—organic, pure, tempered by love.

22

While My Sixteen-Year-Old Daughter Visits Auschwitz

Stephanie Palladino

This is not about a purple parakeet, preening its silky feathers with its hooked beak, nor is it about an apricot-colored cat licking its pink paw with a sandpaper tongue, while lying astride the back cushion on a purple couch.

It is not about terror either, though it could be—the terror of rushing water where streets stood dry a day ago. Or the terror of children at Auschwitz, their blank eyes staring straight ahead as they march two by two to their cremation by gas ovens. Imagine, not even accompanied on the arm of a mother or father, these young strangers walk side by side, sharing only the intimacy of their final footsteps—their innocence soon to be extinguished into ashes along with their flesh.

This is not even about the sudden knowledge of death—your own—any time now. The cancerous cells multiply relentlessly throughout your body, invading your vital organs, your tissues, declaring war on your very life. One day it happens, and the news ripples out to your family, your friends and neighbors, none of whom is as shocked as you—but neither are they immune to your terror, which just as likely might be their own one day soon.

This is about bearded irises, not yet in bloom on this first of May. They lie dormant inside reedy green leaves that will nourish them for the next thirty days. Soon these leaves will thicken at their midpoint, then a stalk will protrude from this bulge and lengthen into a sturdy stem. Early in June a delicate flower will emerge. It will be lemon yellow; its frilled petals will cluster and bend toward the earth.

This is about the season of rebirth and promise—the promise nature makes to yellow irises—this spring and next year as well. Even at Auschwitz.

– 23 –

A Long, Circular Journey

Ellen Narotzky Kennedy

I grew up in Ishpeming, a small town near Lake Superior in northern Michigan. Ishpeming had about 10,000 people and only a handful of Jews, perhaps two or three dozen at most. My family, the Narotzkys, were fairly prominent in that small town—we included doctors, merchants of all sorts, and a professor at the nearby university. Everybody knew we were Jews, because in a small town everybody knows those kinds of things about everybody else. Consequently, I was always singled out at school to "explain" each Jewish holiday. I was the only Jew in my class of Finns and Swedes throughout all my years of school.

When I got married it was to a man with the last name of Kennedy, and I gladly traded the name Narotzky for Kennedy. I had always been uncomfortable with the overtness of my Jewishness when I lived in Ishpeming, and I welcomed the opportunity to lose that particular label. In addition, my husband and I moved from Ishpeming to Burlington, Vermont, where I found that I had not only gotten rid of my label, but I had exchanged it for one that was very commonplace on the East Coast. I felt an enormous sense of relief at gaining anonymity, particularly religious anonymity, after the awkwardness of being Ellen Narotzky, Jew, in that small Scandinavian mining town in Michigan's Upper Peninsula.

For the three years that my then-husband and I lived in Vermont, I knew virtually no Jews. I attended synagogue services only once, at a small Reform congregation that met for High Holiday services in a local church. The crosses and statues of Jesus were carefully draped with sheets for Rosh Hashanah and Yom Kippur. I attended the Rosh Hashanah service alone and cried the entire time, feeling bereft, alone and adrift from the Jewish part of my identity and my family back in the Midwest. I wanted to hear my Uncle Isadore blow the shofar at the High Holidays, eat my Aunt Bea's matzo balls at Passover, and see my mother light the Shabbat candles. But at the same time I was still struggling with what my Jewish identity was all about. For those years in Vermont I struggled, but I did nothing—I never lit Shabbat candles, never said a motzi, never trimmed a sukkah, never ate a piece of matzo.

Then my spouse and I moved back to the Midwest, to Minneapolis, and I reclaimed my Jewish identity. I joined a synagogue, began teaching in the religious school, and developed Jewish friends. Also, most significantly, I returned to the name Narotzky, leaving Kennedy behind me. I shed the covering that had kept my Jewish identity a secret not only from others but also from me.

During this time my husband and I were thinking about having children. This was a profoundly important issue to me, not only because of the obvious implications of life with children compared to life without them, but because I had decided that if I were ever to have a child, that child had to be raised as a Jew. My husband was not Jewish and had no plans to convert, nor did I expect that of him, so raising Jewish children was a momentous issue.

Why was it so important to me that if I became a mother, I became a *Jewish* mother? I think that being a mother was inextricably connected with Judaism. The rituals of Jewish life paralleled, for me, the rituals of mothering. When I imagined raising a child, I envisioned that child waving greggers at Purim, lighting the Chanukah menorah, celebrating confirmation at Shavuoth. But even more than the rituals, it seemed to me that I had an obligation to be a Jewish mother.

To whom did I feel that obligation? Certainly I felt that obligation toward my own mother, who had raised us as Jews in a town where it wasn't easy to raise a Jew or to be a Jew. But the obligation went beyond that personal and idiosyncratic debt. I felt that, because of the fragility of Jewish survival in the Diaspora, I had a responsibility that extended far beyond my personal one. I was directly responsible, with my offspring, for the continuity of Judaism. This sounds like an overwhelming burden and one that has hubris and chutzpah in its very utterance, but that's how I felt. My fear was that if I didn't raise my children as Jews, and if others of my generation didn't raise their children as Jews, we would simply disappear. This was absolutely impossible for me to contemplate. Even during those years when I "passed" as a Kennedy, a gentile, I always thought of myself as a Jew.

The interesting question is how I traveled from wrapping myself in a non-Jewish identity to making Judaism a prerequisite for having children. What we choose for ourselves is one issue; what we do with our children implicates not only ourselves and our children, but becomes a significant historical issue as well.

My spouse understood these issues, and after eight years of marriage we had our first of two children. When Louisa was born she was named in the Ashkenazi manner, for a dear departed relative, and her naming ceremony was held in my hometown synagogue in Ishpeming, surrounded with all the relatives, love, and warmth that I had longed for in Vermont that lonely Rosh Hashanah. And as soon as Louisa was old enough to talk, she identified herself as a Jew.

We celebrated all the holidays and had a very observant Reform household. When Jonathan was born several years later, we shared that joy in a bris at our home. The children are now eighteen and fifteen years old; both have celebrated their B'nai Mitzvah and lead actively Jewish lives. My obligation has been met. I have raised Jewish children. And now that my children are nearly grown, I can reflect on what it has meant to me to be a Jewish mother.

It has been difficult. It's hard, however, to define what has been difficult: being a Jew, being a mother, and finally, or perhaps most significantly, being a Jewish mother.

When I think back on what it has meant to be a Jew, it has meant primarily being an outsider. I moved from that small Michigan town with few Jews to Vermont with few Jews, and then to a Midwest suburb with few Jews. I have used the name Kennedy since my children were born, and ironically I am a professor at a Catholic university. I remain as much an outsider as it is possible to be—female and Jewish at a male-dominated Catholic institution. I live in a community that until the 1960s was one of the most anti-Semitic towns in the nation. Today, although anti-Semitism appears to be only a historical memory, there are still very few Jews; my children can count on two hands the number of Jews in their classes at school. As a Jew, then, in my professional and residential identities, I am the "other."

My role as a mother has been anomalous as well. I am divorced in a community where nearly every adult is married. I have a full and satisfying professional life; many of the women in my neighborhood do not work for a living. I also live in a Lutheran environment where most people have multiple generations of close family nearby with whom to share life events; I am a transplant to Minnesota with no relatives near me. Consequently, I have a very different definition of "mother" than my Minnesota counterparts, and that definition has been one that I have had to construct as time has gone by. Being a mother, like being a Jew, has meant a certain amount of outsider status as well.

However, being a Jewish mother feels different from being Jewish or being a mother. Being a Jewish mother combines pieces of history, ritual, community, and belongingness with loving, nurturing, and teaching. As a Jewish mother I create the celebrations of the ritual calendar that provide anchors and identity for my children and me. The holidays that we share at our small and closely knit synagogue bind our small family together with many others into a communal group that strongly resembles the extended family of my youth. But the community doesn't end at the synagogue door. In fact, that community extends beyond time and space.

Several years ago my children and I spent the month of September in Novosibirsk, Siberia. I was on sabbatical and had been asked to do some lecturing at a university in that city. When our rabbi heard about our upcoming trip, she remarked that we would be away over the High Holidays. A friend in the congregation mentioned that there was a synagogue in Novosibirsk and a Jewish community numbering over 10,000. With a flurry of faxes and e-mails to organizations in several countries, I was able to get information on the Jews of Novosibirsk and names of the leaders of that community. Shortly after we arrived in Siberia I called one of the people on our list and was thrilled to hear a warm and friendly voice speaking halting English, inviting us to attend a Rosh Hashanah celebration. Of course we said yes.

It was almost electrifying to be there in a small, unheated, unmarked garage sharing the New Year with Russian Jews. When my children were asked to say the blessings over the wine and challah, I felt a real fullness in my heart. This is what being a Jewish mother means to me: my children, connecting across the continents, to people with whom they have an unbroken historical tie. My children knew the rituals for Rosh Hashanah, but more than that, they recognized the enormity of the moment. They understood that their ancestors had fled from Russia a century ago searching for freedom. We had come to Russia a hundred years later having been blessed with the opportunity to be Jews. Jonathan and Louisa understood that we were there as part of a chain of history and tradition that was stronger and bigger than we were.

We asked about the denominationalism of the Jews with whom we were sharing Rosh Hashanah apples and honey, and we were told that they were all atheists. Initially we were surprised; then we understood the legacy of Communism. The Jews were all atheists, but they still identified themselves as Jews—not only because the Communists had labeled them as such, but also because their parents or grandparents had transmitted remnants of Judaism to them. We felt inspired by their eagerness to embrace the culture, the rituals, and the ethos of Judaism. We had brought our holiday prayerbooks with us to the cold little garage that day, and we left the books there. For our Siberian friends, these mahzorim were rare treasures.

So my children understand what it means to be Jews. They have heard the Siberians' tales of the personal horrors of anti-Semitism and have seen the poignancy with which these same Jews have clung to Judaism in spite of their suffering.

The most important thing I can teach my children, however, is tikkun olam, repair of the world. I want them as Jews to understand that the world isn't fair, but they have both the privilege and the burden to help make it better. When my daughter organizes food drives sponsored by the synagogue and my son collects items for a crisis nursery, they are embodying the essence of Judaism. They are connecting to others and helping to make the world a bit better than it was.

I have come full circle. I have returned to the life of a committed Jew, and this journey has happened because of being a Jewish mother. We often think of motherhood only in terms of the impact we create on our children's lives, but being mothers has an enormous impact on our own lives as well. For me, being a mother has brought out what is good in me, and that also is the part that is Jewish, the part that has a sense of time and place stretching across centuries and oceans, and the part that sees the possibility of a better world.

SECTION V:
SPIRITUALITY AND RELIGION

– 24 –

A Life in Code

Mira Morgenstern

Being a Jewish mother and a feminist is considerably more complicated than the "classic" dilemma of leading a life that is both emotionally and professionally fulfilled. Being a feminist is generally looked upon askance in traditional Orthodox Jewish circles, and being a committed Orthodox Jew is viewed with distrust in most circles conversant with Western culture, including feminist ones. It is still not entirely accepted on both sides that one can be a fully committed Jew, to say nothing of being a fully involved mother, and at the same time give credence to the implications of the full and equal worth of a woman's life that is championed by feminist thought. How then can I come to terms with the tensions tearing at my own existence, including the challenges involved in transmitting to my own children my unwavering belief in a committed Orthodox Jewish life and practice, as well as my unshakeable belief in the worth of women's lives?

These are not easy questions to pose or to answer. In a very basic sense, it is fair to say that I cannot pose these questions publicly at all: each one of the worlds to which I belong effectively delegitimizes the other, so that at best the fact that I choose to belong to both of these worlds is treated as little more than a smugly tolerated idiosyncrasy. Consequently, in many ways I lead a double life. I am active both in the Orthodox Jewish community within which I continue to live and function, and in the larger "modern" Western community whose cultural and political themes form the substance of my academic work. My insistence on making my life in both these communities, calling both of them home, carries with it much tension that derives not just from the overwhelming demands on my time and energy. Rather, the inner tension that I feel is also because of my own conviction that the identification with both communities need not carry with it overtones of mutually exclusive choice. My insistence on regarding both of these communities—the Orthodox Jewish world and the larger Western political/cultural backdrop—as sources of moral meaning need not mean the denigration of either of them. This certainly goes against the prevailing conventional wisdom. For my part, I have often thought that the sense of intolerance for any other system of thought apart from the traditionally accepted version, whether that be secularly or religiously inspired, is, in a sense, welcomed by the adherents of these respective groups. After all, it is much easier to deal with a potentially unknowable and unstable situation by dividing the world into factions of "us" versus "them," thereby rendering at least a portion of the surrounding environment more susceptible to control.

While I recognize the demonizing tendencies inherent in each of the contemporary manifestations of my respective "worlds," I persist in my claim that their full expressions will serve to strengthen each other. My relation to the demands of Orthodox Judaism does not include merely keeping the minimal legal obligations: I see Orthodox Judaism as a system of profound spirituality and intellectual engagement, made manifest both in the study of its texts and the fulfillment of its commandments. Similarly, I see the world "outside" the strict borders of my religious life as contributing to the larger humanistic goals of Judaism, which for me include realizing the potential of each individual to the fullest degree. In essence, then, the two parts of my life are not separate entities but are two sides of the same coin. Teaching my children the multiplicity of paths to these myriad goals is important to me, so I strive to inculcate this in my children by involving them in the practical fulfillment of the religious commandments as well as in the committed and engaged study of the basic texts.

What I mean by the engaged study of these texts is the sense of not being restricted to a theoretical exercise, but part of the intellectual preparation for the fulfillment of the practices of Judaism. This engaged study holds the key to success in fulfilling the following goals for myself and for my children: to realize the ability to maximize our existence both as Jews and as human beings, and to understand that these enterprises are mutually enhancing. It is no secret that women's intellectual access to Biblical and Talmudic texts has been a relatively recent historical development. I welcome this new openness, and I take great pride in the fact that the Talmud that I was taught surreptitiously by a brave assistant principal in my own girls-only Orthodox Jewish high school, holding our volumes of Talmud literally under the table, is now offered as a matter of course in many religious high schools, including those that are gender segregated. My daughter already studies Mishna in elementary school, and the thought of her being able to make a siyum (a celebration marking the official completion of a portion of Mishna or Talmud) at the occasion of her Bat Mitzvah fills me with gratitude and wonder.

At the same time, I can be dispirited taking note of the very real counterforces that can get in the way of this broadening availability of the text. There is a segment of the Orthodox community that chooses to define itself by its refusal to teach girls any part of the Oral Law, the Mishna and the Talmud. Sociologically this is not difficult to understand: in a society that places a high value on knowledge, control of the acquisition of knowledge is equated with control of the decision-making processes of that society, and thus is a commodity which must be restricted. The religious justification of this decision, however, is less clear to me. To the extent that study of the Torah is linked with redemption, how can one restrict access to that knowledge on a wholesale basis and still profess fealty to the ultimate goals of the Torah? To be sure, many of those advocating this restrictive access to the basic texts of Judaism based on gender may still be unthinkingly applying criteria that they have automatically accepted without questioning. I believe that further education holds hope for this group. Regarding those who continue to insist on the moral and religious appropriateness of gender distinctions regarding intellectual access to religious texts, I wonder whether they are indeed religiously convinced of the morality of this viewpoint, or whether instead they are fully aware of the political implications of this restricted access for their own positions of power within the Orthodox Jewish community, which consequently fuels their advocacy. It is shocking to reflect that for some, the reality of their own power today may be more important than enabling the future redemption of the entire community and indeed, following traditional Jewish thought on the implications of the Messianic Era, of all humanity.

I believe that there is an allusion to this phenomenon in the Torah itself. The reference is a seemingly irrelevant legal passage regarding the indentured servant who, out of affection for his master, refuses his freedom at the end of his period of servitude (Exodus 21:5). In line with the comments of Rabbi Dr. J. B. Soloveitchik who reads this verse as a metaphor for the Jewish nation that by now has lost the capacity even to yearn for freedom, preferring instead to remain in the familiar surroundings of exile, I believe that for many people in the Jewish community, the familiar surroundings of the patriarchal trappings of power can be more seductive than the possibility of liberation for all people. To be sure, there is a fine line between a God-driven sense of self and a selfishly motivated concept of individuality (Morgenstern, 1999, p. 142). Still, to the extent that the full realization of women's intellectual and creative capacities is a prerequisite for the liberation (geulah) as set forth by the Torah, holding back women is retarding the progress of the communities of which they form a part.

In this regard, I have another fear that is less broadly philosophical, but more acutely personal. My fear is that it may well be not just a question of achieving or retarding final spiritual liberation for all of humanity, but of avoiding a spiritual catastrophe among our own people. What will happen to the core of newly maturing young Jewish women now, the girls of my daughter's generation, when they are persistently denied access to the texts that they are being taught to treasure? How will they be able to justify to themselves the denial of a direct connection with Divine teaching? To be sure, it is very easy to claim that truly religious individuals do not seek to aggrandize themselves at the expense of God's will, and that if it is God's will that women remain "educated and ignorant" in Tamar El-Or's (1992) famous phrase, then women will just have to reconcile themselves to their fate.

The problem is that the women of today, and certainly our daughters, are less likely to accept that argument. When women become doctors, when they get PhDs, when they are treated as and are expected to act like fully responsible professionals, it is morally and psychologically dissonant for them to completely give up moral autonomy in their religious lives and understanding. This is not a call for a laissez-faire approach to Biblical and Halakhic interpretation. As an Orthodox Jew, I am well aware of the hermeneutical and philosophical imperatives of a philosophically and intellectually coherent interpretation of Torah and Halakha. I am pointing out, however, that as time goes on, fewer women, and men, will continue to accept what appears to be an arbitrary determination, arbitrary because it is socially sanctioned as opposed to religiously based, of what women are "allowed" to study. People often argue that religious truth is not to be determined by popular poll, and that is certainly true, as far as it goes, but the issue here is that in this case this point doesn't go very far at all. Often these gender-based distinctions are accretions of social practice, borrowed from surrounding non-Jewish communities, and do not express the actual Halakha, or even, in many cases, the actual historical practices in the observant Jewish community. My daughter recently remarked, "When I grow up, I want to be president of our (Orthodox) synagogue. I want to get some respect!" When I inquired into the matter, I found, to my surprise, that the synagogue's constitution, or, more accurately, the constitution of the national organization of which the synagogue is an affiliate, specifically disallows women as synagogue presidents. Upon investigation, I discovered that this was a relatively recent constitutional addition. Apparently, the "threat" of women taking a prominent position in an Orthodox organization was enough to scare the "good ol' boys" into hanging a "boys only" sign on the clubhouse door. Now, it is certainly easy to take the "mature" viewpoint and categorize these tactics of exclusion as "little-boy shenanigans," but I worry about what will happen when these girls discover, as one day they will, that ancient synagogues in locations ranging from North Africa to Italy list women among the heads of the Jewish community and specifically number them as heads of synagogues (Brooten, 1982).[1] What will happen then to the patriarchal claim that women's presence in positions of public leadership runs counter to the religious Jewish ethos? How will the next generation react to the sight of people deliberately presenting their social and gender prejudices as the word of God? My hope is that these women will be able to distinguish between human perfidy and Divine Law, jettison the former and embrace the latter. My fear is that it may not work out that way at all.

In fact, these questions may be a matter not just for future concern, but with direct implication for the present as well. Several weeks after her decision to be synagogue president, Bracha announced that she wanted to become the rabbi of the synagogue as well (she did not indicate whether these positions would be held simultaneously or sequentially). Based upon clearly stated sources in the Shulchan Arukh, the Code of Jewish Law, I told her that Jewish law—although not necessarily contemporary Orthodox Jewish *practice*—allows her to receive rabbinic ordination.[2] I think that it is important to be able to distinguish between the requirements of Halakha and the demands of social practice. If there is to be a dynamic future for the Jewish people, our daughters must be aware of the nonsacral basis of certain social practices, and the openness of these areas for Halakhic change.

I live by a code: the Code of Jewish Law, the Shulchan Arukh, which guides the practices that make up my existence. At the same time, my life often requires that I live *in* code. The people in the different communities of which I am a part tend to look askance at what they perceive as the "outside world," the "strange community." In many ways, the practical necessities of getting through the day or the particular task at hand require strategies that allow me to "pass," to appear to be not too "different" from whichever community I am acting within at the moment. This coded existence goes beyond my practical routine and extends itself to my intellectual activities as well. My intellectual concerns rarely form part of the dialogue with my friends in the neighborhood where I live, and spiritual issues that have come to the fore in life outside the university and that have even shaped my research agenda do not receive an academic airing. The philosophical and spiritual unity that I attempt to achieve in my life rarely, if ever, has the luxury of finding full expression in my writing. At the end of the day, I feel the necessity of living in code if I am to survive with the full complement of the multiple centers in my life that give it meaning. Real-life stresses require that I not always "tip my hand."

One can readily understand the questions that naturally arise at this point. Why bother to be a part of a community that negates a major part of my own identity? Is all this subterfuge worth it? Can I really achieve a sense of personal worth or spiritual authenticity if I am obliged to live in code? These questions are often posed by secularly based friends who can't seem to understand what they consider to be my own involuntary servitude.

For me, the answer to these questions has two parts. First, the notion is firmly embedded in Jewish thought itself, as expressed in the Talmud, that the one clear, undivided expression of truth is not liable to be found by human agency alone. God and His Torah are certainly the quintessence of Truth, but whether that can be grasped at all times by human beings is certainly debatable. That is why the Talmud gives such credence to alternate points of view, minority opinions on Jewish law, and even legal conclusions that the Talmud itself winds up rejecting (Kraemer, 1990). Thus, the attempt to find truth from different sources seems to me to fulfill the dictum of the Torah, following the Talmudic model of using human reason to attain truth and to apply it in the service of God.

Second, my insistence on keeping to my roots in the Orthodox Jewish community stems from a similar desire to cleave to God and His Torah. In spite of all the shortcomings that exist there, the greatest concentration of Limud haTorah and Ahavat haTorah, learning of Torah and love of Torah, is to be found in the Orthodox Jewish community. I see ample evidence of this in the Orthodox community in which I live, particularly among the women in both their more mundane and their self-consciously intellectual pursuits. In terms of inclusivity and sheer loving-kindness, the women of my community are second to none in making sure that needy families have food for Shabbat, are provided with children's clothing courtesy of a clothing exchange, and even have some relief from child care. Participating with them in a weekly shiur, class of Torah study, I have found that their intellectual tenacity and philosophical inquiry reveal a willingness to explore and to question the heroes and heroines of the Bible.

If the Torah that some individuals seem to be propagating bears little resemblance to the Torah received at Sinai and transmitted by the Sages throughout the ages, that is the fault of those individuals and not of the Torah in whose name they claim to speak. In neither case is the Torah to be left to those who least understand it. It is incumbent on all those who love Torah to continue in its study and propagation. As for the question of living in code, this certainly is a difficult issue, but if truth itself, in the Talmudic understanding of it, is not obviously apparent, why should we imagine that the way to truth is easily trodden?

One of the central aims in my life as a Jewish mother has been to cherish the importance of nurturing another human being, and the sheer holiness involved in the enterprise of sheltering and helping to develop another soul, all the while not forgetting the moral imperative inherent in guarding one's own soul and spiritual development. And yet the experience of being "outside," of being prevented from being at the center of things, has been hard to avoid, particularly during religious ceremonies still structured in traditional patriarchical forms. I felt this particularly deeply at the circumcision, Brith, of my first son and second child, who was named after my own father. For me, the most healing part of the ritual came at the end. This is the point when speeches are customarily made, explaining the name of the new baby and thereby explicitly forging the link between the generations. Traditionally, this honor is given to an older man in the family or a rabbi with close links to the family. This time, and for each of the subsequent circumcision ceremonies in our family, I took the opportunity to speak, breaking an old tradition and near-taboo in the Orthodox community. At the same time, I was also forging a new tradition that looks to the future and views the covenant as inclusive of all members of the people, not just an exclusive few. In fact, the question of whether women are included in the covenant was the theme of my talk, and answered in the affirmative, with copious Biblical proof texts, which itself was suggested by my own dilemma of how to present to my own firstborn daughter the seeming exclusion of women from the covenantal promise.

On a personal level, a fuller measure of healing occurred when the children were legally given both of our family names in hyphenated form as their own last names. This was an important step, signifying the refusal to equate motherhood with personal erasure, a practice still widely held not just in religious society, but also in different measure in the larger "modern" Western communities within which these religious enclaves function.

It is obvious that giving a few speeches and attempting to forge new traditions are not to be confused with changing the ingrained perceptions of a patriarchal society. One can even question whether the attempt to be both an observant Jew and a feminist is doomed to failure, resulting not in a dynamic bridge between two cultures but in the static straddling of an irreparable breach. Still, unless one insists on accepting only one model for feminist expression, all of these permutations, even if unexpected, can be viewed as a hopeful beginning. My daughter's generation will be less likely to passively accept their exclusion from Talmudic study and Orthodox rabbinic ordination (Boyarin, 1997). My sons will be less likely to view women fulfilling all aspects of their lives, both professional and familial, as the exception. Being at the beginning of any movement is hard, but as the Mishna in Avot tells us, "You are not responsible for completing the job; but neither are you permitted entirely to disclaim all responsibility for it."

NOTES

1. In this book, Brooten documents the various official positions in the Jewish community held by women and, by careful comparison to how these titles are used in relationship to men (in other inscriptions), is able to prove that these positions could not merely have been honorific and involved, instead, the execution of real power. In Brooten's words, "[t]he view that the titles in question were honorific is based less on evidence from the inscriptions themselves or from other ancient sources than on *current* presuppositions concerning the nature of ancient Judaism" (p. 149; my emphasis).

2. Contrary to the perceived common wisdom, rabbinic ordination was held as early as the eighteenth century to be permitted for Jewish women, as evidenced in the Halakhic response cited by the Pitchei Tshuva to the Shulchan Arukh, "Hilkhot Dayanim"; *Hoshen Mishpat* 7:4, a portion of the Shulchan Arukh).

REFERENCES

Avot, *Ethics of the Fathers* 2:21 (my translation).
Boyarin, Daniel (1997). *Unheroic conduct*. Berkeley, CA: University of California Press (esp. "Talmud study as a system for the exclusion of women").
Brooten, Bernadette, J. (1982). *Women leaders in the ancient synagogue*. Chico, CA: Scholars Press.

El-Or, Tamar (1992). *Educated and ignorant.* Tel Aviv: Am-Oved.

Kraemer, David (1990). *The mind of the Talmud.* New York: Oxford University Press (chap. 4).

Morgenstern, Mira (1999). Ruth and the sense of self. *Judaism,* Spring, 142.

25

You Will Teach Your Children Diligently

Marjorie Hoffman

There is a beginning here. For me it is a great moment, one to commemorate with this writing and to remember always. It is a beginning, and yet it is also a small moment that has occurred before, many times, in a vast continuum of thousands of years. I have taken my place in that continuum.

My two daughters . . . they are sweet gifts given to me to watch over and kvell over. So different from one another they are, but both are bubbly and bright and strong. So strong that together they can set our house rocking. So bubbly and bright that they bring tears to my eyes.

My older daughter became a Bat Mitzvah two years ago. I watched her prepare in awe of the speed, the ease, the comfort she exhibited. At that time I could not read Hebrew and was ignorant of the liturgy. I watched a Jew being born, and she was a mighty inspiration. My pride in her exceeded all boundaries.

It became clear that I needed to learn as well. With my daughter as a model, I set about learning the aleph bet (the alphabet), the prayers, the order of the service, the meaning of the language, and the meaning of the Torah. Oh, what a vast endeavor. With my old head I go at a snail's pace. I cannot remember words and meanings. I must see them hundreds of times. I sit at my kitchen table, at my younger daughter's bedside, in my tutor's home, in my car, in the synagogue, repeating the prayers, the melodies, until they are almost right, but never perfect.

Up from behind me moves my younger daughter. She is also learning the aleph bet and painstakingly learning to read Hebrew. I can feel that her struggle for it is the same as mine. Learning to read English was a terrific challenge for her. So many times we visited that final, silent "e," and I reminded her about its function. For a long time she did not really trust that she would ever learn to read English. Now I understand how she felt.

A few days ago, she found her siddur on our shelf, the one that was presented to her by the synagogue. She'll need it in religious school this week. We began to look through it and she decided to open to the "Shema" and "V'ahavta," perhaps to begin learning it. As our eyes scanned down the page I prepared to read the Hebrew to her, but instead, she began to read to me. Strongly and fluently she read, as if she had been studying the words for weeks. We gazed at each other in surprise.

"Where did you learn this?" I asked.

With wide open eyes she said, "I must have learned it from you. Listening to you singing it over and over again. I listen on Saturday too when everyone sings. I knew it was in me, but I didn't know I could read the words."

That small but great moment was a beginning for me. I have given something to my daughter, without either one of us knowing. I have given her the words of Hashem to dwell in her heart and in her soul.

26

Beresheet, in the Beginning

Rabbi Lenore Bohm

However much I have learned about God from books, lectures, and early life experiences, I have learned even more about God, creation, and humankind from being a parent. Prior to giving birth, I knew to expect pain as part of labor and delivery, but, probably like most women the first time around, I had no anticipation of the ferocity of the birth process. Contrary to what romantics would have us believe, there was nothing gentle or pristine about it. It was raw, crude, and awe-inspiring. The force of life breaking through amidst a deluge of fluid seemed so similar to the way I imagined the creation of the world. The quaking of land—my body. The rushing forth of seas—the amniotic fluid. The thunderous explosions—my screams. Light emerging from darkness—the baby going forth from the womb-cocoon and bursting into life and exposure. The mother first seeing her baby—Va'yhi Or, "and there was light." Thus we read in Genesis on the Sabbath of Creation, Shabbat Beresheet. The text then concludes, "And it was good."

Giving birth made me feel very close to God. And I knew, after giving birth, that I would never read the biblical story of creation in the same manner again. It had become an intimate account of beginnings, which I too could claim as my own—no longer a spectator but a participant.

In the early weeks and months of my infants' development as I watched and held each baby, I felt drawn even closer to God. Each

This sermon was presented in honor of Daniel's eighth birthday, on October 25, 1997, which was Shabbat Beresheet, when the biblical story of creation is read. It was written while Rabbi Bohm served at the Progressive Synagogue in Adelaide, South Australia.

child seemed to evolve in ways strikingly similar to the development of the universe as described in Genesis—from chaos to order. I remember the infants' movements, at first so random and awkward, until slowly, over time, their arms and legs began to function in fluid and purposeful motion. I remember my infants' eyes, at first, so unfocused and nondifferentiating, until slowly, over time, their eyes could begin to hold my gaze and recognize me.

I remember their ability to communicate, in the early days and weeks so animal-like, only cries, yawns, and purrs of satisfaction, and then slowly, syllables, words, sentences. By now, of course, there is nonstop chatter.

From chaos to order in all aspects of their being is how I see this progression, from pudginess to definition of features, from stumbling to graceful strides, from not knowing what they want to knowing exactly what they want, from being totally at the mercy of their environment to affecting their environment with growing sophistication. Yes, I learn about God, creation, and humanity from each of my children.

Creation of the universe and the evolution of a child run parallel in terms of emerging distinctiveness, development of increasing complexity, and a growing capacity to know and understand. Daniel, for example, has become in the last year or two a very intuitive, discerning child. He is not unlike his namesake in the Bible, of whom it was written, "And Daniel had understanding in all visions and dreams" (Daniel, 1:17). Daniel is particularly conscious of nuance and shading. He notices subtle changes in the seasons and in expressions on my face. His instincts are very sharp in this regard, and I enjoy his capacity to observe and discriminate.

When I remember my children as toddlers, I sometimes think of how they reacted when they were particularly frustrated by something they couldn't have or couldn't do. They stood there, tears streaming down their cheeks, fists clenched, stamping their feet, sometimes too filled with rage to speak, at other times able to verbalize, "I don't want to go home now," or "I want that toy and I don't care if it belongs to someone else," or "Why can't I eat this mud soup I made from the backyard, filled with worms and slugs?" or "I'm not tired and don't need a rest."

It often struck me on observing my children in these moments that this is how humanity must look to God: angry, defiant, unreasonable. And God the Parent, unable to explain to our satisfaction why things are the way they are and why we must accept some limits in our lives and actions.

Think of our stance toward that which we cannot control: we are outraged, we don't understand why, nothing will placate us. Even as adults, we act like toddlers and preschool-aged children, shouting: "It's not fair!" We question everything: "Why are there limits—to my abilities, my possessions, my time to play?" And God the Parent responds: "Because that's just the way it is," or "There are reasons and you are just unable to comprehend them."

Think, now, of the opposite side of the spectrum of the parent-child interaction, when we as parents are able and willing to provide what the child needs or wants—food, clothing, hugs, comfort, distractions, diversions, security. We are proud to be so useful, needed, resourceful, and magnanimous with our time or money. Does God share this feeling of fulfilment and self-satisfaction when looked at adoringly through humanity's grateful, satiated eyes?

Does the Source of Life grieve as we do when, like us, God is unable to provide relief for children's wounds, sorrow, losses, despair? My children are always surprised and saddened to see me cry. After all, they view me as pretty much all-powerful. In their eyes I can have or get what I want, no limits, no bedtime, no one to tell me I've had enough ice cream, no restrictions on when and how much makeup I can wear.

As adults we too may look at God and wonder what it must be like to be in control, yet we should realize that being perceived as all-powerful is not the same as being all-powerful. No, it's not what it seems from the other side.

Being a parent has made me more compassionate toward God. I do believe God would love to be there for each of us, every moment, but, like a parent, can't. There are other children, other human beings to attend to, other matters that require attention, so many details to keep life going. As a parent, I'm willing to surmise that God too is sometimes distracted or tired. Perhaps God feels weary of our whining and fighting, annoyed at being asked over and over again for insignificant things, impatient with being told we're bored and have nothing to do in spite of the magnificence of what has been provided.

I imagine that when my children become adolescents, I'll learn different things about God, such as how it feels to be subject to humanity's moodiness and self-centeredness, for example. But for now, I have already learned a lot from my children: about creation, holiness, forgiveness, power, humility, separation, and reconciliation. All these I have learned about God because, as a parent, I too am a source and steward of life.

In conclusion, I want to mention a theological insight that came from Daniel in the form of a conversation we had that he probably doesn't remember and I will never forget. It happened a few years ago when he was five, at an early soccer game on a crisp fall morning. Our oldest son, David, swift as a leopard and graceful as a deer, was already bounding across the field, while Daniel and I cuddled together waiting for the sun to break through the clouds to provide additional warmth. The air was so fresh and the grass brilliantly green. Daniel's eyes drew my gaze like a cloudless sky. I held him close and relished the moment of silence and peace. He turned to me and asked, unexpectedly, "Mommy, what is heaven?" Searching for words to answer him, the ones I found were, "It is this."

Daniel, may you always find a piece of heaven and the reflection of God's love in yourself as I have found these so bountifully in you. Happy Birthday.

27

On Carving a Life

Susan Berrin

> . . . I wither and you break from me;
> yet though you dance in living light
> I am the earth. I am the root,
> I am the stem that fed the fruit
> the link that joins you to the night.

> Judith Wright: extract from "Woman to Child"
> from *A Human Pattern: Selected Poems*
> (ETT Imprint, Sydney, 1995)

This is my gift to you, Noa, my seventeen-year-old, sweet, loving daughter. You are on the cusp of womanhood. As you ready yourself to soar, I am drawn to reflect on our life together and the lives it has produced: My life as a woman irrevocably changed by having you as my daughter, your life endowed with the blessings that only deep and everlasting love can birth.

Weeks after you were born, our family packed up from a four-year stint in a small Maine town and headed west to Vancouver Island, where your Abba would be the rabbi. Victoria, the provincial capitol, is a small, cosmopolitan city on the tip of the island. Of the 250,000 people living in Victoria, about 2,000 are Jewish. Abba was the rabbi of the only synagogue, a Conservative shul opening its doors to the full range of Jewish experience. You and my dad, your Papa, coined the term "character" to describe the array of oddballs passing through our lives, leaving indelible impressions.

The island, off the coast of Vancouver, is a place no one just wanders through. Many sojourners make it part of their spiritual travels; retirees make it their last home. Its temperate climate makes it a haven for the homeless and a shrine for the home botanist and gardener.

Victoria's Jewish community reflects the uniquely integrated diversity of Victoria's larger culture. I write this to you because I firmly believe that we have influenced and been influenced by the culture and community we have lived within for the past sixteen years. And it has been a blessing to share our lives with such an assortment of people, many of whom have touched us each profoundly. Your horizons have been stretched in ways you probably cannot even imagine. The women who have entered your life, as friends of mine and as congregants in our shul, as your teachers and as your friends, have walked along many roads. They dress in an assortment of styles, they work in a variety of professions, and their lives reflect the ways women stretch with experience. They impart wisdom gathered from all directions that the wind blows.

Being the young daughter of the city's only rabbi has certainly affected your life in ways sometimes visible but more often subterranean. That first High Holiday period remains clear in my mind. I brought you to shul in a basket. You kindly slept through most of the services, rousing only to beam your rosy-cheeked smile. As much as I tried to keep your life normal, to refrain from any "model behavior" expectations, to keep our family and your growing-up years out of the fishbowl, you were never an anonymous child. How normal I kept your life is still a mystery to me. In fact, normal is such a relative measure, I hardly know how to use it.

Those early years were devoted to creating a life together. You and I were on a journey to explore new territory: the geography of the city and the interior landscape of a mother-daughter dyad. We set out to establish our place in Victoria and in the synagogue, and to create an extended Jewish community as surrogate for the intense family experience both your Abba and I relished in our youth, with aunts, uncles, and cousins in close proximity.

As a Jewish feminist, I cherished certain values and ideals. Although swaddling you in love, I hoped not to spoil you with material comforts. I encouraged all your activities and hoped the desired Barbie doll you finally received on your fourth birthday wouldn't signal a lifetime ambition. I hoped to ground your feet while fanning your wings. I understand you now wished I'd pushed you in a more athletic direction, but as a woman more endeared to the book than the ball, I never anticipated that desire.

We had to work to create a Jewish life in Victoria. When you were two years old, a few young parents jointly created a preschool through the synagogue so our children's first formal learning experiences would be within a Jewish environment. When you were five years old, we thought momentarily about home schooling you. Without the critical mass for a Jewish day school, we tried to find a way to integrate Jewish learning into the natural rhythms of your day, week, and school year. Approaching kindergarten, together we chose a progressive elementary school that voiced a non-Christian approach to holiday celebrations, a welcoming of diversity.

We tried to shield you from the domination of Christian culture, which manifests itself more stridently in Canada, a country with less separation of church and state than the United States. We tried to prolong your early experiences of living-Jewishly-is-living-normally; to ward off the encroachment of mainstream culture which places Jews on the periphery and which, within that periphery, places Jewish women on the outer edge. And while I acknowledge that life on the margins provides a unique lens for observing the world, I hoped my daughter would not be formed in counterpoint to the culture that surrounded her. But even your progressive kindergarten planned a Christmas concert, and we had to explain why that would be an alienating experience for you. After several meetings, the school agreed to hold a "winter concert" that would celebrate the winter season rather than the winter holidays. As December approached each year, we would meet with the school administration and your teachers to advocate a more multicultural approach to the holiday season. But with all of our efforts, I am sure the sense of "other" filtered down through your innocent and delicate skin. I see glimpses of your discomfort, a tendency to protect your Jewish identity.

Abba and I weighed constantly the advantages and disadvantages of living in such a small Jewish community. Although there was no Jewish day school to provide you with a full Jewish education, we fully experienced the Jewish cycle of time in our home. We also negotiated periods of time to be away from Victoria, when Jewish learning would be more intense and Jewish living more natural. Our first sabbatical was spent in Jerusalem, where you attended grade two. Although the first months were taxing, you eventually welcomed the challenges, enjoyed the exotic, and adapted to the expectations. You are preparing to return to Israel this summer, your first visit back to the place where your Abba and I met more than twenty years ago. I wonder how you will absorb the country's beauty, its history, it majesty, its rudeness, its religious and political struggles. I remember so vividly my own first encounter with this land, and my primal attachment to it. Will you share that sense of deep love?

In Victoria, the challenges you faced at school were coupled with the challenges of living an observant Jewish life in a city that did not include provisions for observance—neither the shops nor the company. I often wondered how, living in a place where open-mindedness and adaptability were the ultimate virtues, we would provide you, and your siblings Yossi and Tzvia, with religious parameters and identity.

Victoria had its charms. We were living in a Garden of Eden, with the Pacific Ocean only blocks from our house, snow-capped mountains ringing the vista. You were blessed with solid roots, a sense of belonging to a community that hovered protectively over you, showering you with the love of an enormous extended family. But, living in the isolation of a chevra was, I believe, a serious obstacle to your happiness. The demographics of the Jewish community were such that there just weren't any other Jewish girls in your age group. You found few other children welcoming and supportive of your Jewish lifestyle.

The pain of loneliness was, I'm sure, only slightly alleviated with our Shabbos facials and manicures, my feeble attempts to keep you occupied and to focus attention on you during long Shabbos afternoons. I'd put aside my feminist principles, the discomfort I felt with such obvious attention to physical adornment, and together we'd apply facial masks, peels, lotions, and hot towels. And then you'd often try out your latest facial enhancements, hoping that maybe you could entice me to wear lipstick, rouge, or a bit of mascara. We'd make Havdalah with the softest skin and a girl-glow between us.

How has all of this affected you? I'm sure most mothers wonder about the consequences of the convergence of their planned child-rearing and the unplanned forces that impact the identity of their Jewish daughters. I am not an exception. I wonder frequently— should we have brought you to a larger Jewish community sooner? Did I protect you from the "expectations" of being the eldest child in a rabbinic home? Have I seeded your Jewish garden so that it will continue to sprout as you grow, hopefully forever learning and seeking on your own? Have we instilled in you a strong sense of self— one that cherishes being a woman and being a Jew?

I know that there have been difficult times, explaining to friends the boundaries of Saturday activity and each fall explaining to teachers your repeated school absences. I don't know how, exactly, these experiences have affected your inner core, your sense of self. On the surface, I detect a certain uncomfortable self-consciousness about being Jewish. But perhaps that is only a surface protection. You are quiet about being Jewish, faintly moving your lips at the Shabbos table while we sing "Shalom Aleichem." Perhaps it's a public shyness that deters you from using the skills you learned so well preparing for your Bat Mitzvah. I miss hearing your voice chanting Torah and Haftorah, as we practiced in the hammock in our backyard.

As your mother, I am the repository of your moods. I know that within the closeness and safety of our relationship I bear your happiness and your sadness, the frustrations of friends, and the anxiety of schoolwork. To say that I have been aware of your every moment, from the time you first wiggled in my belly until today as you prepare to leave for college, is both true and untrue. Before your birth, I longed for you, having lost a baby the year before. I anxiously awaited the moment our skins would touch. We share a closeness, a resemblance. So many of your teachers say as I walk into their rooms for parent-teacher conferences, "You must be Noa's mother."

As a teenager, you are creating yourself anew. Your bedroom is a cluttered haven: music, books, magazines, clothes covering all floor space. You walk with dignity, with a poise well beyond your seventeen years. Your exquisite paintings adorn the walls of our home: the watercolor landscapes of Canada's West Coast, and sunflowers bursting with happiness. Your intelligence, sensitivity, and creativity are obvious, and I am honored to call you my daughter.

But as you grow, I know we share less intimacy. You are making it clear to us that you will walk your own path. And I am grateful for that. While I carved out my own identity, as a woman and as a Jew, distinct from the family I grew up in, so too you will chisel yours. I only hope that we have given you sufficient resources and the gift to carve well.

28

Integrating Feminism, Judaism, and Spirituality

Sharla Green Kibel

A PASSOVER LIBERATION

I've been reflecting on our last three Passover Seders and on my evolution from the Super Jewish, Super Feminist Super Mother who created a Super Seder in 1997. I was simultaneously nursing Andrea, my infant daughter, and dashing over to check and serve the kneidele, matzo balls, made from Granny Esther's recipe. At the same time I was trying to nourish our souls, orchestrating readings from the Haggadah with carefully inserted references to female characters such as Miriam, and the midwives Shifra and Puah, who attended Jocheved, mother of Moses.

This year I delegated food preparation, holding onto my beloved kneidele. I enjoyed and sang the melodies that resonated for me— the beautiful traditional tunes in the benshin after the meal, as well as the modern Debbie Friedman (1988) song about Miriam dancing with her timbrel. I set the table with three special goblets: wine for Elijah, water for the well of Miriam, orange juice for my mother and all other absent family and loved ones. We kleibed nachas, hearing my daughter and nephew competently read from the Haggadah for the first time, and at the last moment accommodated a new member of my temple needing a Seder to attend. I felt supported in the rituals by the presence of the same close gentile friend who had attended the births of both my children. Yes, I mixed in the indispensable ingredient of stress/hysteria at pulling it all together at the last minute, complete with the final dash to buy Afikomen gifts; but somehow I experienced more joy, less a sense of forcing the occasion. It helped to have experimented in prior years, and to

227

have my husband take over the house cleaning! But most of all, I attribute the satisfactions to a sense of inner coherence with the ritual, the food, and my valuing of the event for myself. I could relax, and not be so controlling of how others participated—a new sort of Jewish mother experiencing a liberation!

I have become more comfortable with the doublethink of celebrating ancient wisdom and contemporary sensibilities simultaneously. I am now more hesitant to impose premature censorship on what I pass on to my children. I shall transmit the traditions, warts and all. However, I will just as freely discuss the ways that these sexist or chauvinist warts are addressed in modern midrash. This ancient form of Biblical (or Talmudic) commentary is currently being adapted to contemporary rereading of holy texts with the intent to imaginatively supply the missing fragments. It is with humor, discernment, and passion that I now attempt to freely integrate motherhood, Judaism, and spirituality.

WEAVING IN THE SPIRITUAL
AND FEMINIST THREADS

Despite rabbinical injunctions about a father's duty to teach his children the Law, many mothers today sustain their families' connection to Jewish heritage. My mother and grandmothers provided the emotional links for me and sent me elsewhere, to a Hebrew day school, for the scholastic elements. I think I'm of a unique generation of mothers who attempt to integrate and transmit a synthesis of both, which for me requires the inclusion of a spiritual thread. Deeply immersed in Jewish teachings at school, I struggled to find a spiritual center in the patriarchal, absolutist tradition I was taught. As an adult, I have amplified my own spiritual vocabulary in multiple directions: from astrology to feminism and transpersonal psychology, from Kabbalah to the I Ching, from twelve-step programs to the Jewish Renewal movement.

I now find myself reinhabiting and transmitting a deeper version of my childhood religion. A key element of this synthesis is the spiritual process of weaving women's voices and perspectives into the rich tapestry of existing traditions. For me the "family story" that Jews have told themselves and their descendants is a way of trying to make sense of a discovery of and then a relationship with God. This story has many problematic components. Having received a traditional education, I experience both alienation from aspects of the story and deep resonances. When such stories and traditions are reinterpreted with contemporary, feminist, or mystical sensibilities, those resonances become exquisitely powerful to me.

AN INTERGENERATIONAL CONVERSATION

As a child I felt critical of my mother's approach to religion. I have become more curious about how Esther, my mother, had perceived her own mothering. During Esther's recent visit, my six-year-old daughter, Miranda, and I taped a conversation about my mother's experiences. I was aware from my mother's tone that her granddaughter's presence had an impact on her. In an interesting way, it led Esther to talking as much about being a Jewish daughter as she did about being a Jewish mother:

> **Esther:** For my mother, actually, it was very important to teach her children to be Jewish because she wasn't taught very much about it. When I was a little girl, my mother, who didn't come from a religious home, taught me all the Bible stories, and taught me all the things about being Jewish, and my father, who came from the religious home, taught me about Darwin and Karl Marx, all the people who weren't religious.

> **Miranda:** Your father is stuck to my father.

This is a reference to ways in which Miranda is beginning to categorize fathers as the ones who "aren't religious." I find it an enormous parenting challenge to impart values, but minimize psychic splitting in relation to them. My daughter struggles with knowing her parents have very different attitudes toward religion. Her father's approach is in a way similar to my parents'—nostalgia and respect for customs and traditions, but little sense of how religious community and ritual might have spiritual relevance in his everyday life. He values science and his own immersion in growing plants, while I appreciate the spiritual values that are activated when I keep mitzvoth, the ritual observances, such as saying blessings over food. The intellectual integrity of Jewish tradition invites us to wrestle with received knowledge in ways that are not dissimilar from the scientific method. Recently I deliberately tried to unsettle Miranda's internal categories by affirming my husband's less "religious" expressions of Judaism. I have commented, for instance, on how scientific inquiry fits with Jewish values, and on how much science and agriculture are pursued in Israel!

As I reflect further on our conversations, I find myself retreating from the pain of Esther and Miranda's discomfort about different-ness. They both are children of immigrant parents, something from which I was spared. Esther described the humiliation inflicted on her by her Jewish peers at school when she brought a ham sandwich for her lunch. Miranda's jaw dropped. She kept asking why Esther's mother had made her such a sandwich. My grandmother, Lucia, did not exclude ham from her household, having been encouraged by her doctor to feed up my sickly aunt with ham and bacon! Miranda knows that we have no pork in our own kitchen, and that I prefer that she not eat the pepperoni pizza served at school lunches. It marks for her an area of uncomfortable differentness from her peers. For this six-year-old, hearing that her Nona had violated this prohibition threw her for a loop! Even though they grew up in different coun-tries, they both have experienced the tension between keeping Jewish traditions while engaging with the non-Jewish external culture.

Esther extends this theme as she reflects on her dating experi-ences:

> **Esther:** It was easy to be Jewish in South Africa. . . . There was no question about my identity. It was a given. In fact my interest was in widening my circle—like when I was at Uni-versity, I was expected to date only Jewish boys. And I found this restrictive. So, I knew my mother didn't know and I wouldn't tell her, but I enjoyed very much going out with non-Jewish boys at University; it felt rather naughty, but it also felt important, not to feel constricted and narrowed. And it was also important to me to have girlfriends who remained close friends, who were not Jewish, because somehow it was very cliquey at school—you know, your friends were Jewish and so

forth, and your social life was in a Jewish group, so I liked the widening at University.

Sharla: But you still settled on marrying a Jewish man.

Esther: Yes, I did, because I wanted my children to grow up Jewish. Yes, I settled on marrying a Jewish man. I enjoyed going out with non-Jewish men, but they didn't feel like the kind of people I would want to make a family with, because our cultural backgrounds were so different. So they were interesting but not exactly family material [laughs].

I observe my own children dealing with the stimulations and pressures of a hugely varied modern secular existence. My impulse to transmit the values of my religious tradition feels important, but not simply for the sake of continuity. I question familiar patterns, noticing deeper layers of meaning. In our conversation, I discover new empathy for the way my mother stepped back from some "received wisdoms":

Esther: My God is not necessarily a Jewish God.

Sharla: What's your God?

Esther: He's a much more spiritual being than that chap up in the sky.

Sharla: What's your picture of the Jewish God?

Esther: I'm not nuts for the Jewish God. My image of the Jewish God is the God of the Old Testament who is a wrathful God and a jealous God, and a possessive God and a finger-shaking old gent.

Miranda: My image of God is from imagining him creating the world. He looks all brown with no eyes and a hat, creating a fish.

Sharla: What does your personal God include?

Esther: Well, it's more spiritual than an actual God. There is some spirituality in Jewish tradition, the continuity down the generations, a certain sort of identity and value system, the values of the Torah and Talmud, but I really detest fundamentalism of any kind—especially the aberrations within Judaism.

I have absorbed much of my mother's skepticism. Yet I want to be a mother who evolves a multidimensional frame for spiritual growth, one that can offer grounding through the ebbs and flows of sustaining a coherent connection to the sacred. For me, this requires more active engagement with the full spectrum of Jewish prayer, study, debate, and contemplation.

Esther goes on to address her dissatisfaction with her concept of a typical Jewish mother. We both laugh when I later point out that her feelings about "Jewish Mothers" are similar to her criticisms of a "Jewish God":

Sharla: You said to me once, "I tried hard to be a mother who wasn't a 'Jewish Mother,'" which suggests that you had a picture in your mind about what a Jewish mother was that you didn't want to live out.

Esther: Well, I did want my children to be Jewish, you know, and I did feel I was very fortunate in having a Jewish home and the traditions there because of the grandparents, but I didn't want to be a "Jewish Mother." I think I had a stereotype of the Jewish mother as being possessive, maybe not fitting into the prevailing culture.

Sharla: Being an outsider?

Esther: Being an outsider, being . . . sort of restrictive, overfeeding her children, overprotective of her children, laying down what they could do and what they couldn't do, not very liberal; who they could associate with, and who they couldn't associate with, particularly when they were teenagers—I think I wanted to be more liberal than that, and my children to be more free-thinking than that. But I did want them to know what Judaism was about.

My mother was able to give me an appreciation for tradition and peoplehood, an awareness that choices could vary greatly about one's form and degree of observance. She also conveyed a sense that life should have meaning with spiritual content, leaving me with a much more positive association to the concept of "Jewish Mother":

> **Esther:** Because I did experience some anti-Semitism at school and among other kids, I wanted my children to know about their tradition and to be proud of their tradition. That's why I think I sent them for a Jewish education. I remember you coming home from school and saying why weren't we religious like the other families, because they were doing things; like for Pesach they were changing all their cutlery and their crockery and why weren't we doing all this, and why weren't we being kosher, etc. And I think I conveyed to you then, that when you were older you could be as religious as you liked, that I wanted you to know what religious people did, and then you could choose whether you wanted to be religious or not; but that, you know, that wasn't part of what being Jewish meant to me. I'm delighted that you're more Jewish than I am, in some ways. I'm glad you don't keep a kosher home, but you do keep the tradition. And you do keep the important spiritual things. And that, that gives me a lot of joy to see that, and to see it passed down to my grandchildren.

Esther's approach to passing on her religious heritage was somewhat fragmented, but it left me the freedom to evolve my own synthesis, supported by newer approaches to mining the female dimensions within the fabric of Judaism. I think that each generation will frame different spiritual priorities within Jewish practice.

The survivor experience strongly affected the views of my beloved late grandmother Lucia regarding spiritual responsibilities. She left Poland for Africa in 1938. Her father, sister, and relatives remained and perished in the Holocaust. She wrote:

> Esther was born one year after our marriage. I managed to send home a photo of her when she was a couple of months old and then the war broke out.

I was very fortunate to escape before the war, only missing it by one year. Often I think why should one life be more important than another's. But God gave us four wonderful children and wonderful grandchildren, and with God's help, perhaps they will make a contribution to the betterment of this world. If not our children or grandchildren perhaps our great-grandchildren will do so.

Lucia didn't wait for coming generations, but modeled a life dedicated to powerful service in both secular and Jewish organizations. I have sometimes wondered, though, if my ever-present sense of not being good enough relates to the contribution expected of a survivor's granddaughter.

I would like my own daughters to experience a more coherent exposure to the complex strands of Judaism while still having the freedom to discover their own basis for resonating with their heritage. The physical, sensory experience of observing some mitzvoth can facilitate this resonance. I remember having lit a candle during a recent power outage, and my delight at hearing Andrea, my two-and-a-half-year-old toddler, reflexively start to say "Baruch atah Adonai Elohenu," the first words of the blessing for lighting Shabbat candles. The sensory experience of Jewish ritual can exist in one's bones and under one's skin; but for me, its power is deeper when linked to the mysteries of creation, liberation, moral purpose, and peoplehood. The questions and challenges posed by my six-year-old daughter push me to delve deeper into these very mysteries.

OTHERNESS

"You know, Mommy, yesterday I wished I wasn't Jewish, but then last night I had a dream that even though I was Jewish I was still the best." My children's father and I had just the day before been discussing how Jewish identity formation can unpredictably evoke an oscillation between feelings of superiority and inferiority. Miranda had felt rebuffed when trying to explain to her classmates why Friday night was special. Later, when I asked her about specifics of the dream, she referred to "picking a flower" and knowing that in being Jewish, "I was lucky." This evolution from "being the best" may have occurred after a previous conversation in which I told her that both Christians and Jews have important teachings to contribute to the world.

In contrast to my own experience, my daughter does not attend a Hebrew day school. This raises questions of "otherness" and pluralism at an earlier age, at a time when she is also grappling with basic identity formation.

Shortly before Christmas, Miranda came home from school and described with amazement how the class had downloaded religious symbols during computer time in school. "And the first symbols were Jewish. And I couldn't believe, Mommy, how all the children were listening when the teacher used them. I felt a little funny inside that they were really listening. I couldn't believe it."

My heart clenches as I notice how "funny" I, too, feel inside about those moments of feeling visible, and the unwished-for sense of apology I experience at "imposing" my particularity on others. I am happy that my child's teacher was sensitive enough to begin by validating Miranda's experience. After all, I'd made a point at the parent-teacher conference of Miranda's need for support during December events. Yet I notice my uneasiness with this visibility, and wonder how I can help my daughter escape such constricting self-consciousness, when I am still at least somewhat ensnared by it myself.

What is so compelling to me about these parenting/identity challenges may be the reality that my struggle to nurture my children's functioning and adaptation in oppressive environments makes it excruciatingly painful for me to stay too awake or aware. I believe that other Jewish mothers may have coped with this pain through differing levels of fragmentation; each generation holding some threads of the tapestry colorfully alive, while ignoring or suppressing other equally important threads.

A SPIRITUAL PATH OF ATTACHMENT

I have been surprised at the degree to which Miranda's pain about feeling different has me questioning why I even want to hold on to a particularistic, patriarchal religion. As I posit the question, I have flashes of my attachments to the musically satisfying liturgy, the moral insights, the humanness of the lore of stories, the accents, values, and multidimensionality of my own and my husband's grandparents. Eastern religious traditions emphasize spiritual growth through freeing one's self of emotional attachments. But maybe the very attachments pervading Jewish tradition provide a path to self-awakening; a working with, rather than a relinquishing of, the emotional attachments embedded in our spiritual legacy. "It is a tree of life to those who grasp it" (Harlow, 1985, p. 151). And parenting is about the most fundamental and ambivalent of attachments. How often I find buried, in my own and others' negative reactions to Jewish upbringing, a more personal reaction to the parent or teacher who provided it.

On my birthday, last January, I chanted a Torah portion referring to the dedication of the firstborn. Although this commandment applies to males, I lay claim to this "dedication" by virtue of being a firstborn. I was everyone's first grandchild, a recipient of legacies and a witness becoming entwined within the intricacies of family histories and dramas. I think I found it hard to sustain an awareness of my own self within the richness of absorbing the stories and processes of others. Maybe the path of a true spiritual dedication involves "wrestling" through these thickets, through the joys and sorrows of peoplehood, both embracing and challenging these legacies.

Paradoxically I feel that staying close to my own sacred or spiritual consciousness is an indispensable route to balance, in the midst of pressures from the competing agendas embedded in my heritage. Then my grandmother's wish for contributions from her descendants is no longer an intolerable personal burden, but flows into my engagement with tikkun olam, the commandment to repair the world.

It was my Gaga Lucia who first taught me to say the Shema, the prayer, "Hear, O Israel," before going to sleep. It is her spirit that moves me now to start teaching this prayer to my own children, remembering with gratitude that we are all, separately and together, "works in progress" on this road to healing the world.

REFERENCES

Friedman, Deborah Lynn (1988). Miriam's song (lyrics based on Exodus 15:20-21). In *And you shall be a blessing*. San Diego: Sounds Write Productions.

Harlow, Jules (Ed.) (1985). Torah service. In *Siddur Sim Shalom*, pp. 138-151. New York: The United Synagogue of America.

29

Seeking Serenity
As a Single Jewish Mother

Paula J. Caplan

The clearest, most lasting image of being Jewish that I have, even now when I am over fifty, is of Seder and High Holiday meals in my maternal grandparents' spacious, low-ceilinged living room, where we ate Gram's delicious foods in the company of our small, loving, hilariously funny family. On Pesach, Gram would say to my grandfather as he conducted the service, "Nate, hurry! The children are hungry!" *People* mattered, the little ones mattered, not a claustrophobic, unending, unbending edifice of ritual, much of which seemed (as we raced through it or, in later years, occasionally heard droning voices tell it in other people's homes) to be about battles and sinning and retribution. Storytelling mattered. Laughing at oneself in the healthiest possible way mattered. In the corner of the dining room was the smaller table where we played Scrabble, Jotto, and other games of words and logic. At holiday and many other family meals, there was frequent talk about people in various kinds of need. Those joys of being together and sharing and caring and thinking and questioning were the things that I wanted for my children when I became a mother.

And it felt as though they were inextricably intertwined with being Jewish. Not that I thought non-Jews couldn't or didn't care about the same things, but for me they had an ineluctably Jewish flavor (a food word!).

My son, Jeremy Benjamin, was born in 1973 on Rosh Hashanah, and my daughter, Emily Julia, in 1975. Between their births, we moved from the United States, my home country, to Canada. When the children were five and three years old, respectively, I became a single mother, terrified that I would be such a terrible mother that I would somehow destroy my children's psyches. Trying to provide the right kind of Jewish environment for them was a part of mothering that ended up on the back burner until Jeremy's Bar Mitzvah year was close enough for me to realize that it really would arrive. I knew that I didn't want to immerse them in Orthodox practice, and I had no interest in the Conservative synagogue in Toronto, which looked like a 1950s motel and was so huge they had to pipe the Kol Nidre into a second room to hold all comers. The major Reform temple just looked too imposing for what I sought. I really wanted a Hebrew school where they would learn some Jewish history and culture and some Hebrew and be encouraged to ask questions.

I enrolled Jeremy and Emily in a Hebrew school that was not connected with a congregation and hoped all would be well. They weren't crazy about attending, but everyone said that was a normal part of Hebrew school: *Nobody* actually *liked* to go. As a mother, I hated sending them somewhere they didn't love to go, but I thought maybe as a Jewish mother part of my job was to encourage them to attend anyway. One day, when Jeremy was eleven or twelve, he came home from class, terrified. "Mom," he said, "Ruth," his teacher, "told us about the Holocaust. And she said that it could happen *here . . . at any moment.*" He was so frightened by the way she had said that, that he was looking over his shoulder as he repeated her words to me. I told my children that they would not be returning to that school.

Jeremy was now growing alarmingly close to Bar Mitzvah age. What to do? I had heard about a Reconstructionist congregation from feminist journalist Michele Landsberg, who was a member of that congregation and said it was a group that prided itself on being a warm, welcoming community that was egalitarian and social-action oriented. Sounded like heaven to me. I took the kids and went to the next Saturday morning service, feeling as paralyzed by shyness as I usually did in a new situation.

At that time, the congregation had no rabbi, and a very smart old man gave the d'var Torah (a term I learned there), which was a fascinating historical interpretation he was *pro*posing, not *im*posing, of the ten plagues. Jeremy looked at me, his eyes glowing with delight. We joined up. People were pleasant, but I told the woman cantor—whose gorgeous voice, and the fact that she was a woman, were things I loved for my own sake and for the sake of my children—that I felt strange being the only single parent in the congregation. It turned out that I wasn't, but there weren't many.

The three of us attended services weekly, and I hired a couple of people to prepare Jeremy for the Hebrew parts of his Bar Mitzvah. He and I worked on his d'var Torah. I decided to do it with him myself rather than asking someone else to work with him, because I had heard too many horror stories of people writing their speeches for the kids or telling them what they should say. Jeremy and I used the Socratic method. We read a bit at a time of his Torah portion in English, read every relevant footnote we could find, and then I asked him what he thought about each bit. As we read and talked, he decided that he wanted to talk about the question of why, if God is supposedly omniscient and all-good, there is evil and suffering in the world. All the ideas were his.

Barely a week before Jeremy's Bar Mitzvah, the newly hired feminist rabbi, Debra Brin, arrived. Some combination of her feminist consciousness, her intelligence, her humor, the breadth of her understanding of possible components of spirituality (a word I still cannot define or understand very well), and maybe something else that I cannot identify led me to feel for the first time that Judaism's (or just religion's?) *spiritual* side was important to me. Whatever it was, it had something to do with a sense of wholeness, a sense that everything matters and is intertwined. The first instance of this happened at Jeremy's Bar Mitzvah. The busy new Rabbi Brin was introduced to Jeremy, spoke with him briefly, and heard his one Bar Mitzvah rehearsal. In her address to him the following week at his Bar Mitzvah, she said that what she loved about him was the way his neshamah shone through. It makes me weep even now, when he is twenty-six. She had immediately seen and appreciated something in my son that is special and precious. I also loved her way of combining the political and the spiritual at so many levels. On another occasion, Rabbi Brin organized a small, unpretentious, unforced, deeply meaningful and amazingly effective ritual to help me recover from a physical attack that had left me feeling intensely dehumanized, confused, and invisible, as well as concerned that these feelings blocked my emotional availability to my children. As far as I know, not a word she said came from Jewish prayers, and none of it was in Hebrew, but the spirit and sense she brought to it felt like a perfect combination of the best of Jewish, feminist, and plain old humane practice.

As a result of Rabbi Brin's influence, I actually loved attending services, so taking my children there before and shortly after their Bar and Bat Mitzvah years was a pleasure. They seemed to enjoy much about it, too. I had not yet become disillusioned by the hypocrisy many of the powerful people in the congregation practiced in regard to their professed egalitarianism and social-action orientation.

As the time approached for Emily's Bat Mitzvah, I hired someone to teach her the Torah trope and help prepare her. But a new thought occurred to me. Jeremy had learned what Emily now had to learn, and from his early childhood he had been a natural teacher. I knew there were dangers involved in asking one child to tutor the other, but I sat the two of them down, told them I wondered whether they would want to give it a try—having Jeremy teach Emily her portion—and see how it would work. I said that if either one of them felt it was not working, that would be no big deal. We would just get someone else to teach her. They were eager to give it a try. I told Jeremy his father and I would pay him just as we would have paid anyone else. Some of the stodgier members of the congregation expressed strong disapproval. The implication was that only someone older and more experienced could do the teaching. Frankly, I felt that some ineffable things could be gained from having the children work together that could not come from having Emily taught by an adult she barely knew.

On the day of the first planned lesson, I told Jeremy and Emily I would disappear upstairs and not interfere during the hour. At the end of that time, Jeremy came upstairs and walked into my room. He told me with great seriousness that his sister had done well. "She was pretty active at first," he reported, "so I had her jump on the trampoline for a few minutes to settle down." Anyone who knew Emily then would have recognized immediately the appropriateness of Jeremy's method. So one of the wonderful results of Jeremy's preparation of Emily for her Bat Mitzvah was that, perhaps for the first time in history, someone learned part of her Torah portion while jumping on a trampoline. What wise elder would have thought of that?

I worked with Emily as she prepared her d'var Torah in the same way that I had worked with Jeremy, and she decided to address the fact that there are some kinds of learning you can get from books and others that must be experienced. When she opened the floor to questions, my father asked her a question that she answered by saying, clearly close to tears, that she was learning from the experience of having this Bat Mitzvah that it was a more important thing than she had expected it to be.

In the services we had been attending, besides having a woman rabbi and a woman cantor, women said all the prayers and performed all the functions the men did. During that time, we attended a Conservative service on a visit to California, and afterward Emily asked me, with tears in her eyes, "Did you see the women? Their lips were moving, and they looked like they wanted to pray, but they didn't know the words." Whatever might have been the reality, the point was that, after attending a congregation where women regularly did everything the men did, it was important and disturbing to her to see something so different in a negative way. I felt glad again that she had had so many woman-focused experiences.

As time went on, Jeremy, Emily, and I were deeply disappointed when it became clear that, despite the presence of some good people in the congregation, as a body it was not prepared to live up to its stated commitment to egalitarianism—or even to being a warm, supportive community. Mistreatment of feminists and lesbians was both subtle and blatant. Then, within a few months, I ended a five-year relationship, two dearly loved close relatives died, and Jeremy left home for college. I told the new rabbi (hired after Rabbi Brin left) that I planned to leave the congregation because no one had contacted me to express any sympathy about any of my recent losses or to offer support. He wrote a note, saying that their silence went against ethnic and national type (!) and that I must be communicating some message that made them do that (the myth of women's masochism!). One reason I longed for some support was because I was again worried about not being emotionally available to Jeremy and Emily, bring too preoccupied and isolated in my grief. My rabbi's and my congregation's unavailability caused me to withdraw from any kind of public Jewish practice, and, once Rabbi Brin had left, the soul had gone out of services for me. I hoped that my sense of alienation would not interfere with whatever positive things my children might have gotten from being Jewish. But I wondered about that and sometimes worried.

When the children and I lived on our own, we sometimes had tiny Rosh Hashanah dinners or Seders with just the three of us present. I remember thinking that strangers looking in might feel that that was pitiful. I did not. I felt peaceful, but I did worry that I might be depriving the kids of something. (Some years, of course, we had friends or visiting relatives at holiday dinners with us.) The best Jewish celebration I have had since my childhood of having Seders and Erev Rosh Hashanah dinners at my grandparents' house in Springfield was the Seder the kids and I had alone one recent year in my sunroom, the day *after* what was supposed to be the First Seder. We had to have it then because I had a performance of a play I loved during First Seder night. No question of our being observant Jews in any traditional sense. The three of us made the various dishes, had a great time setting the table, eating our special meal in the sunroom, and having a peaceful time with no prayers whatsoever, not even a Haggadah in sight. But we had food we had always shared at that time plus some different foods, we were together on a Jewish holiday, and that was what mattered. This time I felt completely serene and full of joy, because I was finally quite sure that nothing was missing.

Perhaps that is spirituality.

30

Oranges and Cinnamon

Marlena Thompson

Three is not a number usually associated with Jewish traditions. It certainly doesn't appear in the Bible as often as seven or forty. But when my daughter Jenny was born, the number three loomed large in my mind's eye, foreseeing a trio of future life-cycle events: a naming, a Bat Mitzvah, and a wedding.

The naming went according to schedule. But other milestones, specifically those having to do with development, were markedly delayed. Jenny was four and yet to engage in the prattle typical of children newly able, however simply, to report their impressions of a freshly discovered world. There were other things as well, telltale neurological indicators that hinted at the undeniable fact that all was not well. Even after allowing for the fact that children do not always progress according to predetermined timelines, it was apparent to both my husband and me that Jenny was—different. In fact, we held onto that adjective for a long time after it ceased to be entirely accurate, because it was infinitely easier to accept than that other word that described our daughter, autistic.

Though still not high on the list of well-understood disorders, in the early 1980s, when Jenny was born, autism was an even more esoteric label than it is today. It commonly evoked the image of a spinning child totally out of touch with her or his surroundings. In fact, autism is a syndrome of neurological abnormalities affecting the use of language, ways of relating to others, and sensory perception. The level of impairment varies significantly among those afflicted with the disability.

When the doctors relayed Jenny's diagnosis, my husband and I were devastated. As parents, we grieved for the death of dreams we had nurtured for our daughter. But the more Jenny developed into her own person, the more we saw behaviors symptomatic of autism as simply characteristics of her own unique self. We rejoiced in the special talents she possessed in abundance. The heightened sensory perception that added to her distractibility had its "up" side as well, that is, the making of an artist of no small magnitude. Her drawings revealed colors so brilliant, it was clear that only someone who could see beyond the spectrum visible to the normal eye could have produced them. As sounds were equally acute to Jenny, music became an important part of her world long before she was able to string three words together. Like many parents of disabled children, I too grappled long and hard with issues of belief. But if ever I doubted the existence of God, living each day with this child, whose very being seemed dependent on the endless creation of beauty, restored my faith.

When Jenny approached the age when a Jewish girl usually prepares to become a Bat Mitzvah, I began to think about what would, and would not, be appropriate for her. I would necessarily be making most of the decisions concerning the liturgical and ceremonial aspects of the Bat Mitzvah, as my husband is not Jewish. I knew instinctively that the standard ceremony, a Torah service necessarily modified to accommodate Jenny's "deficits," would not do. I sought a service that would highlight her gifts and validate her unique essence.

It seemed to me that the Havdalah service, during which we bid farewell to the Sabbath and welcome the coming week, would be perfect for my daughter. In that ceremony, all five senses are involved: We are delighted by the pungency of fragrant spices, cheered by the taste of sweet wine, warmed by the heat of the flame, inspired by the sound of ancient melodies, and comforted by the sight of family and friends. This service would not only open a window of accessibility through which my daughter could embrace an aspect of Judaism already sanctioned by custom, but with its joyful celebration of the senses through which she lives so intensely, Havdalah would confirm Jenny as she is, a perfect creation of God.

But the rabbi of the synagogue to which I belonged did not share my conviction. Because the Bat Mitzvah ceremony I envisioned did not include a Torah service, I was told it could not be held in the synagogue. I still recall the interview I had with the rabbi, because it brought to the surface a truth I had been trying to hide from myself for years.

I explained why I felt that a Torah service, though typically the focus of the Bar or Bat Mitzvah ceremony, would be inappropriate for my daughter:

> What Jenny knows about Judaism, she knows through her senses, and not through law and intellect. And because a Torah service would have no real meaning for her, it could, perhaps, even be said to trivialize Torah.

After pausing, I continued with words that I had, until that moment, kept locked within the depths of my being:

> Rabbi, it is unlikely that my daughter will ever stand beneath the bridal canopy, or that I will ever attend the baby naming of a grandchild. Jenny is my only child. This will be the only major Jewish life cycle event she will ever remember. Can it not be one that will be the most meaningful to her—and to those who love her?

After uttering these words, I was momentarily overwhelmed by a vision of my family tree, the one our tradition enjoins us to nurture so that it will continue to flourish m'dor l'dor, from generation to generation. The branches on my tree were truncated and shriveled, cruelly amputated even before they had had a chance to bloom. I would not dance at my daughter's wedding. Nor would I ever hold a grandbaby in my arms.

But rules prevailed. I could not hold the Bat Mitzvah in the synagogue if I opted to forgo the Torah service.

When I got home, I cried. I wept out of anger, frustration, and self-pity. It was recognition of that last sentiment that dried my tears for good and all. I'd indulged in more than my share of self-pity when my daughter was first diagnosed with autism. Thus, I knew well that beneath the superficial solace it offers its subscribers, self-pity only encourages emotional and psychological paralysis.

And I could not afford immobilization of any sort. I had a job to do. I knew that the Bat Mitzvah service I had in mind was well within the boundaries of tradition. It did not contradict Halacha, Jewish law, but merely challenged the rules of a particular synagogue. A Torah service, though customary, is not mandatory. If I could not bring my daughter to a sanctuary, then I would create a sanctuary for my daughter.

The Havdalah service does not require the presence of a rabbi—it is, after all, usually performed at home. However, because I wanted the event to be as special as possible, I asked a friend and colleague, who happens to be an ordained Orthodox rabbi, if he would consent to conduct the service. He agreed without a moment's hesitation, declaring that it would be "an honor."

I had decided to hold the ceremony in a nearby hotel. The room, simple but elegant, was festively adorned with purple, pink, and white flowers. These were Jenny's favorite colors and ones that represented her well. Pink symbolized her budding womanhood, purple, her passion for art and music, and white, an innocence that can only belong to someone who does not have the capability to deceive.

I had also scattered oranges pierced with cloves and cinnamon sticks throughout the room, on tables, serving trays, and even in planters. The tangy perfume that mimicked the scent of the Havdalah spices filled the air.

When it came time for the ceremony, the rabbi called Jenny to his side. He then called those who were of particular importance in my daughter's life: her parents, grandparents, two half-brothers, and teacher.

Because this was a Havdalah and not a Torah service, Jenny's father and two brothers, who are not Jewish, could be full participants. This proved to be a serendipitous blessing, for the pride that lit my husband's face as he stood close to his daughter almost outshone the glow of the flame atop the braided candle.

The lights were dimmed. The rabbi, also an inspired cantor, began to chant the blessings. The radiance emanating from the Havdalah candle seemed to expand and intensify, creating incandescence around Jenny and those whose lives she touched most deeply.

As the rabbi chanted, Jenny sang with him in Hebrew. She was frightened at first, and her fear was reflected in a brief bout of giggles that disappeared as the singsong of the melodies familiar to her from home worked their magic and calmed her.

Singing at first timidly and then in a surer, stronger voice, she thanked God who creates the fruit of the vine, the fragrant spices, and the lights of fire. We sipped the wine, inhaled the sweet-smelling condiments, and felt the warmth of the flames that illuminated our gathering.

With the lights still dimmed, everyone locked arms and sang Eliyahu haNavi, the song about the Prophet Elijah customarily sung during the Havdalah service. According to folkloric tradition, if not biblical testimony, Elijah is renowned for visiting the spiritually pure and virtuous throughout the ages. And, gazing at my daughter's lovely face, luminous with the joy of achievement, and hearing her remark, "Being Jewish smells like oranges and cinnamon," I had no doubt that Elijah had indeed made his way to our self-styled sanctuary. His presence would be a fitting tribute to the sanctity of innocence and my unwavering belief that, differences and disabilities notwithstanding, God simply does not make mistakes.

SECTION VI:
THE REAL WORLD

31

Dealing with the Real World: Our Children, Ourselves

Shulamit Reinharz

When my second daughter, Naomi, was only a few weeks old, I had to stop at a massive discount store to purchase something. I took her out of the car seat, put her in a little holder, and then placed the baby holder in a shopping cart. As I walked through the store with my precious baby looking up at the gargantuan ceiling, I found myself crying silently. I immediately knew why. I realized that I had kept my baby at home until then, and now for the first time I was having her meet the real world. That world consisted of overly bright fluorescent lights that buzzed and flickered; of oversized people in undersized clothes; and miles and miles of shelves with junk that nobody needed but everyone wanted. I had hoped to keep all of that away from her, but I was never able to. I also realized I was launching her on her education—and this education did not conform to my sense of Jewishness.

"Who is wealthy?" Jewish tradition asks. "The person who is content with his or her portion." But our economy and psychology move us in the opposite direction. "Who is wealthy?" the ad asks. "The person who can afford to buy the latest, biggest, best, and most exclusive thing," the ad answers. My experience as a Jewish mother to a certain extent has meant dealing with the conflicts between what I think Jewish values are and what I know reality is.

In her Jewish day school from kindergarten through eighth grade, Naomi received important books when she and her classmates reached special milestones—a siddur, a Tanach, a Megillat Esther. In fourth grade, she received a weekly planner! There were daily in-school sessions on how to use the planner for shul. Although the sessions have served her well, I had the feeling that this was as serious as the other elements of her Jewish cultural heritage. How do we choose when the choice is between a sports achievement and Shabbat? One friend told me, "I resolutely expect my kids to keep their own calendar and own appointments. And I raise hell if they miss any appointment I have to pay for." Another friend, Rabbi Moshe Waldoks, told me that if I wanted my child to grow up to be a soccer star I should take her to soccer games on Saturday morning, if I wanted her to grow up to be a Jew I should take her to shul on Shabbat."

In fifth grade, Naomi became active in Girl Scouts, an organization that, among other things, trains American girls to be door-to-door salespeople and fund-raisers. The girls push cookies, not the healthiest item to begin with, and then compete for prizes based on the quantity of sales. A little uniformed salesgirl was not my image of a Jewish daughter, but to oppose it was to make her very unhappy. Jewish tradition says, "Do not separate yourself from the community" (*Pirkei Avot*, 4/7).

When Naomi left grade school, I realized I had to teach her about *bureaucracy*. I had to show her how to follow through on a need for information, how to complain to the right people, how to fill out forms and know which forms you don't really need to fill out, and how to treat time like money, to be spent wisely. As she grew older (she's now seventeen), I was aware of moments when I felt I was introducing her to "my world" or "the real world," the world of contemporary adults in our particular culture. I noticed how I was training her to be part of that world, how I was reproducing that culture despite myself. I was teaching her how to schedule, how to watch her little watch, to squeeze things in. I taught her how to "keep in touch with friends," to write thank-you notes for gifts she had already given away, and to plan for next summer's vacation at the end of this one, in order to "get what you want." None of this is terrible, but all of it together compelled her to be less of herself and more like everyone else.

Naomi is now well socialized. She has filled out college applications, created a résumé, and learned to present herself in different ways for different purposes, just as everyone else does. She has gotten her driver's license and has even gotten a credit card. She schedules dentist appointments and orders her own medications on the pharmacy call-in line. She travels by bus to New York, although I do not yet think she can schedule air travel and purchase tickets (have I failed?). Should she have an ATM card, like many of her friends? Should she be investing in the market? Is she behind? Ahead? Age-appropriate?

When my older daughter, Yael, reached the age of ten in 1986, we gave her a telephone extension in her room so she could have a phone of her own (not her own number). When my younger daughter turned ten in 1991, she got a computer so she could communicate with the whole world via e-mail! She is in her room right now, filling out forms, applying for something, making calls, and becoming bureaucratically efficient. I am proud that she has mastered these tasks and dismayed that she has had to do so. The real world is becoming a very large world and it's all at her fingertips—literally.

One of the tasks of motherhood in our society is to train children for bureaucracy. To me, this entails a certain tension. Can't we expect motherhood to be a relief from the bureaucratic ways of relating to one another? Motherhood, after all, is the "female," the spontaneous and emotional component of society, whereas bureaucracy expresses the "male," rational, organized component. Is this a stereotypic way of thinking? Has motherhood disappeared?

Feminist psychologists and sociologists have yet to define motherhood. Jewish feminist sociologist Nancy Chodorow made a breakthrough by overturning Freudian psychoanalytic assumptions and focusing on girls' attachment to their mothers (rather than their fathers), giving the mother-daughter bond center stage in explaining why "motherhood has been reproduced" since the beginning of time (Chodorow, 1978). But the theory did not explain what mothering actually was. Jewish feminist psychologist Rhoda Unger made the interesting observation that "much early feminist research in psychology was on achievement rather than motherhood, whereas fatherhood and the family have been major concerns of psychologists within the men's movement" (Unger, 1988, p. 188). Early feminist theorists, including the Jewish poet Adrienne Rich, challenged the Hallmark image of motherhood (Rich, 1976) without specifying an alternative definition.

Interestingly, many sociologists and organizational consultants are now trying to help bureaucratic organizations become more "female" by introducing flextime, parental leave, casual dress days, National Secretary Appreciation Day (analogous to Mother's Day?), and other features. Organizations are called families, and they are supposed to mother their employees. At the same time, and conversely, actual biological or adoptive motherhood is becoming more organized and bureaucratic. Perhaps we are moving into a new era when organizations and motherhood will both be androgynous!

An essay on the "androgynization" of Jewish motherhood or the feminization of the workplace would be out of place in this volume. So I return to the topic of the creeping (and creepy?) bureaucratization of motherhood. And in typical Jewish fashion, I have to begin with a question: Is mothering *particularly* bureaucratized among Jewish women? I believe it is, for several reasons. First, Jewish women are more highly educated than any other group of women in the United States. Educational attainment is a result of achievement orientation, deferred gratification, and rational planning. Education is linked to a belief in science and order, and leads to an appreciation of differences in rankings and prestige. Second, Jews in the United States are leaders and trendsetters. Patterns of behavioral change in society at large are frequently foreshadowed by changes in the life of the Jewish community. Examples are a decline in birthrate, a rise in age at marriage, and an increase in divorce. Third, Jewish families in the United States cluster in the middle class. Data for all three patterns are readily available in the *Data Book About American Jewish Women*, prepared by the National Commission on American Jewish Women (1994). Because of Jewish women's place in U.S. society, Jewish motherhood is likely to become professionalized and bureaucratic.

This process begins early and is pervasive. Many women from a variety of backgrounds turn to professionals for help with all aspects of their reproductive lives, but Jewish women who want to become pregnant and are experiencing difficulty have become avid consumers of reproductive technological aids (Kahn, 1998). When Jewish women do become pregnant, they turn to physicians to confirm the pregnancy, to monitor the pregnancy, to treat the pregnancy, and to deliver the baby. Jewish women are themselves likely to be professionals.

Before the child is born, in some cases, the Jewish mother investigates the options among pediatricians and obstetricians, and also the options available among schools, day care centers, in-home baby-sitters, and other forms of child care and education. Placing the child in the *best* environments and providing the child with the *best* opportunities become the tasks of the mother. The mother must explore social options, must rank-order them, and must compete with others to secure a space. She must develop social contacts that will ease the way and will provide useful information. She then has social capital that she can use to increase the value of the child. Children are beyond value, of course, but a child who plays the piano, speaks several languages, and attends the right school is even more "beyond value."

In the hospital, the mother is banded, as is the child. The child is cared for according to a regimen. The rules may be minimal, but they are there. Forms must be filled out to take the baby home. There are tests, such as the APGAR, to determine how well the baby is doing. The APGAR test is one of the first "social encounters" the baby has—he or she is ranked, evaluated, and scored. The Jewish mother sees in her child the future successful outcome of her labors—he or she is a genius, so bright, so smart. Reinterpreting the infant's behavior in terms of this cherished goal is part of what she does, even if she does it with some embarrassment. The newborn infant leaves the hospital with many forms signed—the birth certificate, the insurance forms, and instructions, perhaps, on how to care for the baby.

When I entered the hospital about to deliver Naomi, the receptionist asked, "While you are here having a baby, is there anything else we can do for you?" I presume that this bizarre question reflected the form she was filling out. Some women experience motherhood as a set of tasks to be learned. Instructions can be found in the books women purchase about how to raise their children. In addition, there are groups or classes in which you can develop "parenting skills."

Various companies hook the mother and child into the market by providing free "trial" products. The trip from the hospital to the waiting car must be taken in a wheelchair, in many cases, to prevent the hospital from being sued should the mother slip or the baby fall. The child comes home from the hospital—new forms appear. There is a series of vaccinations, which must be carefully monitored and recorded. There is weight to watch and formula (unless breast-feeding) to purchase. There is also the day school or nursery to enroll in, to research. There is the pediatrician to select. The health insurance forms to fill out. The will to modify. The announcement cards to send out. The new passport to purchase, and perhaps even the Social Security card or at least number for the child. I found it disheartening that my file cabinet had to have a file labeled "Yali," and five years later, another file, "Naomi."

When Yali was five months old, my husband and I planned to spend the summer in Israel. Our passports were in order, but it never crossed my mind that a baby needs a passport. A baby is a baby! Not a legal entity, I mistakenly assumed. Somehow on the first leg of the trip, driving from Michigan to New York, I realized I might be wrong. Arriving in New York a day or two before our flight, I called a passport office and learned I was indeed mistaken. So began our frantic activity to obtain an instantaneous passport for a little girl who could not yet walk or talk but clearly needed to be identified as a U.S. citizen. This stressful experience reminded me of a story my own parents had told me about my arrival in the United States as a ten-month-old child born in Amsterdam a year after the end of World War II. The immigration officer asked my parents if I was a prostitute. Alarmed, my parents wondered what kind of a country they were entering. In hindsight they realized that the officer was only "doing his job," an awful reminder for these Holocaust survivors.

As children grow, so does the paperwork. Health maintenance organizations offer the opportunity to enter bureaucratic mazes. Then, too, the mother must locate a dentist, and if the mother is working part-time or full-time, she must begin the complicated task of scheduling her life and her child's to mesh efficiently. The choice to nurse her baby while working requires the "rationalization" of her milk flow, including breast pumps, storage, and measuring. The day care center personnel report on the toddler's behavior in terms of performance charts, indicating napping behavior, eating, and perhaps bowel movements. Time and information are carefully managed commodities that accommodate various schedules and needs. The soccer mom is born.

When I was in this phase of my life—working full-time and not yet tenured—with two young children, I had fantasies of new Olympic sports. Every week, on the drive to piano lessons with my two daughters, we stopped at a clothing discount store. The sport was to see how quickly we could locate the items we needed, select the best line to stand in at the checkout counter, and write out a check or use a credit card. Typically I had under ten minutes for this fly-through shopping trip, before rushing to show up at the piano lesson on time, with the right piano books and paraphernalia. If all went well, I could grade a few papers and figure out my next day's schedule while "listening" to the piano lesson. Efficiency was always my goal. Mapping out the shortest routes, figuring out clever ways to do two or even three things at once—these were the contests that I, and countless other mothers, were engaged in. Remarkably, these tasks were accomplished before we all had car phones or cell phones.

With all this experience behind me, I was ready for the true challenge, the ultimate test—the Bat Mitzvah. In some ways, the Bar or Bat Mitzvah is also a coming-of-age for the mother and/or father. The ability to spend a lot of money on the Bar/Bat Mitzvah demonstrates that the parents are mature, successful, and fully adult. All the child has to do is learn to chant the Haftorah (or read the Torah portion, lead the service, or make a speech). The parents have to accumulate disposable income and demonstrate their success tastefully to friends and relatives.

Much of the burden falls on the shoulders of the Jewish mother. She has to develop an invitation list, select the invitations, keep records of RSVPs, arrange seating, and define how many activities there will be. She must select the date, the caterer, the hall, the band, the flowers or centerpieces, the entertainment, the hotels, the photographer, the videographer, the display of the child's life story in photos, the sign-in book, the goody bags, and whatever else she considers appropriate. She must have her hair done, her nails done, her clothes bought, and arrange the same for the rest of her family. At the same time, she must manage her household, and most likely her job. She has to monitor the child's thank-you notes and be ready to reciprocate appropriately to all the children who are having their Bar or Bat Mitzvah celebrations. One way of sidestepping these issues is to hire a "Bar/Bat Mitzvah planner," or rely heavily on a "Bar/Bat Mitzvah planning guide."

College Boards, AP exams, strategic selection of courses—these are all issues that must be dealt with as well, by Jewish mothers. We are our children's mentors. We provide them with connections and career counseling. A Jewish mother is not one who suffers in silence, as the jokes about us claim. Rather, she is a woman who stakes out and creates opportunities for her children. In the last few years of their adolescence, I have tried to impress on my daughters the value of acquiring business skills, particularly documenting and packaging themselves. Clearly, they have had to accumulate "lines on their résumés" that show how active, multitalented, balanced, and achievement-oriented they are. Some items have to be exaggerated to sound better than they are.

My daughters (sadly) have learned to put a spin on their experiences in order to sell themselves in various competitive situations. I am happy to report that their résumés for college were several pages long. At a young age they had to learn the bureaucratic skills of calling in advance for clarification of issues, keeping receipts, filling out forms, making Xerox copies of everything, and keeping files. They might even have a file on me!

Our household is a busy one. Being a good Jewish mother in my house means taking messages, paying bills, attending award ceremonies, planning vacations, and doing all the other organizational activities that are the blessed tasks of our lives in this safe and comfortable period in Jewish history.

Jewish tradition talks about the task of each age. What are the tasks of childhood? The task of childhood is to be different from adulthood, just as we divide the sacred from the profane, the weekday from the Sabbath. I believe that as Jewish women, we might consider the cause of letting our children be children. I think we can restore childhood, just as we have begun to restore the mitzvah in Bar Mitzvah, and the "holy" in holiday. It is a strange, new task for Jewish mothers who have been stuck with the label of pushing their children. To the extent that this pushing did occur, perhaps it related to insecurity within a hostile environment. Now that our environment is not hostile, we can relax, perhaps, and let there be a season for everything, including a season for childhood.

REFERENCES

Chodorow, Nancy. (1978). *The Reproduction of Mothering: Psychoanalysis and the Sociology of Gender.* Berkeley, CA: University of California Press.

Data Book About American Jewish Women (1994). National Commission on American Jewish Women, p. 3.

Kahn, Susan M. (1998). Rabbis and Reproduction: The Social Uses of New Reproductive Technologies Among Ultra-Orthodox Jews in Israel. *Working Paper 3: Hadassah International Research Institute on Jewish Women.* Waltham, MA: Brandeis University.

Rich, Adrienne. (1976). *Of Woman Born: Motherhood As Experience and Institution.* New York: Norton.

Unger, Rhoda. (1988). Psychological, Feminist, and Personal Epistemology. In M. M. Gergen (Ed.), *Feminist Thoughts and the Structure of Knowledge* (pp. 124-141). New York: New York University Press.

32

No More Family Secrets

Marcia Cohn Spiegel

One afternoon in the fall of 1957 I recognized that I was turning into my mother. It was an ordinary day. Horrible. Hearing a strange noise in the kitchen, I rushed in and found water pouring from the washing machine all over the floor. In my panic I couldn't remember the location of the shutoff valve. My frantic calls to plumbers went unanswered. I watched the laundry room and kitchen turn into a swimming pool before I was able to stop the flow. After I soaked up the mess with every towel available and I was ready to sit down with a cold drink, I found that someone had left the freezer door ajar. Ice cream had melted and dripped over everything, and all of the meat was defrosting. I had just stocked the freezer from a sale and now everything was ruined.

I was barely holding myself together, when the kids started acting up. Three little girls, two, four, and five years old, began fighting over a toy. The details are lost in history; I could feel the tension rising and knew that an eruption was near. I was terrified of the feelings of rage and violence that engulfed me. I didn't want to lose my temper. I didn't want to explode. I wanted to be calm and rational, and settle the matter quietly. But the fighting escalated, as did my fury. Desperately I phoned my parents and told them that I needed them to come, before there was an outburst I knew I would regret.

"Well," was my father's response, "if you would stay home more often and take care of things, you wouldn't have these problems. You need to pay attention to your house and family and not be running around amusing yourself."

What had I done that was so terrible? I spent one morning each week at the park, and while the girls were in child care I took tap dancing lessons with a group of other mothers. Was that so bad? Occasionally I attended a sisterhood meeting at the synagogue. Not exactly a hectic social schedule.

"Sorry," my mother said, "I have a bridge game. We'll come over on the weekend. Maybe we'll play some cards and you can relax."

The weekend was three days away, but I needed help immediately. By five o'clock the house was in a state of bedlam. The girls were fussy and hungry, but I wouldn't let them snack so close to dinner. It would ruin their appetites. That was how I was raised and I knew it was the right thing to do. I was tired, depressed, and in tears.

"Please, behave yourselves," I pleaded. "I'm very angry and upset. If you don't stop it this minute, I don't know what will happen."

When I was little my mother would become furious, scolding me, screaming at me, sometimes even throwing things at me. I never knew what I had done to provoke her. The outbursts came from nowhere. I promised myself then that I would always remember the feelings and never treat my children like that. Now, when I was on the verge of just such an explosion, I would at least warn them and make perfectly clear what they were doing to make me angry. As if a hungry, fidgety two-year-old would understand my rational explanations. I could feel the knot in my stomach grow, my pulse race, my head pound. I couldn't hold it in any longer. I dumped their toy box out on the floor and started to throw the toys at them.

"Now are you happy?" I shrieked. "You pick up each of these things and put them away neatly. I don't want to hear another sound from any of you." The girls became ashen. They looked terrified. What had happened to their mother? Who was this witch who was screaming and throwing things? They cowered in fear. But I couldn't stop myself. I shouted things at them that even now, more than forty years later, I don't want to think about or repeat. When I finally came to my senses, I was horrified at my behavior, deeply ashamed. I had no idea how to apologize for what I had done.

I couldn't wait until my husband, Sid, got home to give me a hand smoothing out some of the calamities. He was always home by six. Dinner was cooking, the table was set, but he didn't come. At seven I called his office; the switchboard was shut down for the night. At seven-thirty I decided to break our long-standing rule of sitting down to dinner together, and fed the children and put them to bed. I was frantic with worry. This had never happened before. Should I call the police? The hospitals? At eight he arrived with a silly grin, staggering. Drunk! I couldn't believe it. There had been a meeting with the salesmen. It ended late and they decided to stop for a drink. I didn't know whether to laugh or cry.

"But why didn't you call? You knew I was expecting you."

"No one else called their wives. I didn't know I needed your permission to go out for a drink."

That was how it began.

Sid got a better job. We were able to pay off all of his loans for college and graduate school and move to the suburbs. Soon there were five children. I was in a constant state of exhaustion from housework, child care, and carpools. Sid's drinking continued. At first there were more late nights at work, then daily drinking at home. A sixteen-ounce "martini" of vodka or gin before dinner, a highball, sixteen ounces of straight scotch after dinner, then he passed out, or, euphemistically, went to bed early. Despite the heavy drinking, he got up every morning and went to work. Apparently he functioned well at the office, because he got raises and frequent promotions. But at home it was a different story. No one else seemed to be aware of his drinking problem. We kept the secret hidden behind closed doors, along with my escalating anger and violent explosions toward the children.

I knew where to turn for help. "Dear Abby" advised reaching out for help to your family, your clergy, and/or a therapist. I figured it was worth a try. First I turned to my parents, who assured me that if only I would change, everything would be fine. Sid was a good man, successful and quiet. "After all, he married you, didn't he?" Their response left me feeling worthless and ashamed. I knew I would not be able to trust them to help me salvage my marriage. When I went to my rabbi, I got a lecture on Jewish drinking patterns: Jews were not alcoholic. Therefore if Sid had a drinking problem, it was my fault. When I changed what I was doing to trigger his drinking, things would improve. In desperation I turned to a psychologist. Once more I was reminded that since Jews don't drink, Sid couldn't be an alcoholic, but was only responding to my actions. Everything was my fault. Sid was not responsible.

I felt betrayed by everyone I counted on for help. I couldn't trust anyone with my feelings of confusion. How could I tell anyone what I did? No one to whom I had turned asked how I was doing, how I was coping with the children. I was certainly not going to volunteer any information knowing that it would lower me even further in their esteem. No one else saw what happened when I was alone with the children. I was deeply ashamed of my loss of control.

The pattern of the episodes continued as they had begun. First there would be some incident, a fight, a household emergency, an emotional scene, usually when we were all hungry and tired. Then I would warn the children to behave. I would tell them what was making me angry. However, they wouldn't stop what they were doing. I would try to contain myself before I exploded in a fury of screaming, cursing, throwing, tearing, and breaking things. I was left with feelings of overwhelming, unexpressed remorse.

The world saw us as a close-knit family, active in sports, Scouts, synagogue, and community activities. Sid and I went out to dinner and to the theater regularly, and often played bridge with friends. We had an active weekend social life with his business associates. His public behavior was appropriate, even exemplary. He was rarely seen drunk. He did most of his drinking at home before we went out, and after we returned. The children, however, were nervous when their friends came over. Would their dad be drunk and do something to embarrass them? Would it be safe to drive with him? They could never anticipate what would happen. Meanwhile I played "Let's Pretend," acting out the role of the happy suburban housewife. With five children and no way to earn a living, I knew I had to stick it out and make the best of it. There was no place to turn.

Because of our shared predicament, the children and I grew very close. At night after Sid passed out, we sat around the family room table playing games, doing puzzles, and just talking. We talked about our problems, friendships, relationships, and activities. However, I shared more with them than I should have. My parents, rabbi, and therapist had all denied the truth of my life, but here was an audience who knew what was really happening and understood my concerns. The secrets and feelings I kept bottled up needed to be released, and the children became my unwilling confidants. I told them about my disappointments and despair but reassured them, and myself, that I really loved their father despite it all.

While our lives seesawed between emotional extremes, my sense of isolation, depression, and worthlessness grew. One morning I spotted an article in the local paper describing a group for families of alcoholics. Even though I knew that Jews weren't alcoholic, I cut it out and stuck it in my wallet. More than a year passed before I could open that wrinkled piece of paper and phone the number to ask for help. I was given the time and location of the next meeting.

I was shaking with fear and nervousness as I drove to the meeting. As I walked into St. Peter by the Sea Presbyterian Church, I heard a woman saying, "If you are in a relationship with an alcoholic, remember: you did not cause his drinking. He has freedom of choice, and no matter how much he blames you, it is his choice."

I couldn't believe what I had heard. Instantly I knew that I had found a home. Here were people who shared my experiences. They lived the same life, with the hidden secrets and shame, but they were happy, giggling, smiling, and joking. I was eager to learn how they survived, and the process changed my life forever.

I was the only Jew in this close-knit community, and each week I struggled with the discomfort of sitting in a room dominated by a simple large cross, reciting the Lord's Prayer. But I needed the support of the other women, so I was faithful in my attendance. Trying to find a way to deal with my distress, I began to look for answers within Judaism.

Our meetings utilized the Twelve Steps of Alcoholics Anonymous, which at first were totally alien to me. The first two steps, "admitting that we are powerless . . . our lives have become unmanageable, . . . that belief in a Power greater than ourselves can restore us to sanity," were counterintuitive. How could a belief in anything alter what was going on? The third step, which requires that we turn our will and our lives over to the care of that Higher Power, negated everything I had learned about being a Jew. As I understood our religion, we do not turn our lives over to anyone or anything. We must always remain vigilant and in control. Relying on God could be dangerous. We can only rely on ourselves. I went back to the rabbi to discuss these contradictions, and he assured me that the Twelve Steps were based on Christian dogma and could not be reconciled with Jewish beliefs and practice. Despite his admonitions, I continued attending meetings. I felt as if my survival depended on the support I received from the other women. They were the only people who accepted and believed in me.

In the synagogue each week I examined the prayer book closely, searching for answers to the questions I was wrestling with, trying to find some connection to the Twelve-Step program. One Saturday morning I had a great awakening. It was as if I were reading the prayers for the very first time: the first three steps were right there in the prayer book. In our early morning prayer we say "modeh ani lefanecha," we give thanks to God for restoring our soul to us. Later in the Amidah, the ancient standing prayer, we pray " . . . Our lives are in your hands; our souls are ever in your keeping. . . ." In the familiar closing hymn, Adon Olam, we turn our soul over to God. Many of the Psalms describe how God will restore us to wholeness. What could be a clearer expression of our belief in a Higher Power to whom we trust our souls and our lives, and who can restore us to sanity?

I began to understand that it wasn't Judaism that didn't believe; it was Jews. Most of us recite prayers by rote without examining their content. Persecution, pogroms, and the memory of the recent Shoah, the Holocaust, reinforced the idea that we can only trust ourselves. We certainly could not turn our lives over to anyone else, even to a God who might betray us. It was clear to me that in order to survive I had to find a way to believe in a Higher Power, to understand God not as a great puppeteer who manipulated us in history or who abandoned us when we needed Him. I needed a God who was a creative force in nature, who nurtured and surrounded me and accompanied me through the day. As I studied Jewish thought, I found that feminists had reclaimed just this mystical aspect of God, the Shechinah, the indwelling presence of divinity. The spirit of Shechinah permeated my life, enfolded me with love, protection, and guidance.

Turning my life over to the Shechinah allowed me to give up control of everyone around me. I would be accountable for myself, but I could let my Higher Power run the world; I didn't have to be responsible for everyone and everything else. I was able to separate myself from other people's opinions of Sid, or me, or the children. Haircuts and clothes stopped being a source of contention between the boys and myself. One of the major causes of family battles had always been neatness. I wanted the house to be immaculate. Everything had to be put away at night, beds neatly made in the morning, nothing left on the floor. Dishes were done after every meal and the kitchen left spotless no matter what time of night it was or how tired I felt. I lived as if *House Beautiful* magazine might arrive at any moment to take pictures for a double-page spread.

I learned to close doors. In a flash of understanding, I realized that God didn't care if there were socks on the floor or dishes in the sink. Unfortunately, by the time I had this awakening, the girls had left home for college, and didn't get to enjoy this more relaxed atmosphere. Sometimes they remind me that they would have preferred this new mother to the one who raised them. The paradox was that in accepting my powerlessness, I began to find my power.

The fourth through tenth steps are probably the easiest ones for many Jews to accept because, like me, we assume guilt for everything that happens around us. These steps require that we make an inventory of our wrongs, admit them to God and to ourselves, ask our Higher Power to remove our shortcomings, and then make amends to those whom we have harmed. These steps to repentance are mirrored in Judaism. Moses Maimonides, the twelfth-century sage, taught that there are four steps to teshuvah, turning our lives around: first we must acknowledge what we have done wrong, and we must go to those whom we have wronged, ask their forgiveness, and make atonement as best we can. Then we must change our behavior so that when confronted with the same situation, we do not repeat our wrongdoing. Each year the High Holy Days are focused on these concepts. From Rosh Hashanah to Yom Kippur we are enjoined to ask forgiveness, not only of God, but from all those whom we have injured. I learned that the month preceding the Days of Awe, the Hebrew month of Elul, is to be spent in introspection, examining our lives so that we can cleanse our souls in preparation for the Days of Atonement. It is a month dedicated to healing relationships with family and friends.

Although I found that it was easy to admit what I had done wrong in some areas, I still could not face what happened between me and the children. At St. Peter's, where women shared with one another the deepest secrets of their relationships with their spouses and families, no one disclosed how they acted against their children with words or deeds. I was not ready, even in this safe haven, to reveal to myself or to anyone else my shameful truth. It took many years of slow growth before I could make this final admission. When I finally achieved enough strength and self-assuredness, I was able to write a letter to each of the children in which I admitted what I had done and asked their forgiveness. It was enormously painful to do so, because it meant that first I had to acknowledge my actions to myself.

I realized as I wrote my letter that many mothers, my own mother included, acted as I had. They did not lash out at their children because they hated them or wanted to destroy them; these mothers lashed out because they were helpless, alone, unsupported, powerless, frustrated, and exhausted; just as in my house, there were no witnesses—only mother and children. The ancient rabbis created an image of the Jewish family that is harmonious, loving, and protective, where there is shalom bayit, peace in the house. Contemporary religious leaders reiterate that image. If the family is not like that, we judge ourselves failures. What was meant as an ideal has become the yardstick by which we measure ourselves and come up wanting. We don't hear other women talking about how angry they become, how they hit their children or scream at them. So we don't share our stories. We remain isolated while we present a happy face to the world.

Writing to my children was only the first step on our road to healing as a family. I went to therapy with some of my daughters and spoke at length with the boys. It meant that I listened to their memories without denial; memories that often made me cringe. It also meant that they heard my story and began to understand who I was. Although I couldn't take back events of the past, I could acknowledge that they took place. I struggled not to be defensive or put the blame on someone else. I had to admit my behavior. The process was different for each child. Some of our relationships are still fragile. But we can come together now as a family openly, with no secrets.

The Twelfth Step tells us that as a result of our spiritual awakening, we carry the message to others. I have dedicated my life to seeing that in the future, no one who turns to the Jewish community for help will be rebuffed as I was. No one who seeks help should be told by a professional, "Jews don't do that." Through writing and workshops I began to address dysfunction in Jewish families.

When I first considered writing this story, I had to ask myself why I was prepared to expose myself to a large audience using my own name, to tell a secret that I had kept hidden all of my life. I realize that I am respected by many people and could risk losing their respect. I am writing for every woman who has felt the rage and turmoil that I felt, and didn't know how to stop, and was too ashamed to ask for help. Nowadays, families have an opportunity to learn more about their feelings and behavior, as well as techniques for coping with their children from books, courses, television, and therapy. Newspapers and magazines provide information about nutrition and its relationship to mental health. Because hunger can be an emotional trigger, we are taught to eat nutritious snacks between meals and to give them to our children. We know about biofeedback, yoga, and meditation to help us relax. Even high schools provide training in parenting skills and child development. But there are still those moments when the demons rise, when the fears and emotions grow, and we are terrified of what will follow. I wrote this story for those mothers—to tell them not to keep the secret hidden. Open the closed door. Don't wait. Find someone who will listen. Find help.

I also wrote this for other women, whose children are grown, but whose relationships still bear scars from long ago. Among my friends I see adult children who repress their angry memories while trying to maintain family relationships, or who choose to avoid family gatherings and sever connections. I know the pain of both parents and children. I want to tell them that we all lose out if energy is spent in concealment and denial when healing is possible. It will take more than just saying a perfunctory "I'm sorry." It won't be easy. You will have to listen to each other without judgment or blame. Some may be able to do it alone; others may need to do this work with the help of a therapist or spiritual counselor.

I believe that this is a story of hope and even of redemption. As I watch my daughter, Linda, raise her children, I know that it is possible to break the cycle of abuse. My children and I have struggled to come to terms with the past so that we can move forward. We have managed to come back to each other with love and support. Before that could happen, I had to name what I had done and rebuild my children's trust in me. I have grown and changed. I barely remember the angry woman who terrified her children. But there are times that I flinch when I see a film or read a story, because I recognize myself in the character of the abusive parent. I cry for who I was, for the mother I could have been, for the mother my children deserved but didn't have. Now my children and I can be friends, but when they close their eyes and remember *mother,* only they know whom they see.

33

If I'd Known How to Be a Jewish Mother, I Would Have Been One

Helen Gardner

I have set out to tell my own story as a Jewish mother, rather than my mother's story. Yet I feel strongly that nothing I say or am as a person, a Jew, or a mother can be understood without reference to my relationship with my mother, so I will start with a brief account of that before proceeding to myself.

I was born in Melbourne, Australia, in October 1939. My adult brother was in the army at the time, and my father had just been placed in a psychiatric hospital. My mother left me in the hospital for ten months while she worked to earn a living. She brought me home to live with her when she found a woman she considered suitable to look after me. When I was two, she arranged for me to live in the country about 100 miles away, with the pious Christian woman who had been caring for me in my mother's home. I lived there as a devout Baptist until I was nine, when I was brought back to Melbourne and sent to an Anglican boarding school for two years, after which I rejoined my mother in her home. My mother visited me two or three times a year during my seven years in the country, and I spent two-week holidays with her every Christmas. My father had died when I was eight, without my ever having known him. When I was thirteen, my mother remarried and I went to live with her and my stepfather. Some months later, they had the first of what became their ongoing fights. This one was over me. My stepfather threatened to burn my clothes and throw me out, and to protect me, my mother sent me to live with my brother and his family for a year or so, after which I returned to the intermittent battlefield that was their home.

My mother did not like the child she got back. She had expected me to be like her and had no idea why I was not. She was, however, quite clear that she had done nothing to deserve such a dreadful child. There was something wrong with me. I was wicked and ungrateful. Who did I think had paid for my food and my clothes and my piano and dancing lessons? Who had brought me beautiful presents? I was unnatural, giving my love to the hired help instead of to her: she, who had slaved for years to see that I got proper care. She set about remaking me in her image, and I fought her tooth and nail. She lived in an enmeshed family situation, to which she wanted me to belong. I felt suffocated and found her intensely intrusive, and I struggled for distance. She was fashion-conscious and immaculate. I set out to be a frump. She wanted me to leave school at fifteen and be a secretary. I went to University as a science student. She wanted me to get married at seventeen to a nice Jewish boy in Daddy's business and swan around with a live-in maid to look after the house and the children while I played cards. I got married at twenty-three to a teacher and worked as a scientist. But I did marry somebody Jewish. Although we argued over many things, being Jewish was not negotiable. She was not going to have any "Christian nonsense" in her home. She had made it crystal clear that she would sit shivah if I married out, and I couldn't cope with being abandoned again. My particular form of revenge was to decide, together with my fiancé, that we would become Orthodox when we married. She didn't like it, but she could hardly complain.

There was nothing malicious about my mother. She believed all her life that the decisions she made on my behalf were what was best for me. She never meant to hurt me, but her decisions have reverberated throughout all aspects of my life in ways small and large, conscious and unconscious.

SO! I had four children, and I tried to bring them up Orthodox, but every one of them picked up my ambivalence about Judaism. I believed that I had given up being Christian and become Jewish, and it took me a long time to realize that I had done neither; that, like many children who are forced to change cultures in their formative years, I had essentially wound up with neither one nor the other; that my Orthodoxy was empty. It had no content. The externals were all there, but something was missing on the inside. I began to study Judaism, to look more deeply at its philosophy and beliefs, its values, its laws and practices, its ways of looking at the world. As a child, Christian beliefs and values had given form and substance to my world and it took a long time for Jewish beliefs and values to fill the void left when Christianity disappeared from my life.

By the time I came to terms with Judaism and learned to untangle it from my rage at my mother, by the time I began to find my own identity and stopped having knee-jerk reactions to the values my mother imposed on me, it was too late to give my children a positive approach to Judaism. And somehow, what I remember are the disasters. Friday nights, for instance, were usually dreadful. After a long hard week, tempers were short. The kids became more reluctant to participate in the rituals as they got older. "Do I have to (come for kiddush, say benshen, go to shul . . .)" became the identifiable catch cry of Shabbat. Though I do remember one Friday night when I won. I'll leave you to put the aggression into the voices. The dialogue went like this: Child 1 to one of the others: "Shut up!" Child 2: "You shut up!" Child 3: "Leave him alone!" Child 4: "You keep out of this!" I said I wished it wasn't Shabbat so I could have tape-recorded it, and I proceeded to say it back to them just the way they had said it, and everyone laughed, and the tension went and we had a nice evening, for a change. But I didn't manage that often.

We sent them to a Jewish school, but most of the other children came from nonobservant families, and we had tears and resentment over the parties on Shabbat or Yom Tov (Holy Days), or the trips to MacDonald's to which they couldn't go. Our shul had few children their age, the Jewish youth groups met some miles from our home, and our children weren't interested enough to make the long walk. Most of all, I think, we didn't know how to make Shabbat something positive for them. For us, it was a welcome time-out from the working week. But they didn't want time out. They wanted activity and fun and to do the things their school friends were doing, and we weren't able to compensate for what they were missing out on. Only Pesach has positive memories: the time we all trooped outside to look for Halley's comet; the time we opened the door for Elijah and found, poised to knock, our daughter's best friend, who had decided to drop in. On second night we have always had our close friends, whose children are their close friends. The tradition of a fun-filled second night Seder has remained as they have grown and found partners.

Of course there was also the yearly cycle of festivals. Purim (thank goodness for my mother-in-law's magical abilities with a sewing machine and her inventiveness with ideas for costumes), Rosh Hashanah with its apples and honey, Yom Kippur with its solemnity and fasting, Chanukah when we always seemed to be the only family that sang all the verses of Maoz Tsur. But they seem to have passed by in an indiscriminate blur, with nothing to distinguish one year from any other.

My children are all grown up now, and Judaism doesn't really figure much in any of their lives. If I talk to them about Jewish groups, they ask why they should join something they couldn't invite half their friends to. My eldest daughter married out. Her husband was hurt by our distinct lack of welcome, and although we have tried to heal it since, a rift persists to this day. Daughter number two married a Jewish partner, but it was more accidental than planned. My youngest son has just become engaged to a non-Jewish girl from England. I hope we will manage a better welcome the second time around. My other son is also unlikely to marry a Jewish partner. I don't know if my sons will say Kaddish for us, apart from maybe a couple of days for minyan. Maybe they will. Maybe they won't. They don't know either. My grandchildren are unlikely to have much connection with Judaism. It makes me sad to think that the unbroken chain of Jewish generations that produced my husband and me as Jews may well end with us. I have struggled so hard to be Jewish, and I have not managed to pass the identification on. Judaism will continue, but my descendents are unlikely to be a part of it. If being a Jewish mother means having children and grandchildren for whom being Jewish matters, then my mother succeeded better than I did. If I'd known how to be a Jewish mother I would have been one. But I refused to emulate my mother's methods, and mine didn't work.

But I have great kids, who have great values, and I'm proud of them. I succeeded in other ways. Sarcasm and put-downs were never part of our interactions with them, and grounding or other forms of punishment were rare. If they did things we didn't like, we talked to them and explained why we didn't like it and asked them not to do it again, and by and large they didn't. We didn't have daily battles about making beds or cleaning up messes, because I didn't worry about these things. I didn't make my own bed, beyond straightening it up at night, so I didn't see that they had to make theirs. I found it easier to learn to walk through the mess without noticing it than to have daily hassles about cleaning it up. My cleaning lady came once a week and made the beds and cleaned and tidied, and I let the house deteriorate until she came again. Interestingly, as adults, my children all seem quite capable of keeping a clean, tidy house, and they are all better cooks than I. Self defense, probably.

If I said "yes" or "no" to something, and they could show me why I should change my mind, I would. When my second daughter was turning twelve she wanted to have her ears pierced, and I said *absolutely not.* She said, "You won't let me, only because you never wanted to have *your* ears pierced," and I knew she was right. I was trying to make her be like me, which is what my mother did to me. So I let her get her ears pierced, and I also began to understand that looking nice was not a betrayal of my integrity. I began to care more about my own appearance as well.

When my children went to stay over with friends, they would come home and give me a cuddle and tell me they were glad they didn't live in that house, and their friends would often say they wished they lived with us. Although the children sometimes told lies to get out of the house, there were times when I was the only mother in the group who knew where they really were and what they were really doing. I wasn't comfortable with that secrecy, but since no mother ever asked me, I never had to decide what to say.

My children think I'm a wonderful mother, and my friends thought so too. Only I, who suffered the incongruence between the caring outside and the struggling inside, felt that it was all a sham. But when I watch my eldest daughter with her own children I can see that I must have been OK. My children are all loyal, caring, compassionate friends. They care about society and the underprivileged. My eldest daughter and her husband and kids, together with my youngest son, have recently taken a year out to teach about sustainable agriculture to people in third world countries. On their own time and money.

My mother was the last person in the world I would have turned to for help, and I had a quite conscious expectation that when my children turned nineteen or twenty they, too, in the natural process of growing up, would go away and lead their lives with little reference to me. I was quite shocked to find that long after they reached that age they continued to come home to discuss important issues. I came to see that as a sign of success as a mother. More recently I have come to understand something even more significant. When I was a young wife and mother, I thought it was something of an advantage to be able to maintain a distance from my mother. It meant I could be relatively impervious to her constant attempts to lay a guilt trip on me for the things I did not do for her. Now that I approach the mother-adult child relationship from the other side, I see that no matter how old they get, at significant moments of their lives my children, especially my daughters, still want their mother. My mother knew that she was missing out on something fundamental. I did not. In her usual fashion she ascribed this to her rotten luck in having given birth to a daughter like me. But until I saw it in my own children, I did not realize that in having never wanted my mother I, too, had missed out on something fundamental. If my mother succeeded in having a Jewish child where I failed, I have succeeded in creating a deep relationship with my children where she failed.

OK, so my children aren't very Jewish. But they don't have to be like me, and they don't have to be the way I'd like them to be. They're fine people just the way they are. I think I'm a good person, a good Jew, and a good mother. I'm not too sure about the combinations, though.

34

Chopped Liver and Sour Grapes:
Jewish but Not a Mother

Sharon L. Siegel

Picture the expression on the faces of those who accidentally bite into a sour grape. They hardly know how to get rid of the taste quickly enough, especially if they cannot spit it right out again. The lips pucker, the eyes dart around the room, the body language screams: "Yech, this cannot be!" I've seen this many times. One typical instance is when a friendly temple-goer, doing "outreach" to welcome me, a stranger, asks my name and immediately follows it up with: "So, are you married?" to which I reply, "No, I am divorced," and the other comes right back with, "Do you have children?" The answers being negative on both counts, I feel the sour-grapes energy begin to rise. "Oy!" it seems she is thinking. "Now what can we possibly talk about after I proudly show pictures of my own children and grandchildren?" She wants me to know she has lived a respectable life and is a good Jew. Since we are sharing intimate details of our lives, shall I mention now or later that I am a lesbian feminist, too?

The Jewish community fails to value me as an individual. Wife, mother, and the centrality of the home with children are the only validated and understood "norms" for Jewish women. Like Vicki Lindner (1989, p. 284), I always ". . . wanted to be a normal female, part of a world of close, fertile families, joyfully reproducing themselves and being able to talk about my sameness." For conversational

I wish to express my appreciation to Rachel Josefowitz Siegel for her mentoring and support during many years, and to Gil Schorr for decades of constructive, loving criticism in editing my written creations.

purposes, it does not matter that I am "a doctor," which carries pride primarily if it is bragged about by one's parents; nor that I am an excellent psychotherapist and an activist for peace in the Middle East; that I built sections of my home with my own hands; have sat on numerous boards of directors; or that I am simply a very nice person and a mensch (an honorable person). The die is cast if I am barren; I fail to exist as a person one would want to know better. I am chopped liver—or maybe chopped liver in the Jewish community is even more respectable than a Jewish woman who does not mother.

I am a Jew whose core vibrates with the unavoidable patriarchal teachings, including the command to "be fruitful and multiply" (Genesis 1:28). Yeah, right. Would I have any other choice for selection of a first commandment? I am not a biblical scholar. It would be more accurate to say I am antibiblical. Yet this command runs through my mind despite grand efforts to ignore it. I have not complied; I am considered pitiable, or bad, recalcitrant, obstinate, or perhaps even mentally unstable. In 1986, Menachem Brayer wrote: "Children are the most cherished blessing . . . a childless couple is considered poor, even dead" (p. 60). None of the patriarchs told our Jewish community to see the childless woman as having other substantive rights or respectable alternative interests.

The approval of my immediate Jewish family was never really palpable, but when I divorced, a rare thing to do in 1966, and then ten years later told them that I was a lesbian, my parents could not continue to acknowledge me to their Jewish community. Presently, Mother still agonizes about introducing me to her friends, even though I assure her that I will not mention lesbianism. But her Jewish friends, thoroughly delighted to "try to be friendly and get to know me," are struck dumb after I am introduced as only a doctor, and without a husband or children. This has happened not only in my mother's Jewish world but in countless other Jewish settings. I throb with a longing to feel genuinely welcome in the greater Jewish network. I personally wish that this societal dynamic simply reflected a dysfunctional family, but it is the opinion of the Jewish majority, rather than of only a small fringe group of nonthinkers.

The always inadvertent ostracism from Jews is far more painful to me than from society as a whole because I so need alliances with my culture, tradition, ethnicity, and Jewish family. I am considered childless because the untimely death of my only child qualifies me as barren in the Jewish world. Although many women consciously choose to remain childless, I did not. I am blessed to have birthed a baby even though he died at the age of three days. His life and his death shaped the adult—and now the aging—woman that I am. When people ask if I have children, they become uncomfortable, even if compassionate, as I explain that my only child is deceased. This is more than they want to know. I am keenly aware, especially on Mother's Day, of my belief that a woman earns the right to call herself a mother by mothering responsibly twenty-four hours a day, seven days a week—and not simply by having been pregnant and delivered offspring. Yet I cannot deny that my son Sandor Marc Siegel was born. Bearing Sandy touched my soul, even though his birth does not count for much in the Jewish community, where one must produce and raise live issue. But every Mother's Day, I secretly celebrate the moments that I was a mother.

My fear of losing another child, or having a seriously sick baby to raise alone, also contributed to my lack of courage to bear or adopt a child, although I now wish I had done so. I have wanted to join in the deeper understanding and sharing that mothers have, not only to hold status in my Jewish culture, nor just for ego gratification and "identity," but because I have always overflowed with maternal yearnings to love and raise a child. My feelings of protectiveness about children have not changed throughout the years. One might ask how a woman can keep that "I don't care what happens to me as long as my baby is OK" mentality when there is no baby. I don't know, but I have.

I am among the many Jews who cannot imagine life without children, even though this is a picture of my life. I therefore have inner pain as I manage my envy and jealousy of Jewish women who are able to engage happily in long diatribes about their children and grandchildren, or family dynamics. Various authors, some of whom are listed in the references at the end of this chapter, address this issue of relationships among Jewish women. Susan Weidman Schneider (1984, p. 377) quotes Vicki Rosenstreich:

> It is not in the banks of Wall Street or the halls of Ivy that women created the bonds and harmonies that resonated

through all walks of life. The nature of birthing and nursing and caring for dependent creatures shaped the nature of our relationships to each other and our gender capacities for empathy and sympathy.

I have problems relating to mothers in casual conversation or for friendship, especially when I can feel their uneasiness that children are not a part of my life experience. At Jewish events, such as parties and weddings, even the professional women prefer to discuss their children rather than careers or other interests. The lesbian-elders community can often be a refuge, as so many of us did not raise children. But this community rarely includes substantial numbers of Jews.

Regardless of the fact that my life has been truly abundant—with a career, friends I love, spiritual connections that are important to me, education, domestic partners who have significantly altered my life, joy and prosperity—what I have wanted more than anything else throughout my life has been to be a wife, including to a woman, and a mother. It is possible, although not entirely likely, that my own feelings about being unmarried (according to religious and civil law) and childless are reflected back to me by people I meet in the Jewish community. However, when first meeting people I always find it enormously refreshing if they neither tell me their proud heterosexual marital status nor mention their children. When a Jew asks the question "Do you have children?" it begs for an affirmative answer. Perhaps this is also related to the post-Holocaust consciousness—the imperative to make up for those lost or never born (Schneider, 1984; Siegel, 1995). I argue that there are other very interesting things to talk about when encountering a stranger instead of limiting ourselves to the images and accomplishments of children.

Societal norms have significantly changed over time, and as we now move into the new millennium, more women than ever are choosing to be single mothers. Yet others for many reasons cannot, or choose not to, bear or adopt children. Fifteen years ago, the word insemination was not known except as it related to animal husbandry; in vitro fertilization was unheard-of. Children of lesbians were being taken away by almost any challenger, including state departments of children's services, families, and neighbors. Until relatively recently, ex-husbands and almost anyone else could sue and win custody of lesbians' children based on "unfit mother" accusations. Now, of course, many lesbians and gay men are having or adopting children, especially among the young and even the single people in our community. Do I wish I had been born later? Of course! And I would have been a carpenter, but that is another story.

My relationships with mothers in the generalized Jewish sisterhood, with the women of Hadassah or in my own lesbian and gay synagogue, suffer because of the absence of children. I identify with Naomi Bluestone's withdrawal from Judaism. She states: "Every woman is preoccupied by children and grandchildren . . . it becomes uncomfortable, embarrassing and inconvenient to participate . . . *Latkes? Dreidels? Esrog?* [Jewish pancakes; toy tops; a festive citron for the holiday of Sukkoth] . . . these are the toys of childhood, resurrected for each generation only when the generations continue, otherwise they are of no value!" (1981, p. 933). My lack of offspring separates me from Jewish participation. I am in galut, albeit inadvertently or unconsciously caused, during holidays that are centered on children's activities.

Just five years ago there were rarely any children in attendance at our lesbian and gay synagogue—we might all have been arrested for contributing to the delinquency of a minor. Imagine! Now there are multitudes of young ones at temple, and extensive programs to meet their needs. The majority of lesbian women there are mothering or have plans to do so. I am glad to celebrate the births, Bar and Bat Mitzvahs, and holidays with the young, but it is also a wrenching experience. Not only will I never be the proud parent at B'nai Mitzvahs, I will also never receive the gift of that delighted acknowledgment that people shower on the blessed new parents; never enjoy people cooing over my baby; never feel the awesome bond that new parents describe upon first eye contact with a newborn. I will never have the involvement in my synagogue that I would have had through raising children there.

I do not mean to say that my joys are not celebrated in the temple, but the effect is very different, and cannot be compared. And I am not saying that my temple or my own self-worth are completely tied to having children. But my self-esteem shatters and reshatters when

I see younger lesbians and other single women bearing, adopting, and in various ways raising children in our temple, and I have learned to restore and rebuild it by my own sheer will.

Nothing I can ever do, however wonderful or life-improving for others, allows membership in the elite and unacknowledged clubs of "real" mothers. My pregnancy stories, which are about great health and preparation for the baby, are not welcome because the end of that story is so tragic. However valid my advice regarding children, it is not based on personal experience. People do not want to hear about my very interesting cats, or about the clients whom I have surrogate-mothered and helped to restructure into healthy adults, nor about my wise counsel to parents. My friend and esteemed colleague, Dr. Lillian Klempfner, insists that I have "mothered plenty," but other "mothering," including therapeutic, just does not count when mothers are talking.

Faith Benedetti (1996, p. 22) quotes Terry Madden: "We give birth to relationships, to works of art, to hope, to children, and to each other." Faith comments further, "These words include the many possibilities of what it means to give birth." I feel caustic and angry as I read these and many other such accounts in literature that try to equate the idea of birthing something other than children with being a mother. I have given birth to relationships, creative works of art, hope, good work toward world peace, political and altruistic agencies, and I love my two dear god(dess) daughters. However, with the wisdom of a Crone and as a lifelong Jew, I know that if a woman has not given birth or at least raised a child, the Jewish community does not hold her in esteem.

Will the Jewish community ever honor the childless woman as a source of joy and strength rather than as a nonentity or burden? Worse, perhaps, is the fact that due to sexism, homophobia, and ageism, being a lesbian "older woman" is a curiosity and/or cause for prejudice, even among more "liberal" Jews. In addition to not being able to talk about a husband or significant other, I also cannot put the other at ease by discussing mothering or grandmothering. As a Jew, being childless causes even more invisibility than solely being a lesbian-elder.

When I first began to share the excitement about writing this essay, my own mother's response was that the Jewish community is very accepting of everyone, and the problem I describe does not exist. But my experience is not so unique. I believe my mother is protective of how the Jewish world is seen. She does not want Jewish dirty linen shaken in public, and is upset that I will not join in her adamant denial that there is a problem.

I suggest, for Jewish disbelievers, that you walk a mile in the shoes of a nonmothering woman. Go to Sabbath services at an unknown synagogue and introduce yourself as a woman who does not have children; share and explain other aspects of your life. Try to carry on a conversation. If you want to add spice, say you divorced thirty years ago or mention that you are a lesbian. I will be interested to hear you say, in response to the treatment you receive: "What am I, chopped liver?"

I dream of a Jewish community that challenges misogyny and offers a wholehearted welcome to all women, one that counts all women equally. Women should always be lauded for their contributions to the world, including mothering, but not excluding other achievements that make the planet a better place.

It is possible that the Jewish response to childlessness is not significantly different from that of gentile communities. However, I expect so much more from my people. I want us to stop oppressing women who for any reason do not mother, normalize and acknowledge the frequency and acceptability of childlessness, and talk about it openly. As Jewish women, I want us to develop and discuss many aspects of our lives in addition to talking about our children— or lack of children—in a world that gives equal honor to all lifestyles. And I want to be here to celebrate it in this lifetime.

Finally, will my individual identity, rather than an identity as a mother and grandmother, ever suffice in my own heart? I hope and I pray for inner peace. I should live so long.

REFERENCES

Benedetti, Faith (1996). Reflections on the untried womb. *Sage Woman*, #36, (p. 22).

Bluestone, Naomi (1981). Exodus from Eden: One woman's experience. In Jacob R. Marcus (Ed.), *The American Jewish woman: A documentary history* (p. 933). Hoboken, NJ: Ktav Publishing.

Brayer, Menachem M. (1986). *The Jewish woman in rabbinic literature.* Hoboken, NJ: KTAV Publishing House.

Lindner, Vicki (1989). Saying no to motherhood. In Carol Diament (Ed.), *Jewish marital status* (p. 284). Northvale, NJ: Jason Aronson.

Schneider, Susan Weidman (1984). *Jewish and female: Choices and changes in our lives today.* New York: Simon & Schuster.

Siegel, Rachel Josefowitz (1995). The Jewish woman's body: Her sexuality, body-image, self-esteem. In Kayla Weiner and Arinna Moon (Eds.), *Jewish women speak out: Expanding the boundaries of psychology* (pp. 41-53). Seattle, WA: Canopy Press.

35

My Two Lives

Barbara D. Holender

I learned to be a Jewish mother from my Jewish mother, a role model par excellence. She was a conventional housewife, mother of three, secretary for my father, community activist, artist. She was an ardent Zionist and gave me a love of Israel. Quite an act to follow.

I have given of myself to the Jewish community in my role as writer, program coordinator, and performer. Zionism has been a major focus of my life since childhood and Judaic studies a lifelong concentration.

Married to my childhood sweetheart, I, too, was a conventional homemaker, in the sense that I did not work outside the home. I certainly worked hard learning my craft as a poet, studying, writing, and illustrating stories for my children. My rewarding experiences as a mother were tempered by the challenge and heartache of coping over a thirty-year period with my husband's increasingly disabling rheumatoid arthritis, with all the attendant anxieties, adjustments and frustrations, and finally by his early death. Trouble can bring you together or it can tear you apart. We faced and endured everything together, right to the end. Looking back, I don't know how, but one does not live thirty years at a time. A day is a day, and that is manageable. Our kids saw that we didn't run from problems and that we loved and respected each other.

Being a mother was a great joy to me. I have had naches (pleasure) from my son and daughter all their lives, and they rarely gave me cause to worry. Of course there were occasional clashes, and like all kids they had growing pains. I often thought of my grandmother's saying, "kleine kinder kleine tzorres, ganze kinder ganze tzorres"—little children little troubles, big children big troubles. I considered it normal for four distinct personalities living together to disagree. We insisted on mutual respect, but not unquestioning submission.

Once when my son was about six, he objected violently to one of his father's arbitrary decisions. Loud stomping up the stairs. Much banging overhead. Down came Fred, marching around the dining room table brandishing a sign tacked to a yardstick: DADDY IS UNFAIR. Daddy *was* unfair; Daddy relented.

Unconditional love, high expectations, and a sense of humor seemed to work for us. Our concentration was on giving our children as stable a home as possible, and it was no martyrdom or sacrifice on our part, but the best work we ever did. Fred, born in 1952, and Judith, born in 1955, were children of the protest era. While many of their contemporaries were experimenting with drugs, and college campuses were erupting with violent demonstrations and sit-ins, our kids were occupied with music, athletics, and studies. They were politically aware, and our dinner table was a place for discussion. But they were not rebels.

If I could state in a word the most important lesson of parenting, it would be "listen." Listen, and you will learn from your children who they are, who they are becoming, what moves them toward or away from you. I had no idea who my children would be, and each stage of their lives was an illuminating surprise. They have always been interesting, lovable, and loving people. I had no careers in mind for them, no plan except to make sure they were well educated and exposed to as many experiences as possible, especially given the limitations of our family situation.

My husband showed great courage despite his constant pain and confinement to a wheelchair. An active, independent man, forced to change in mid-career, he adjusted to a sedentary profession and worked until a few months before his death at the age of fifty-five. Our life grew increasingly restricted, but we knew and our children knew what was important. They both graduated from fine colleges and became successful in their chosen professions. Along the way the family had many good times, even when things were toughest, and my husband and I were there for our children's performances and games and shared all important occasions. At the end of my husband's life they were there for us constantly. For that I am immeasurably grateful.

As adults they have continued to be a source of satisfaction. Both married Jewish partners whom I love, and both have passed on their strong Jewish identity to their children.

Widowhood is a bizarre experience, impossible to understand unless one has been through it. It is a total dislocation. I was fifty-five, reeling from years of excruciating stress, the first of my circle to be bereaved. Surrounded by good friends, I tried to keep from imposing my emotions on them. I did what I've since found new widows commonly do—I ran from one thing to another, just kept going. My daughter was living at home, in her third year of law school, and we grieved together and separately. It was hard for her because she was very close to her father and because she was an adult child living at home after four years away at college. It was difficult for me because I tended to mother her. We solved that shortly after her return home by finding a code word, which she let fly when I was overmothering. That was all it took, that one word. I backed off, we both laughed, and a potential flare-up was defused.

That first year of widowhood was unreal. I went to temple every week to say Kaddish with my children, but I never really registered what had happened. I learned that being "beside oneself" was a literal description, as I watched myself in action as if from a distance. I was not a candidate for a support group, being a very private person, too spent to receive others' grief and having nothing to give. So I found a therapist who helped me through. And I wrote poetry, almost unconsciously. It was healing and clarifying for me. Often I did not know what was going on inside me until the poems came out. I called them my "bullet poems," because they erupted with such force. *Shivah Poems: Poems of Mourning* (Holender, 1986) was the outcome, my first book. It has resonated with people who have suffered losses of all kinds, and I feel gratified that my words help. Just a small illustration:

> Your dying sheared off my life
> like an earthquake the side of a building
> leaving all the rooms exposed, in which
> the comings and goings are as usual,
> there being no other place to live.

My son was extremely helpful. He and my attorney acquainted me with business details related to my husband's death and encouraged me to handle things myself, guiding me when I needed help. I had been taking care of the monthly bills and other household affairs for a long time, so I was not an uninformed widow all at sea. Now I became competent and independent in a new situation.

After my husband's death, I continued to have the holiday celebrations in my home, because it helped me maintain my role in the family. Gradually my children began to invite me to their homes and to host the holidays. At first I thought, "Wait a minute, that's my Rosh Hashanah, that's my Seder." It didn't take me long to realize that they had assumed their natural place, and that it was my turn to let them take over. It is a relief, actually. We all pitch in, but the generational roles have changed.

The widow's state opened up what I call my second life. I didn't know how long and painful the adjustment would be, but after so many years of repression, I knew just what I wanted to do, and I was free to fly. I have always had a desire to travel. So when I found myself on my own, with likely half my life yet to be lived, I said, "Look out world, here I come."

I had wanted in my youth to make aliyah, which did not work out, and all my life Israel had a special attraction for me. The summer my husband died, I said to my daughter, "You know, honey, next year . . . ," and she said, "Mom, I was going to take you." "No," I said, "that's your graduation present." That was the entire conversation. We knew where we were going, and go we did, first to Egypt for a few days, then on to Israel. August 1983. I thought I would feel totally at home, but to my surprise I felt intensely American in a foreign country.

In the years after, my wanderlust took me on tours to Greece and Japan, to Italy and Kenya. I did not travel with anyone I knew, preferring to meet the tour group en route, and on one trip to France I was totally on my own. Being a lover of languages, I learned something of each in order to meet the inhabitants face to face. Even a little Japanese, even a little Swahili, a good deal of Italian, and traveler's French (beautiful accent, limited knowledge). I found the world a friendly place and the people welcoming and responsive. The new me was coming into her own. My children were wonderfully supportive, a little bemused by the adventurer in the family. It was good for them that I was not socially or psychologically dependent on them and a blessing that my husband had provided for me economically.

In my mid-thirties I had started a Bible study group to share my interests and to learn. We are a minyan of women who have become close friends and serious students, all of us with our various translations and commentaries. We are still learning after more than thirty-five years.

My book of midrash, *Ladies of Genesis* (Holender, 1991a), was a direct outgrowth of my interest in Torah. In reading Genesis, I realized how little had been said about the women, these remarkable, influential women. I felt that I knew them, that I had lived long and deep enough to put myself in their places. And I began to write the stories hidden in the white spaces. All the years I was writing, no one else was paying attention to these women. Now everyone seems to have discovered them.

I have always been dissatisfied with translations, especially of biblical poetry, and had wanted for years to study Hebrew. It just seemed like such a monumental undertaking. After my return from France, in celebration of my sixty-fifth year, I wrote a ceremony of passage (Holender, 1991b). On my birthday I shared it with my study group. By this time I had lost my husband, then my father and mother, and I had begun a new life. It was truly a time to mark. In the context of my new direction, I committed myself to begin at last the serious study of Hebrew.

I started at once to take private lessons and fell in love with the language. If I have three words in a language, I am ready to speak. So I learned quickly to say what I wanted to say, though I couldn't understand for some time what was said to me. Backward learning, I suppose. My biblical Hebrew was put aside for a later date while I immersed myself in modern Hebrew.

After a year of serious work I learned about Ulpan Akiva Netanya, the famous center for international living founded and directed by Shulamit Katznelson. Primarily for olim (immigrants) who then were coming mostly from Russia and France, it is an intensive language program as well as an introduction to living in Israel. I went in 1993 for a month of study. In a totally nonpolitical atmosphere I lived and studied with students from all over the world, and with Arabs learning Hebrew and Israelis learning Arabic. The force of Shulamit's personality brought together diplomats and olim, dignitaries and ordinary students like me, learning from exceptional teachers and learning from each other. In 1995, back I went for another month. And the next year for two months. By that time I was writing poetry in Hebrew, talking with everyone I met, and finding myself totally at home in the country and the language. I had translated one of my children's books into Hebrew, and it was illustrated and published in Israel in 1996. The English version is still waiting to be discovered. No matter, *Ani Cli-Zemer* (*I Am a Musical Instrument*) (Holender, 1996a) is alive and well.

That same year, my third book of poems, *Is This the Way to Athens?* (Holender, 1996b) was published, after twenty-eight rejections. I am a stubborn woman. It was quite a year.

You want to know what language can bring? People, first of all. Because I became fluent in Hebrew, I also became the honorary "American Grandma" to a group of gifted young Russian-Israeli musicians who came to Buffalo on their U.S. tour. They spoke no English and I no Russian, so we conversed solely in Hebrew. After the tour we kept in touch, and since 1995 we have been close friends. I see them every year in Israel, and two of them have stayed with me on return engagements. Without the language, I would have missed a rare experience. I am blessed to share their lives and to watch their progress.

I did, after all, study biblical Hebrew at the State University of New York at Buffalo. I can't say I know enough to read Psalms without a translation for reference, but I can read text, and I laid claim to the language with all my heart.

Being a celebratory, rather than ceremonious, person, I felt that my approaching seventieth birthday warranted some special marking. An adult Bat Mitzvah seemed appropriate. I chose the one perfect portion that by some miracle had not been designated for a young student. Nitzavim, Deuteronomy Ch. 30, contains Moses' farewell advice to the Israelites. When I read, "choose life, that you and your seed shall live," I knew I'd come home. And the Haftorah portion from Isaiah, "rejoice in Adonai" completed the circle. I learned trope, and chanted the Torah and Haftorah portions, regardless of the panic throat infection that had seized me ten days before. I knew the meaning and construction of every Hebrew word, and the deepest implications of the text.

It was a glorious event. I did not work with a group because I was already an advanced student, so the day was mine. My children and grandchildren took part in the service, as I had in theirs. I wore my grandsons' Bar Mitzvah tallith, and my kids gave a beautiful kiddush after the service. I will never forget the feeling of taking the Torah in my arms, the absolute certainty of possession and of being possessed. That "tree of life" was my own spine, on which my life was braced. It was one of the best things I've ever done.

I ended my D'var Torah with these words:

> These two words—b'charta b'chaim—choose life—led me to choose this parasha. This is what I wish to give my children and my grandchildren, because although I hope to live many years after this, my seventieth year, they will go on for many more years without me. We do not live in a constant state of heightened awareness, but I would hope that you will make conscious choices, and live fully in whatever way you choose, that you will live joyously, that you will find something so worth doing that you will use all your heart and all your being, and that your lives will be filled with love and with giving. For this, I can give you no better inheritance than the words of Moses, the words of Torah.

I'm fortunate in having good health. The aging process has not bothered me particularly, except that there's too little time ahead, too much behind, and too much still to do. I resent having to slow down now, although my body does occasionally insist that I give myself the pleasure of curling up with my books and music and a good cup of tea.

How has all this affected my children and grandchildren? It has certainly kept me out of their hair, which can be a big problem with aging parents. But more than that, it has shown them that getting old can have great rewards, that life can open up in unanticipated ways, and that once life's major obligations have been met, there's a great big exciting world out there just waiting to be experienced. I'd like to think that, at the time of their greatest concerns with children and careers, it gives them hope for their own future and a sense that this period can be one of fulfillment. I'm very fortunate that my children live close by. We are a loving family, proud of each other and supportive. I've been blessed with a close relationship with my son and daughter-in-law's two teenage sons and my daughter and son-in-law's eight-year-old boy. It keeps me young to share their lives. When my oldest grandson went to college, I got e-mail to keep in touch, and we have more contact now than we ever did when he was home. His high-school-age brother also answers my messages. They get a kick out of Grandma keeping up. Which is what grandmas do these days.

I've never liked the term "senior citizen." It's inelegant and patronizing. In Italian, we are known as *terza età*, literally "third age." That has a ring to it. But my littlest grandson really hit it one day in casual conversation. "You know, Grandma," he said, "when you get to the grand age . . ." "That's it!" I yelled. "I'm at the Grand Age! Thank you, Sam."

Sam and I have a special relationship. He loves books, and he loves Hebrew, which he has recently begun to learn. He is teaching his mother. I write and illustrate a book for him for each birthday, a Sam and Grandma adventure. We have done some crazy things in those stories. Sam is always the voice of reason, while Grandma seems increasingly bent on mischief.

Now in my seventy-second year, in a time of losses, I have a sense of mortality breathing down my neck. I'm ever conscious of the preciousness of each day and the sheer good luck of waking up in the morning. I hope I have given my children and theirs something of that awareness and desire for life.

What is this Jewish mother connection? I find with aging that I am more and more like my mother. I look in the glass and think, Mother, what are you doing here? Intentionally or not, we leave our imprint. I only pray it will be for the good.

A MESSAGE FOR MY CHILDREN

I will be busy when I die
leaving messages in several languages
along your possible paths,

clues you may not understand but
will recognize as mine, and therefore
meant to encourage.

I will never be done with this world—
I will leave my tracks, not to follow
but to know, when you feel most at risk,
no life is entirely without precedent.

You will find me when you least expect
in your words and gestures and, with the years,
in your morning face in the mirror.

My leavetaking will be a leave-giving.
Take to yourselves what possessed me—
The Tree of Life cries out, Eat, eat!
Be hungry.

REFERENCES

Holender, Barbara D. (1986). *Shivah poems: Poems of mourning.* Hartford, CT: Andrew Mountain Press.

Holender, Barbara D. (1991a). *Ladies of Genesis.* New York: Jewish Women's Resource Center.

Holender, Barbara D. (1991b). A ceremony of passage on my 65th birthday. In Rabbi Debra Orenstein (Ed.), *Lifecycles*, Vol. I. Woodstock, VT: Jewish Lights Publishing.

Holender, Barbara D. (1996a). *Ani Cli-Zemer.* Kiryat Gat, Israel: Dani Sfarim Ltd.

Holender, Barbara D. (1996b). *Is this the way to Athens?* Princeton, NJ: Quarterly Review of Literature. Poetry Book Series, Vol. 35.

Glossary

Notes:

Hebrew and Yiddish words often have multiple spellings in English transliteration (alternate spelling in parentheses).

Literal translations are in italics.

We indicate h, for Hebrew; y, for Yiddish terms. All other languages are spelled out.

Abba, h. *Father.* Diminutive for Father, Daddy.

Adon Olam, h. *Lord of the Universe.* Hymn sung at conclusion of many synagogue services.

Adonai, h. *Our Lord.*

Adonai Elohenu, h. *Our Lord, Our God.*

Afikomen, Greek. *Dessert.* Ritually a special piece of matzah signifying the end of the Passover Seder, set aside for that purpose. Children are playfully encouraged to hide the afikomen in order to exchange it for a small gift.

Aggada, **Aggadot** (pl), h. Nonlegal rabbinical narrative.

Ahavat haTorah, h. *Love of Torah.*

Akedah, h. *Sacrifice.* Usually refers to the story of Abraham's readiness to sacrifice his only son, Isaac.

Aleph bet, h. *A, b.* The Hebrew alphabet.

Aliyah, **aliyot** (pl), h. *Ascent.* The honor of being called up to the bima during the Torah reading. Also immigration to Israel.

Amidah, h. *Standing.* Important prayer in Jewish liturgy, said while standing up.

Ashkenazi, h. Jews of Central and Eastern Europe.

Avot, Pirkei Avot, h. *Sayings of the Fathers.* A section of the Talmud.

Baal Kiddushin, h. *Master of marriage ceremony.*

Baal Shem Tov, h. *Master of the divine name.* Generally refers to the founder of Chasidism (ca. 1700).

Ba'al teshuvah, h. *One who repents.* Commonly describes a newly religious Jew.

Baruch atah Adonai Elohenu, h. *Blessed art thou our Lord, our God.* First sentence of most traditional Jewish blessings or prayers.

Bat/Bar Mitzvah(ed), B'nai Mitzvah (pl), **Bar/Bat Mitzvoth** h. *Daughter/son of the commandments.* The religious ceremony marking adult membership in the community at age thirteen. The first girl's Bat Mitzvah was led by Rabbi Mordechai Kaplan for his daughter Judith in the early 1920s.

B'chaim, h. *To life, with life.* In life.

B'charta, h. *With blessing.* Choose with blessing.

B'charta b'chaim, h. Choose life.

Beit midrash, h. *House of study.*

Benshen (benshin), y. The act of chanting grace after meals.

Beresheet (B'reshit), h. *In the beginning.* First word of the creation story in Genesis, first word in the Torah, the Five Books of Moses.

Beshert, y. *Fated.* Often refers to the person(s) fated to become a life partner.

Bima, h. Podium at which Torah is read.

B'not Esh, h. *Daughters of fire.* Name of a small group of Jewish feminist leaders and innovators.

Bobbe (bubbe, bubby), y. Affectionate diminutive for Grandmother.

Bracha, Brachot (pl), (**Barucha**), h. *Blessing.* Prayer of praise or thanks.

Bris, y. **Brith**, **Brith Milah**, h. *Covenant of circumcision.* Ritual male circumcision eight days after a Jewish boy's birth.

Bund, y. *Association of loyal members.* Refers to a Jewish Socialist Organization. **Bundist**, y. One who belongs to the Jewish Socialist Organization.

Bund, German. *Association.* Refers to Deutscher Bund, a Nazi Youth Organization.

Chabad, h. Name of a Chasidic organization reaching out especially to young people.

Challah, **challot** (pl), (**Hallah**), h. Braided egg-bread traditionally served on Sabbath and Holy Days.

Chametz, h. *Leavened bread.* Refers to all foods not allowed during Passover.

Chanukah. *See* Hanukkah.

Chasid, **Chasidic**, **Chasidim** (pl), h. *Faithful follower.* Member of ultrareligious Chasidic group.

Chavurah (**havura**, **havurot** [pl]), h. *Groups, friendship groups.* Often an independent study or prayer group functioning with lay leadership; or a subgroup within a particular congregation.

Chevra, h., y. *Circle of friends.*

Chochmat haLev, h. *Wisdom of the heart.*

Cholent, y. *Derived from French "chaud lent."* A stewlike dish kept warm for the Sabbath meal when cooking is forbidden.

Christkind, German. *Christ child.*

Chupa (Chupah), h. *Wedding canopy.*

Chutzpah, h. *Insolence, effrontery.* In common usage, being pushy, arrogant.

Dayenu, h. *Sufficient unto us.* A song traditionally sung during the Passover Seder.

Days of Awe. Ten days of penitence and reflection between Rosh Hashanah and Yom Kippur.

Dreidel (dreidl), y. *Four-sided top.* Game played with a spinning top during Hanukkah.

D'var Torah, h. *Word of Torah.* A brief talk on a theme or insight from the Torah reading.

Eins zwei drei, German. *One, two, three.*

El, h. *God.* Short form of Elohim, the name of God, also the sacred.

Eliyahu haNavi, h. *Prophet Elijah.*

Elul, h. *Month of Elul.* The month preceding the High Holy Days of Rosh Hashanah and Yom Kippur.

Erev Rosh Hashanah, h. *Eve of Rosh Hashanah.* All Jewish holidays begin at sundown on the eve of the holiday.

Erev Shabbat, h. *Eve of Shabbat.*

Esrog, y, h. *Citron.* Citrus fruit used in Sukkoth ritual.

Fabrangen (Farbrengen), y. *Enjoy time together.* Also name of a havura.

Four Questions. Four questions traditionally asked by the youngest person at the Passover Seder.

Galut, h. *Exile.* Commonly refers to exile from the promised land to Diaspora, the world outside of Israel.

Gefilte Fish, y. *Stuffed fish.* An appetizer or main course made of chopped fish, traditionally served on Jewish holidays, especially Passover.

Geulah, h. *Liberation.*

Glatt kosher. A more rigorous set of rules than those governing ordinary kosher food.

Goy, goyim (pl), h. *Non-Jew(s), nation.*

Gregger, y. *Noisemaker.* Traditionally used by children to drown out the name of the infamous Haman during the reading of the Book of Esther on Purim.

Ha-Aretz, h. *The Land, the earth.* Refers to the Holy Land, also used in blessings, as in "who brings forth bread from the earth."

Haftorah, h. *Conclusion*. Portion of Prophets read after the weekly reading of the Torah portion and interpreting or illustrating that Torah portion.

Haggadah, **Haggadot** (pl), h. *Telling* or *legend*. Most commonly the story of the exodus from Egypt, read at the Passover Seder.

Halacha (Halakha), **Halachot** (pl), h. *The proper way*. Jewish law(s). Legal part of postbiblical Jewish literature, religion, and morals.

Halachic (Halakhic), h. In strict adherence to Jewish law, according to Halacha.

Haman, h. The name of the villain in the Book of Esther, which is read on Purim.

Hamantaschen, y. *Pockets of Haman*. Three-cornered pastry filled with poppyseed paste or other sweets, eaten during Purim.

Hamotzi, **Hamotz**, h. *Brought forth*. Refers to the blessing over bread at the beginning of every meal, thanking God who "brought forth bread from the earth."

Hanukkah (Chanukah), h. *Feast of Lights*. Eight-day festival commemorating the Jewish rebellion and victory over the Romans, celebrated by lighting an additional candle every night and gifts for children.

Hanukkah gelt, y. *Hanukkah coins*. Small coins or chocolate coins given to children at Hanukkah.

Haredi, h. *One who trembles before God*. A specific ultraorthodox community in Israel.

Hashem, h. *The name*. The name of God, commonly used instead of pronouncing the word "God."

Hashomer Hatzair, h. *Youth Guardians*. World Zionist Youth Organization.

Hasid, **Hasidic**, **Hasidim** (pl), h. *See* Chasid, Chasidic, Chasidim.

Havdalah, h. *Separation*. Ceremony at conclusion of Sabbath and festivals, indicating the separation between holy and mundane, observed with candles, spices, and wine.

Havura. *See* Chavurah.

Hazor b'shalom, h. *Return in peace*. Farewell greeting before a long or dangerous journey.

Hora, h. Israeli dance.

Judische Selbsthasse, German. *Jewish self-hatred*.

Kabbalah (cabala), h. The mystical tradition within Judaism.

Kaddish, h. *Sanctified*. Memorial prayer of sanctification traditionally recited only by male mourners, recently allowed to women mourners.

Kartoffelpuffer (Erdapfelpuffer), German. *Potato pancake*.

Kashrut (cashrut), h. Adherence to Jewish dietary (kosher) laws and practices.

Keinanhora, y. *No evil eye*. A phrase used to ward off bad luck.

Ketuvim, h. Third and last division of the Bible.

Kibbutz, **Kibbutzim** (pl), h. Collective community in Israel.

Kibbutznik, h. Kibbutz member.

Kiddush, h. *Blessing*. Blessing over ceremonial wine.

Kislev, h. Month during which Hanukkah falls in Jewish calendar.

Kleib(ed) (past tense) **naches**, y. *Gather(ed) joy*. Take pride and pleasure, usually about children or grandchildren.

Kleine kinder kleine tzorres, ganze kinder ganze tzorres, y. *Little children, little worries, whole or grown children, whole worries*.

Kneidele, y. *Dumplings*. Usually refers to matzo balls.

Knish, y. A savory pastry filled with meat, mashed potato, or other filling.

Kol Nidre, Aramaic. *All Vows*. Most solemn prayer chanted on the eve of Yom Kippur, asking forgiveness of all unfulfilled promises to God.

Kosher, h, y. According to Jewish laws; primarily pertaining to preparation and consumption of food.

Kotel, h. *Wall.* Wailing Wall in Jerusalem. Remnant of the Jerusalem Temple now used as a special place of worship, also referred to as Western Wall.

Krapfen, German. *Doughnuts.*

Kugel, y. *Pudding.* Usually but not always a noodle pudding.

Kvell(ed)(ing), y. *Feeling and expressing pleasure.* The opposite of complaining.

Kvetch(ed)(ing), y. *Complaining.* Expressing discomfort, pain, displeasure.

Latkes, y. *Pancakes.* Potato pancakes served during Hanukkah.

L'chaim, h. *To life.* A toast.

L'dor v'dor, h. From strength to strength.

Lechlecha b'shalom, h. *Go in peace.* Farewell greeting usually followed by "Hazor b'shalom" *(return in peace).*

Limud haTorah, h. *Torah study.*

Lubavitcher, h. *From Lubavitch (town in Lithuania).* Members of a Chasidic ultrareligious sect, followers of the rabbi of Lubavitch.

Lubavitcher rebbetzin (rebetsin), y. *Wife of the Lubavitcher rabbi.*

Lulav(im) h. *Palm branch(es).* Used during the festival of Sukkoth.

Mahzor, mahzorim (pl), h. High Holy Day prayerbook(s) used on Rosh Hashanah and Yom Kippur.

Mandelbrot, y. *Almond bread.* Almond cookie.

Maoz Tsur, h. *Rock of Ages.* Hanukkah hymn sung after lighting the Hanukkah candles.

Masorti, h. *Traditional.* Name of Conservative movement in Israel.

Matzah, h. **matzo**, y. Unleavened bread eaten during Passover.

Matzo balls. Fluffy matzo meal dumplings, usually served in chicken soup.

M'dor l'dor, h. *From generation to generation.*

Megillah, h, y. *Scroll.* A story, an account.

Megillat Esther, h. *Scroll of Esther.* Biblical story of Esther read on the holiday of Purim.

Mehitzah, mehitza, h. Curtain separating women from men in Orthodox synagogues.

Menorah, h. *Candelabra.* Usually refers to the Hanukkah candelabra.

Mensch, y. *Human being.* A person of highly developed human qualities, a good person.

Meshuggene(r), meshugene, y. *Crazy.* Eccentric, odd, weird person or thing.

Mezuzah, h. Tiny scroll containing the Shema prayer encased in a decorative fixture, attached to the doorposts of a Jewish home.

Midrash(im), h. Biblical legend(s) interpreting or adding to biblical texts.

Mikvah, h. **Mikveh**, y. Body of running water used for ritual immersion after menstruation or as part of conversion; also a body of water used for immersion of utensils to be used in a kosher kitchen.

Minhag, h. *Custom.* Usually refers to local adaptation of Jewish customs or songs.

Minyan, h. **minyon**, y. A quorum of ten Jews required for significant parts of religious service, only recently beginning to include women.

Mishnah, Mishna, h. Rabbinical collection of Halachot (laws) compiled in the third century.

Mitzvah, mitzvoth (pl), h. *Commandment of God.* In popular usage a good deed; also the precepts, duties, good acts mandated in Torah; the performance of Jewish rituals.

Modeh ani lefanecha, h. *I am thankful before you. I admit to you.*

Mohel, h. *Circumcisor.* A person trained in the rituals and procedures of Brith Milah, circumcision.

Mohnnudeln, German. *Poppyseed noodles.*

Moishe Rabbenu, h. *Moses our Teacher*. Respectful and affectionate apellation of the prophet Moses.

Motzae Shabbat, h. *Exit of Shabbat*. The time after sundown when Shabbat is over.

Motzi, h. Abbreviation for the blessing over bread, which contains the word "Hamotzi."

Naches. *See* Kleib naches.

Neshama, neshamah, h. *Soul*. Jewish soul, spirit.

Nevi'im, h. *Prophets*. The biblical book of Prophets.

Nitzavim, h. Name of Torah portion in Deuteronomy, chaps. 29-30:9.

Nona. Affectionate term for grandmother.

Olim, h. *Those who ascend*. Refers to immigrants to Israel, the Holy Land.

Omayn v'omayn, h, y. *Amen and amen.*

Oneg, h, y. *Pleasure*. Refers to reception or entertainment, especially after Sabbath services.

Papa, Greek. *Orthodox priest*. (*Daddy* in other languages.)

Pappou, Greek. Affectionate term for grandfather.

Parasha, h. Weekly Torah portion.

Passover (Pesach), h. Holiday celebrating and commemorating the Jewish people's liberation from slavery and the exodus from Egypt.

Pirkei Avot, h. *See* Avot.

Purim, h. Feast of Esther, commemorating how Queen Esther outwitted the evil Haman and saved the Jewish people from persecution.

Pushke, y. *Box*. Alms box, also any tin box or can of food.

Rebbetzin, y. Wife of a rabbi.

Rogalkes, y. Rolled-out pastries filled with raisins, nuts, and other goodies.

Rosh Hashanah, h. *Head of the year.* Jewish New Year, birthday of the world.

Rosh Hodesh (Rosh Chodesh), h. *New moon.* Celebration of beginning the lunar month, has become the focus of women's spiritual groups.

Rugela(ch), y. From rugel (royal), same as rogalkes.

Sabra, h. *Fruit of cactus.* Slang for Israeli-born, prickly outside and soft inside.

Salzteig, German. *Salt dough.*

Schaloch manos, h, y. *Sending gifts.* Assortment of sweet edibles exchanged as gifts during the Purim festival. Also known as Purim baskets.

Seder, h. *Order of service.* Ceremonial feast on the first (two) nights of Passover that includes reading the Haggadah.

Sephardi(c), h. Jews of Mediterranean origin including Spain, Portugal, and Morocco; migrated to Holland, the Americas, and other countries during the expulsion from Spain.

Shabbat, h. **Shabbos**, y. Jewish Sabbath, day of rest, beginning at sundown Friday night and ending at sundown Saturday night.

Shabbat shalom, h. *Peaceful Sabbath.* Sabbath greeting.

Shabbaton, h. *Work stoppage.* Commonly refers to an all-day Sabbath gathering or celebration.

Shaina punim, y. *Pretty face.*

Shalom Aleichem, h. *Peace to all.* Name of introductory song at the Friday night dinner table.

Shalom bayit, h. *Peace in the home.* The ideal of domestic harmony.

Shavuoth, h. Feast of first fruits, celebrating the giving of the Ten Commandments.

Shechinah, h. *Heavenly spirit, Divine presence, immanence of God.* Also seen as God's female presence.

Shehehyanu, h. *Who has kept us alive.* Blessing said on special occasions, thanking God for allowing us to reach this season or event.

Shema (Sh'ma), h. *Hear.* "Hear O Israel, the Lord is our God, the Lord is one." Central prayer of the Jewish people.

Shiksa(s), y. Non-Jewish girl or woman, usually derogatory.

Shikun, h. *Public housing.* Housing complex.

Shiur. Class of study, lesson.

Shivah, h. *Seven.* Seven days of mourning.

Shoah, h. *Holocaust.*

Shofar, shfarim (pl), h. *Ram's horn(s).* Ritual blowing of ram's horn signifying call to repentance on Rosh Hashanah, and Yom Kippur.

Shtetl, y. *Small town.* The Jewish towns, neighborhoods, and ghettoes of Eastern Europe.

Shul, y. Synagogue, house of prayer.

Shulchan Arukh, h. *Prepared table.* Authoritative code of law of Orthodox Judaism.

Siddur, h. *Order, arrangement.* Daily and Sabbath prayer book.

Simhas Torah (Simhat Torah), h. *Rejoicing in the Torah.* Holiday celebrating the completion of the annual cycle of Torah readings, immediately followed by reading the first verse of the Torah. Last day of the Holy Day season that began with Rosh Hashanah.

Siyum(im), h. Celebration(s) when a portion of Jewish learning is completed.

Succah (Sukkah), h. *Shelter.* Harvest hut constructed for the Jewish holiday of Succoth.

Succoth (Sukkoth), h. *Hut(s).* Harvest festival commemorating the forty years of wandering in the desert.

Tallith, tallit(ot) (pl), h. **Tallis**, y. Ritual fringed prayer shawl(s) worn by men and lately also by women.

Talmud, h. *Study* or *learning.* Two-thousand-year-old compendium of Oral Law, philosophy, and legends that comprise the central body of Jewish teachings and guidance for Jewish life.

Talmud Torah, h. *Torah study.* Religious Jewish elementary school, also study of Torah.

Tanach, h. Old Testament, Hebrew Bible, Five Books of Moses.

Teitsch-Humash, y. Yiddish translation of Old Testament.

Terza età, Italian. *Third age.* Midlife.

Teshuvah, h. *Return to Jewish thought and practice.* Also, repentance.

Tikkun olam, h. *Repair of the world.* Jewish people's responsibility to help repair or heal the world.

Torah, h. Literally, the parchment scroll that contains the handwritten Five Books of Moses; in the broadest sense, all of Jewish law and teachings.

Torah trope, y. Musical cantillation for chanting Torah or Haftorah.

Tsores (Tzorres), y. Worries, problems, concerns.

Tzedakah, h. *Charity, justice.*

Ulpan, h. *Studio.* Intensive Hebrew classes, mostly for immigrants to Israel.

V'ahavta, h. *And you shall love.* First word of the prayer: "And you shall love the lord your God" (part of the Shema prayer).

Vashti, h. *Queen Vashti.* Was divorced from King Ahashuerus after she refused to dance naked before him and his guests. In the Book of Esther, read on Purim.

Va'yhi Or, h. *And there was light.* In Genesis, the story of creation.

Vayishalchahoo, h. *And he sent us forth.*

Wailing Wall. *See* Kotel.

Yarmulke. Small head-covering worn by Orthodox and some Conservative Jewish males.

Yeridah, h. *Descent, going down.*

Yeshiva, yeshivot (pl), h. Talmudic academy, school of Jewish studies for young men only.

Yeshiva bocher(s), h. Young man (men) who pursue(s) Jewish studies in a yeshiva.

Yiddish(e) Mamme, y. *Jewish mother.* Idealized Jewish mother who nurtures, comforts, and sacrifices herself for her family.

Yom Kippur, h. Day of Atonement, holiest day in Jewish calendar, celebrated ten days after Rosh Hashanah.

Yom Kippur War. The war that started on Yom Kippur, October 6, 1973, when Syrian and Egyptian forces attacked Israel by air.

Yom Tov, **Yomtov**, h. **Yontef**, y. *Holy Day.* Any Jewish holy day.

Yored, **yoridah**, **yoredet**, **yordim**, h. *He/she/they who descended.* Those who leave Israel.

Yossel der Roiter, h. *Joseph the red-haired one.*

Order Your Own Copy of
This Important Book for Your Personal Library!

JEWISH MOTHERS TELL THEIR STORIES
Acts of Love and Courage

_____ in hardbound at $59.95 (ISBN: 0-7890-1099-2)

_____ in softbound at $24.95 (ISBN: 0-7890-1100-X)

COST OF BOOKS_____	☐ **BILL ME LATER:** ($5 service charge will be added) (Bill-me option is good on US/Canada/Mexico orders only; not good to jobbers, wholesalers, or subscription agencies.)
OUTSIDE USA/CANADA/ MEXICO: ADD 20%_____	
POSTAGE & HANDLING_____ (US: $3.00 for first book & $1.25 for each additional book) Outside US: $4.75 for first book & $1.75 for each additional book)	☐ Check here if billing address is different from shipping address and attach purchase order and billing address information. Signature_____
SUBTOTAL_____	☐ **PAYMENT ENCLOSED: $**_____
IN CANADA: ADD 7% GST_____	☐ **PLEASE CHARGE TO MY CREDIT CARD.**
STATE TAX_____ (NY, OH & MN residents, please add appropriate local sales tax)	☐ Visa ☐ MasterCard ☐ AmEx ☐ Discover ☐ Diner's Club
FINAL TOTAL_____ (If paying in Canadian funds, convert using the current exchange rate. UNESCO coupons welcome.)	Account #_____ Exp. Date_____ Signature_____

Prices in US dollars and subject to change without notice.

NAME _____

INSTITUTION _____

ADDRESS _____

CITY _____

STATE/ZIP _____

COUNTRY _____ COUNTY (NY residents only) _____

TEL _____ FAX _____

E-MAIL_____
May we use your e-mail address for confirmations and other types of information? ☐ Yes ☐ No

Order From Your Local Bookstore or Directly From
The Haworth Press, Inc.
10 Alice Street, Binghamton, New York 13904-1580 • USA
TELEPHONE: 1-800-HAWORTH (1-800-429-6784) / Outside US/Canada: (607) 722-5857
FAX: 1-800-895-0582 / Outside US/Canada: (607) 772-6362
E-mail: getinfo@haworthpressinc.com

PLEASE PHOTOCOPY THIS FORM FOR YOUR PERSONAL USE.